The New Age

The New Age

The History of a Movement

Nevill Drury

Page 1: Detail of *The Ascent of the Blessed*, Hieronymus Bosch, *c.* 1450–1516.

Pages 2–3: Burning Desire, Mariko Mori, 1998. Glass with photo interlayer, five panels. The artist depicts herself both as a levitating deity and as her four divine attendants.

Page 6: Start Here. Fractal graphic image suggestive of mystical aspirations and intent.

Page 7: Yoga at sunset on a beach in the Maldives.

© 2004 Thames & Hudson Ltd, London
Text © 2004 Nevill Drury

First published in 2004 in paperback in the United States of America by Thames & Hudson Inc., 500 Fifth Avenue, New York, New York 10110

thamesandhudsonusa.com

Library of Congress Catalog Card Number: 2004102817
ISBN 0-500-28516-0

Printed and bound in Singapore by CS Graphics

Contents

Truth is a pathless land.

Krishnamurti

When the individual feels connected
           to the cosmos as a whole,
it becomes clear that ecological
           awareness is truly spiritual.

Fritjof Capra

We are now in the process of learning
           to see with our souls –
combining our life's experience
with our deepest archetypal knowings.

Jean Houston

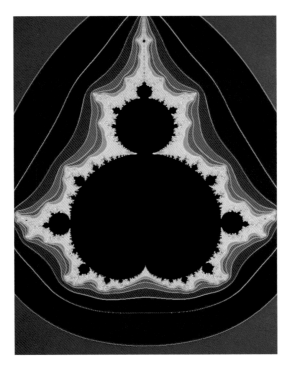

Introduction

The New Age movement may well reflect the future face of Western religion. Its fusion of spiritual practices is grounded not only in experiences of higher consciousness and personal growth, but also in the perennial wisdom traditions of East and West. In a welcome contrast to fundamentalist extremism, the movement argues for a spirituality without borders or confining dogmas, and for a tolerance in religious belief that does not exclude through doctrinal difference. It is also searching for a paradigm that builds on new scientific insights, while recognizing that the foundations of life remain a mystery. In holding to the view that there are many ways to self-realization, that no religion or philosophy holds a unique key to spiritual enlightenment, the New Age takes the middle ground between institutional Western religion and the secular, often sceptical, materialism of modern times. And although it began as a substantially American phenomenon, it is now rapidly gathering momentum internationally.

How the New Age is perceived depends very much on how it is defined. In popular usage such expressions as 'the human potential movement', the 'personal growth movement' and the umbrella term of the 'New Age' itself, are all to some extent interchangeable. But they also need some clarification.

The four key precursors of the New Age – Emanuel Swedenborg, Franz Anton Mesmer, Madame Helena Blavatsky and George Ivanovitch Gurdjieff – represent much of what the New Age now sets out to achieve. They are, however, only a starting point, and there have been many twists and turns along the way. Historically the New Age movement builds on the idea promoted during the late nineteenth century by Madame Blavatsky and the Theosophists that there is a universal wisdom tradition uniting the spiritual teachings of both East and West.[1]

Much of the inspiration driving the New Age derives from ancient and perennial wisdom teachings – from the Vedas, Hindu sacred texts, including hymns, chants and mantras, dating from around 1800–1200 BCE; from Yoga; from the Mahayana tradition (the so-called Great Vehicle of Buddhism) in northern India and Tibet, which places emphasis on *bodhisattvas*, spiritual beings close to achieving complete enlightenment; from Sufism, the mystical tradition within

Sikh Yogi Bhajan teaching Kundalini Yoga, summer solstice, Tesuque Reservation, New Mexico, 1969.

Islam; and from 'indigenous spirituality', the spiritual traditions of native peoples around the world.

At the same time the New Age movement is also a creative fusion of metaphysics, self-help psychology – especially the psychology of self-realization and integration advocated by such pioneering thinkers as Carl Jung and Abraham Maslow – and holistic approaches to self-awareness. The term 'transpersonal' – which refers to states of awareness beyond the human ego – is an expression that has been used by Jungian and humanistic psychologists alike, just as the expressions 'personal growth' and 'human potential' were originally associated with the rise of humanistic psychology in the 1960s.[2] Esalen Institute in Big Sur, California – the model for all experiential 'personal growth' centres – was founded on the very idea of fusing self-help psychology with the perennial wisdom traditions, and Esalen has helped define the New Age movement around the world today.

The New Age, of course, has its critics, and this overview, while concentrating on its undoubted strengths and originalities, also deals with its eccentricities and shortcomings – including its commercial aspects. It is also important to stress, however, that contrary to the popular media image emphasized by its detractors, the New Age is not just about hedonistic self-help and sensory indulgence. Many of the most progressive ideas feeding through to the New Age from the transpersonal movement are at the forefront of modern thought and demand our attention. Some first-rate thinkers – including Aldous Huxley, Krishnamurti and Joseph Campbell – have presented their ideas at Esalen. Thinking of a high order continues to feed into the New Age from the international transpersonal movement, a progressive group of psychologists, physicists, biologists, anthropologists, philosophers, spiritual scholars and social theorists. Their ideas have contributed to the possibility of a new paradigm: a worldview that includes both science and spirituality. Among these prominent thinkers and academics are Stanislav Grof, Ken Wilber, Jean Houston, Fritjof Capra, Rupert Sheldrake, Ralph Metzner, Kenneth Ring, Jean Shinoda Bolen, Danah Zohar, Charles Tart and Frances Vaughan, all of whom feature in this book. My view is that the best ideas from the transpersonal movement gradually find their way through to the New Age, although in a more popular and accessible form, and then help shape the New Age movement as it moves forward.

I think it will become increasingly clear in the following pages that the New Age does indeed have a tangible history and that it hasn't simply burst on to the contemporary scene in a random flurry of metaphysical enthusiasm. The strong influence of Eastern mysticism that pervades the New Age movement has been present in the West since the pioneering days of early Theosophy and the visits to the United States by Vivekananda more than a hundred years ago.

As increasing numbers of Indian gurus began visiting the United States in the late 1960s, many within the counterculture began exploring Buddhism and techniques of meditation. At the same time, consciousness researchers like Ram Dass and Timothy Leary turned their attention to the ancient *Tibetan Book of the Dead* as an experiential guide to transcendent states of human awareness. The Eastern influence on the personal growth movement continues to the present day with the visits of gurus and spiritual teachers, and the 14th Dalai Lama, Tenzin Gyatso, enjoys unparalleled popularity as an international ambassador for Tibetan Buddhism. Sales of his publications compare very favourably with those of leading New Age authors with similar Eastern perspectives, and maybe this should come as no surprise. Increasingly, people are looking beyond their own cultural traditions in the search for meaning and spiritual renewal.

In the rise of the New Age movement there is, in addition, the important historical link between the British novelist and philosopher Aldous Huxley, who was attracted to Vedanta after moving to Los Angeles in the late 1930s, and Krishnamurti who was based at the time in nearby Ojai – they became close friends. Later Huxley influenced and encouraged the founders of Esalen Institute in Big Sur, the organization at the very heart of the personal growth movement, and Krishnamurti had constructive dialogues with Professor David Bohm, an influential thinker in the study of quantum physics. Both Huxley and Krishnamurti championed the universal aspects of the perennial wisdom traditions, and both considered the relationship between science and spirituality extremely important, basing their ideas on a deep exploration of human awareness. Huxley and Krishnamurti are now iconic figures in the history of the 'new consciousness'.

There are clear historical links, too, between nineteenth-century Theosophy and such modern researchers as John Lilly and Stanislav Grof whose transpersonal studies also support the view that credible belief systems should encompass both science and spirituality, and that belief systems based on dogma alone provide limited insights into the nature of experiential 'reality'. And while orthodox Western religious traditions have had much to say about an afterlife based on specific doctrines relating to Heaven and Hell, the transpersonal science of thanatology described in Chapter 11 takes us beyond belief into a science of death itself. Near-death studies transcend the continuing debate about religious doctrinal differences and provide insights into the nature of dying and the possibilities of post-mortem existence. Here the emergence of data based on medical and scientific enquiry is having a considerable impact on the nature of spiritual belief itself. As consciousness researcher Robert Monroe has said, the challenge now is to convert our beliefs into 'knowns', so that our paradigms of belief can finally be grounded in a body of knowledge that reflects a broad range of human experience.

The fusion of East and West continues, for the New Age is strongly committed to eroding the barriers between religious traditions, concentrating on the trans-cultural dimensions of human awareness rather than on beliefs that divide human beings into competing camps or, in extreme situations, into opposing fundamentalist factions waging 'holy war' on one another.

The New Age is essentially about the search for spiritual and philosophical perspectives that will help transform humanity and the world. New Agers are willing to absorb wisdom teachings wherever they can find them, whether from an Indian guru, a renegade Christian priest, an itinerant Buddhist monk, an experiential psychotherapist or a Native American shaman. They are eager to explore their own inner potential with a view to becoming part of a broader process of social transformation. Their journey is towards totality of being. Their essential quest – one that I also happen to share and endorse – is for a holistic worldview that offers both insight and hope for the challenging times that lie ahead.

1

Wisdom from the East, Wisdom from the West

It is often said that many of the precepts of the New Age have been with us for some time, that there is nothing especially 'new' about it. While I think this is basically true, it is also apparent that the New Age is unique to its own time. In drawing on both Eastern and Western spiritual and metaphysical traditions and then infusing them with influences from self-help and motivational psychology, holistic health, parapsychology, consciousness research and quantum physics, the New Age has characteristics that are all its own. Nonetheless, among the influences on the movement it is possible to identify several important precursors.

01.01 Scientific visionary Emanuel Swedenborg (1688–1772), a key precursor of the New Age.

THE VISIONS OF SWEDENBORG

Emanuel Swedenborg (1688–1772), born in Stockholm, was the third of nine children. His father was a distinguished professor of theology at the University of Uppsala, and Emanuel spent his formative years in Uppsala. His early inclinations were clearly towards science rather than theology. In 1716 he was appointed special assessor to the Royal College of Mines by Charles XII of Sweden, and this remained the only professional appointment of his career. He made experimental drawings for a flying machine and for studying the properties of light, and published works on mathematics, chemistry, astronomy, magnetism, psychology and human anatomy. He wrote on the pituitary gland and the cerebral cortex as well as on cerebrospinal fluid, and was the first to discover the function of the cerebellum. In 1734 he proposed the 'nebular hypothesis' to account for the formation of the planets, anticipating the theories of Immanuel Kant and the French astronomer, Marquis de Laplace.

In 1744 Swedenborg published *On the Infinite and Final Cause of Creation* which discussed the relationship between the soul and the body. Still very much a scientist, he was drawing closer to the deep involvement in spiritual matters that would characterize the later years of his life.

At the end of 1744 he recorded in his diaries a number of vivid dreams about his sinfulness and his intellectual pride, which had a profoundly humbling effect on him. Then, in 1745, he had a decisive experience at a London inn. 'Towards the close of the meal I noticed a sort of dimness before my eyes; this became denser, and I then saw the floor covered with horrid crawling reptiles…. I was amazed, for I was perfectly conscious, and my thoughts were clear.' Swedenborg noticed a man sitting in the corner of the room who said to him, 'Eat not so much'. The darkness intensified and then cleared, to reveal that he was alone in the room.

> Such an unexpected terror hastened my return home…and during the same night the same man revealed himself to me again, but I was not frightened now. He then said that he was the Lord God, the Creator of the world, and the Redeemer, and that he had chosen me to explain to men the spiritual sense of the Scripture and that He Himself would explain to me what I should write on this subject; that same night were opened to me so that I became thoroughly convinced of their reality, the worlds of spirits, heaven and hell, and I recognized there many acquaintances of every condition in life. From that day I gave up the study of all worldly science, and laboured in spiritual things.[1]

In 1747, at fifty-nine, Swedenborg resigned his position with the Royal College of Mines and accepted a half-pension in order to dedicate himself to exploring the realms of spirits and angels. 'Many will say that it is all a phantasy,' he wrote in his *Arcana Coelestia*, 'But by all this I am not deterred, for I have seen, I have heard, I have felt.'[2]

For Swedenborg, his new spiritual quest meant factual, scientific observation within an unfamiliar domain – the visionary exploration of a world rarely glimpsed by a mortal. He seems to have used a form of meditative trance to enter these states of consciousness, and would startle his servants by engaging in conversations with spirit-beings who were visible only to him.

In his voluminous mystical works, Swedenborg describes a universe in which everything emanates from the One God, or Creator who sustains the universe through the spiritual sun – the primal source of love and knowledge.

The Lord (One God)

Celestial Heaven
Spiritual Heaven
Natural Heaven

The world of spirits

Humanity on earth

The world of Nature

Above humanity and the natural world in the hierarchy is the realm of spirits – the world accessed at death – and above them are the three levels of Heaven (each of which has an equivalent Hell). According to Swedenborg, all the angels and spirit-beings residing in these heavens once lived in the world, but they were now functioning in realms appropriate to their level of spiritual realization and development.

In Swedenborg's cosmology, all forms in the natural world come into existence through impulses from the spiritual realm. God's spiritual sun of love and wisdom, for example, has its counterpart in the natural sun, whose light and warmth sustain Nature. The cosmos operates through a spiritual hierarchy of cause and effect. He refers to the symbolic relationship between spiritual and natural forms as 'correspondences'. The hierarchy of beings in the different heavens represent different orders of spiritual existence and act in 'correspondence' with each other. The Lord acts through his celestial angels, who correspond on a lower level to spiritual angels, who correspond to angels in the third natural heaven, who in turn correspond to the world of humanity below.

Within Swedenborg's greater scheme of things, 'free will' is a comparatively narrow option since all individuals are subject to the interactions of good and evil spirits who represent positive and negative causality in the universe. As American psychologist and Swedenborg scholar Wilson Van Dusen has expressed it, 'In effect, good and its opposite evil rule through this hierarchy of beings down to man who stands in the free space between them.'[3]

For Swedenborg, 'good' people can be recognized through their willingness to work in harmony with the natural world, thereby accepting this shared destiny of souls, whereas 'evil' people remain isolated and self-centred, and through arrogance take full credit for their personal achievements. He maintained that most people have two good spirits and two evil spirits in permanent attendance.[4] Today, we might be inclined to speak of these spirits more as forces or polarities within the subconscious mind. The real message that he was conveying, however, was that every human being is subject to potent forces beyond the scope of normal ego-based awareness.

Swedenborg claimed that angels had taken him through death on several occasions, and he was able to observe in great detail what took place in the afterlife. He maintained that Heaven and Hell both exist but 'they are states rather than places.' All human beings become discarnate spirits and then, after being greeted by friends and family who have preceded them in death, they are drawn towards the good or evil realms that correspond to the true inner nature of their soul. Death is nothing other than a state of transition in which we continue to perceive

01.02 William Blake, *The Resurrection*, 1805. Blake was influenced by Swedenborg's mystical revelations. Here Christ's shroud, representing the body, has been removed to reveal the 'true man'.

and interact with other beings just as when we were alive. Many people do not even realize that they have died.[5]

In seeking passage to Heaven the apparently 'good' acts we perform in life are not in themselves sufficient; it is the character of the inner person that is really significant. Referring to the process of afterlife transition, he writes:

> Almost all of them desire to know whether they shall come into heaven, and many believe that they shall, because they led a moral and civil life in the world, not reflecting that both the wicked and the good lead a similar life outwardly, doing good to others in the same manner, going to churches, hearing sermons, and praying; and not knowing at all that outward deeds and outwards acts of worship are of no avail, but the internal states from which the external acts proceed.[6]

We will all enter the Heaven or Hell we deserve. Indeed, we are even living in these realms now, for the polarities of good and evil control our everyday lives on Earth.

Athough Swedenborg was strongly Christian, he had a universalist view of religion and believed that many different spiritual traditions had a valid interpretation of 'truth'. He claimed to have heard from the angels themselves that 'churches which are in a variety of goods and truths are like so many jewels in a king's crown.'[7] He also wrote that 'varieties in matters of doctrine and or worship are like the varieties of the senses'[8] and maintained that 'the church of the Lord consists of all those, whosoever they are, who are in truths derived from good'.[9] As Wilson Van Dusen has observed, 'Swedenborg was speaking of the heart of religion that transcends the boundaries of creeds, nations, cultures, times, people. All who act in the good that they know will be saved.'[10]

MESMERISM

Franz Anton Mesmer (1734–1815) was another major forerunner of the New Age movement. Quite apart from his role in the development of what later came to be called hypnotherapy, he advocated a life-energy approach to healing through the transmission of 'animal magnetism' to his patients, an idea that continues to flourish in a many forms of spiritual healing. And although Mesmer could not have anticipated the findings of twentieth-century quantum physics, he similarly emphasized the interconnectedness of all the heavenly bodies and natural life-forms in the universe, a holistic view now widely accepted by New Age devotees keen to explore the apparent parallels between mysticism and the New Physics.[11]

Mesmer was born in Germany, near Lake Constance, and originally intended to enter the Church. He was, however, drawn to mathematics and science, and studied medicine at the University of Vienna. Here he absorbed the prevailing sci-

01.03 Franz Anton Mesmer, engraving by von Meyer.

01.04 The act of projecting magnetism and 'mesmerizing' a patient. Engraving from E. Sibley's *A Key to Magic and the Occult Sciences*, *c.* 1800.

entific view that a magnetic fluid permeates all aspects of life. The idea of 'magnetism' as a form of vital force was an idea of long standing – Paracelsus and Van Helmont shared a belief in a fluid that pervaded the universe. In his dissertation at the University of Vienna – *De Planetarum Influxu* (On the Influence of the Planets), written in 1766 – Mesmer wrote that the sun, moon and stars not only influenced each other in a way similar to the movement of the tides, but that they also 'affect in similar manner all organized bodies through the medium of a subtle fluid, which pervades the universe and associates all things together in mutual intercourse and harmony'. For Mesmer this natural flow of energy equated with health and vitality. Blocking the flow of energy in the body would lead to disease and ill-health.

Mesmer's thesis attracted the attention of a Jesuit priest, Father Maximilian Hehl, who was court astrologer to Empress Maria Theresa, and also a professor of astronomy at the University of Vienna. Professor Hehl believed in the impact of planetary magnetism on physical health, and used magnets to 'correct' imbalances in the human organism. When Mesmer graduated from the University of Vienna, he, like Hehl, used magnetism in his medical treatments. His first patient, Fräulein Oesterlein, was an epileptic. Mesmer attached three magnets to her stomach and both legs, and was greatly encouraged when she claimed that the painful energies she had been experiencing were now subsiding to the lower part of her body. Her convulsive symptoms disappeared after six hours.

Mesmer soon discovered that he could produce equally effective cures by transmitting healing energy to his patients through touch, by pointing his forefinger or making passes over his patients with his hands, or by using iron rods or wands that he had personally 'magnetized'. He referred to this healing force as 'animal magnetism' and considered it an innate human quality – quite different from the 'mineral magnetism' utilized through Professor Hehl's magnets. Mesmer noted that during his treatments some of his patients lost control of their limbs, while others went into convulsions, began speaking in strange voices or sank into states of catalepsy or coma, but he seems to have thought that these unusual symptoms were all part of the healing process.

Not surprisingly, Mesmer fell out of favour with Professor Hehl and the Viennese medical profession. In 1778 he moved to Paris, and was soon treating large numbers of patients. Many were wealthy aristocrats, and he took care to create an ambience that would impress them. His consulting rooms were softly lit, and decorated with paintings, mirrors, clocks and crystal objects. A chamber orchestra played gentle music as he and his assistants moved among the patients, waving their wands in order to stroke and 'magnetize' the patients. Mesmer himself wore a shirt of leather, lined with silk, to prevent his personal 'magnetic fluid' from escaping from his body.

Mesmer soon had so many patients that he had to develop a method for treating them collectively. He created a device called a *baquet* – a round wooden bath tub that he filled with magnetized water and iron filings. A number of iron rod conductors protruded from the tub, and the patients were asked to hold these while also being attached by a moistened cord in a continuous circle to close 'the force'.

Mesmer's first convert in Paris was Charles d'Eslon, physician to Comte d'Artois, brother of King Louis XVI. In September 1780, impressed by what he regarded as a revolutionary approach to healing, d'Eslon asked the Faculty of Medicine to investigate Mesmer's methods. The proposal was rejected, however, and the authorities threatened that d'Eslon would be struck off the rolls if he did not recant.

Mesmer's unconventional successes continued to attract hostility from the Medical Academy. Finally, in 1784, a Royal Commission was set up by Louis XVI to investigate Mesmer and his claims of 'animal magnetism'. The Commission was chaired by Benjamin Franklin – at the time United States Ambassador to France – and included the distinguished chemist Antoine Lavoisier; Dr J.-I. Guillotin, a physician better known as the inventor of the guillotine; Jean-Sylvain Bailly, an astronomer and future mayor of Paris; and the botanist Laurent Jussieu. Mesmer declined any direct involvement, but the committee was able to investigate Mesmer's colleague Charles d'Eslon and the controversial *baquet* in operation. By this time d'Eslon had developed a technique for inducing states of trance in some of the patients. This is Jean-Sylvain Bailly's account of what he observed:

> The sick persons, arranged in great numbers, and in several rows around the *baquet*, received the magnetism by means of the iron rods, which conveyed it to them from the *baquet* by the cords wound around their bodies, by the thumb which connected them with their neighbours and by the sounds of a pianoforte, or an agreeable voice, diffusing magnetism in the air. The patients were also directly magnetized by means of the finger and wand of the magnetizer, moved slowly before their faces, above or behind their heads, or on the diseased parts. The magnetizer acts also by fixing his eyes on the subjects; by the application of his hands on the region of the solar plexus, an application which sometimes continues for hours. Meanwhile the patients present a very varied picture. Some are calm, tranquil and experience no effect. Others cough and spit, feel pains, heat or perspiration. Others, again, are convulsed.[12]

01.05 Mesmer's patients gather around a *baquet* to receive animal magnetism. Engraving *c.* 1780.

The investigating committee did not dispute that many of the patients gained great benefits from the unconventional treatment, but it established that when the patients were blindfolded and unable to tell whether or not they had been 'magnetized', nothing happened one way or the other. It therefore decided that it was the patients' own imaginations producing the healing benefits, and found no evidence to support 'animal magnetism' or the presence of a magnetic fluid. The committee recommended that members of the Faculty of Medicine who adopted Mesmer's method of healing should be expelled from professional practice.

Although Mesmer and his colleagues continued to practise magnetic healing in Paris, the report of the Royal Commission had the effect of temporarily diminishing its appeal. Nevertheless, an influential ally rescued the cause. Armand Chastenet, Marquis de Puységur, a former artillery officer who had studied with Mesmer, began demonstrating his own animal magnetism cures in Busancy in 1784, the year the Royal Commission rejected the concept out of hand. He did not employ a *baquet* but instead magnetized a tree, fastened cords around it and invited patients to tie themselves to it. Puységur also discovered he could induce a state of trance in some of his patients simply by making 'passes' over them and lulling them into what he called 'magnetic sleep'. He found that this trance could eliminate convulsions.

One of Puységur's patients, Victor, a twenty-three-year-old peasant, talked aloud while 'asleep', obeyed words or signs, and also seemed to respond to unspoken commands, but remembered nothing on waking. Puységur thought that perhaps Victor was clairvoyant, and attributed the phenomenon to animal magnetism. This was a breakthrough of a quite different order, however. As the parapsychologist Dr Nandor Fodor has observed, this represented the discovery of the somnambulistic state.[13]

Mesmer's fortunes were not helped when one of his strongest supporters, Antoine Court de Gébelin, best known for his now discredited theory that the Tarot was of Egyptian origin, died while sitting in a *baquet*. But Mesmer continued with his practice in Paris until 1789 when the French Revolution forced him to leave France. He went to Karlsruhe, and then to Vienna in 1793. He was accused of spying for France and was jailed for two months. After his release he returned to Lake Constance, dying in 1815.

After the French Revolution, interest in mesmerism was revived by a curator at the Paris Jardin des Plantes, Jean Philippe Deleuze (1753–1835). In 1812, after four years of research, Deleuze published his *Histoire Critique du Magnétisme Animal*, in which he sought to establish the reality of mesmerism and to describe how subjects behaved in a somnambulistic state. Alexandre Bertrand, a young French physician, was attracted to the study of animal magnetism through Deleuze's work. Bertrand made a study of induced trance, and published two important works, *Traité du Somnabulisme* (1823) and *Du Magnétisme Animal en France* (1826). He believed that the cures resulting from treatment in trance states derived from the suggestions of the practitioner acting on the imagination of the patient, whose suggestibility was increased while in a state of trance. This theory was supported by a Portuguese priest, Abbé J. C. Faria. He gave public demonstrations in Paris in which he put subjects into a state of somnabulistic trance, and in 1813 he also ascribed the magnetic phenomenon to the imagination. Abbé Faria and Dr Bertrand laid the basis for the later development of hypnotherapy.

THEOSOPHY: DIVINE WISDOM

A leading founder of modern occultism, Madame Helena Petrovna Blavatsky (1831–91) was born in the Ukraine, growing up on large estates near the Volga. She was the daughter of Colonel Peter von Hahn and Helena Fadeyev, a well known novelist – her mother died when she was eleven. She received no formal schooling, but learnt several languages from her grandmother, Princess Elena Dolgorukov, and was a gifted artist and pianist. She also liked to ride horses that had not yet been fully broken in. Just before her seventeenth birthday she married a widower in his forties, Nikifor Blavatsky, Vice-Governor of the Province of Erivan in Armenia. A few months later, and without consummating the marriage, she left her husband to lead the life of a bohemian.

Count Witte, in his memoir, recorded that Helena Blavatsky pursued a range of exotic activities after abandoning her marriage, among them riding horses in a circus in Constantinople, giving piano lessons in London and Paris, managing an artificial flower factory in Tiflis, and wandering around Europe with an opera singer.[14] Her travels also took her to Egypt, and when the American artist Albert Leight Rawson met her in Cairo in 1850–51, she was dressed as an Arab, smoking hashish and taking lessons from a snake charmer.[15]

In 1873, aged forty-two, now very overweight and a chainsmoker, Helena Petrovna Blavatsky arrived penniless in New York from Paris, and found accommodation in a tenement house for working women. She later claimed that she had been urged by her spiritual Masters to come to America to explore spiritualism.

At this time, two brothers, William and Horatio Eddy, were holding seances in Chittenden, Vermont, and claiming to materialize discarnate beings who had once lived on Earth. These spirits included soldiers from the Civil War and a number of drowned sailors and Native American squaws. The seances were held in a room that was dimly lit, separated from the audiences by a wooden barrier. In 1874 the New York *Daily Graphic* sent one of its feature writers, Colonel Henry Steel Olcott, to report on the Eddy brothers. Colonel Olcott (1832–1907) had been a Union officer in the American Civil War, as well as a farmer in Ohio, and then became a successful lawyer in New York while also working as a journalist. He had a lifelong interest in spiritualism and psychic phenomena, and as a youth had experimented with mesmerism.

Olcott's articles on the Chittenden seances in the *Daily Graphic* caused a sensation.[16] Madame Blavatsky read them and immediately went to visit the Eddy farm in Vermont. Colonel Olcott later recounted that when he first saw Madame Blavatsky at the Eddy residence in September 1874 he was amazed by her unconventional and ostentatious appearance. She had frizzy blonde hair and large blue eyes, and was wearing a scarlet Garibaldi blouse. She was speaking loudly to another woman in French. After dinner, when Madame Blavatsky went outside to roll a cigarette, Colonel Olcott lit it for her. As they talked, Olcott became even more interested when Madame Blavatsky told him she was a Russian aristocrat and a spiritual medium in her own right. Not only was she thoroughly familiar with what was taking place at the Eddy farm, but some of the discarnate beings had now begun speaking to her in Russian.

Back in New York, Colonel Olcott arranged to interview Madame Blavatsky for the *Daily Graphic*. She claimed to have spent three nights in the Pyramid of Cheops, and said she had also witnessed the English psychic, Daniel Dunglas Home, levitating out of a window in London – claims now thought to be fictitious. Olcott described her in the *Daily Graphic* as 'handsome, with

01.06 Madame Helena Petrovna Blavatsky and her 'chum' Colonel Henry Steel Olcott – co-founders of the Theosophical Society.

[a] full voluptuous figure, large eyes, well-formed nose and rich sensuous mouth and chin.'

Within a year Olcott, for some time estranged from his devout wife, had moved into Madame Blavatsky's apartment in New York City, taking care to point out to his friends that he was sharing her premises but not her bedroom.[17] Soon their apartment on West 47th Street became known as the Lamasery, and was a meeting place for mystical seekers, esotericists and bohemians, with a succession of parties and lectures. Madame Blavatsky was now claiming regular psychic contact with spirit guides. She referred to them as Brothers or Masters – they were similar to the beings known in India as Mahatmas ('the Great Souls'). Madame Blavatsky claimed she had met her personal guide, Master Morya, face to face at the Great Exhibition in London in 1851, although she had known him on the inner planes for many years.

To formalize their meetings and lectures, the Colonel and Madame Blavatsky formed a society to promote what she termed Theosophy, meaning 'divine wisdom'. Colonel Olcott, as president, gave his inaugural address on 17 November 1875, and Madame Blavatsky was corresponding secretary, working primarily as a channel for the spiritual Masters who would guide the new organization. The preamble to the by-laws of the Theosophical Society made it clear that the aim of

01.07 Sketch of Madame Blavatsky's spiritual guide, Master Morya.

its members was to 'obtain knowledge of the nature and attributes of the Supreme Power, and of the higher spirits by the aid of physical processes' – a well focused and practical approach to occultism and metaphysics.[18] Early members of the New York branch included the celebrated inventor Thomas A. Edison, and General Abner Doubleday, the inventor of baseball.

HPB, as she liked to be known, wrote *Isis Unveiled*, on the nature and origins of the divine wisdom itself, as a guiding credo for the Theosophical Society. Published in New York in 1877, it had taken her two years to write, and covered Neoplatonism, Pythagoreanism, Alchemy, Masonic symbolism, Hinduism and Zoroastrianism. It commended the pioneering work of Mesmer, and included references to the ancient Egyptians, the Chaldeans and the Kabbalah. It also compared the lives of Krishna, Buddha and Jesus. Although in one sense the book was a text in praise of Western Gnosis – esoteric spiritual knowledge of the sort that had become heretical with the rise of institutionalized Christianity – *Isis Unveiled* looked to the East for its ultimate source of inspiration, asserting that the wisdom of the West's profoundest mind was but a compendium of 'the abstruse systems of old India' which were thousands of years older.[19]

In *Isis Unveiled* HPB alluded to the existence of a brotherhood of adepts who continued to transmit the secret science of the ancients to those worthy of it. HPB claimed to be personally in touch with the Tibetan section of this group, and maintained that two Masters from the Great White Brotherhood – Master Morya and Master Koot Hoomi – had chosen her for her awakened intuition and far-ranging psychic powers, and had trained her as an agent through whom the wisdom of the East could be channelled to the West.

HPB, however, soon came to the conclusion that the United States was too materialistic for the new spiritual movement. She was drawn instead to India, home of the Mahatmas and the universal wisdom tradition, and she invited the Colonel to accompany her. They embarked for India via London, establishing the London branch of the Theosophical Society in January 1879. It later attracted such notable figures as the poet W. B. Yeats, the Gnostic scholar G. R. S. Mead, and Oscar and Constance Wilde.

In mid-February they were met in Bombay by the local representative of the Arya Samaj, or Society of Men of Good Will, with whom Colonel Olcott had already been in contact. Led by Dayananda Sarasvati, whom Madame Blavatsky soon declared to be an incarnation from the Great White Brotherhood, the Arya Samaj had been founded in 1875 to reform Hinduism on the basis of the Vedas, and included the young Mohandas Gandhi among its followers. Olcott and HPB at first wanted to align the Theosophical Society with the Arya Samaj – it had, after all, provided them with an opening to India – but Olcott later came to view it as too conservative, and not sufficiently 'universal'. Increasingly Olcott and HPB would find themselves drawn to Buddhism rather than Hinduism, but for the moment they were spiritually and psychologically open to all things Indian. They soon became so pro-Indian that they were perceived locally as being both anti-British and anti-European.

In October 1879, Olcott and HPB sank much of their capital into a magazine called *The Theosophist* – a journal devoted to Oriental philosophy, art, literature and occultism. The tone of *The Theosophist* was distinctly pro-Indian and equally anti-Christian, stating plainly that Theosophy was an 'ancient Wisdom-Religion dating back to Ammonius Saccas and Plotinus of the Neoplatonic School at Alexandria, and far beyond, as far back as the sacred Indian Vedas. It consisted of mystical and esoteric knowledge – brutally suppressed in the Christian era – of the 'single Supreme Essence, Unknown and Unknowable.'[20] *The Theosophist* sold surprisingly well, and helped Colonel Olcott and Madame Blavatsky make many new contacts. Local Christian missions, however, viewed the newcomers with intense suspicion.

01.08 Front cover of Blavatsky's and Olcott's journal, *The Theosophist*, October 1879.

In 1882 the Colonel and HPB bought Huddlestone's Gardens, a mansion on the banks of the Adyar River, eight miles south of Madras. Set in 28 acres of lush tropical landscape, the Adyar complex remains the world headquarters of the Theosophical Society to this day. The Colonel soon embarked on a programme of intense prose-lytizing activity, attracting many new converts to the Theosophical cause. In 1883 he established a connection with Ceylon (now Sri Lanka) to promote Theosophy. He also assisted with reforms in education and agriculture for which he is still remembered.[21]

Meanwhile, HPB and Olcott maintained that they were still in regular contact with the Masters. Olcott said that, as he travelled around India, from time to time Koot Hoomi would give him advice on a particular matter, and then vanish into thin air. For her part, Madame Blavatsky remained deeply engaged with the Great White Brotherhood. As Theosophical scholar Jill Roe has written:

Blavatsky stressed particularly the superior possibilities of Theosophy as compared with spiritualism, now proven not only narrow, but dangerous to its practitioners, amateur manipulators of powerful unseen forces. The findings of spiritualism could be comprehended only if they were recognized as but feeble repetitions of what had already been seen and studied in former epochs, indicated by a formidable collection of references to ascetics, mystics, theurgists, prophets, ecstatics, astrologers, 'magicians' and 'sorcerers' in times past.[22]

01.09 The world headquarters of the Theosophical Society on the banks of the Adyar River, south of Madras (Chennai).

In 1884, delighted with the progress of Theosophy in India, Madame Blavatsky decided to return to Europe, staying first in Nice in the palace of Marie, Countess of Caithness (who supported theosophists and occultists and also claimed to be a reincarnation of Mary Queen of Scots), and then travelling on to England. Olcott was also coming to London on behalf of the Buddhists of Ceylon. While HPB was in England, however, a scandal broke that could have been fatal for the Theosophical movement. HPB had left the Adyar headquarters in the care of Emma Coulomb and her husband Alexis whom she had first met in Cairo. Then the Coulombs had become involved in an internal quarrel at Adyar during HPB's absence, and in league with a group of Christian missionaries in Madras who were strongly opposed to Theosophy, they revealed that Madame Blavatsky's rooms at Adyar had been altered to assist her mediumistic performances and materializations. In an article published in the *Madras Christian College Magazine* in September 1884, Madame Coulomb described how she herself had been involved in a fraudulent collaboration to produce 'marvellous phenomena', helping to drop forged letters from the Mahatmas through a slit in the rafters while her husband donned robes and did Koot Hoomi impersonations.

In response, the scholarly British Psychical Research Society – established in 1882 and highly regarded for its systematic investigations of paranormal phenomena – suggested they should conduct an inquiry into the matter. With Madame Blavatsky's blessing, the Society despatched Richard Hodgson, a young Australian lawyer, to investigate. Following an examination of the premises at Adyar, Hodgson was able to confirm Madame Coulomb's claim that sliding panels had been made and that there was a hidden door linking the so-called 'shrine room', where many alleged miracles occurred, with Madame Blavatsky's bedroom. These secret entrances made possible a variety of deceptions, including claimed spirit-manifestations of flowers and the mysterious transmission of messages from Tibetan masters.

The conclusions of the Psychical Research Society were nothing less than damning: 'For our own part we regard her neither as the mouthpiece of hidden seers, nor as a mere vulgar adventuress; we think she has achieved a title to permanent remembrance as one of the most accomplished, ingenious, and interesting imposters in history.'[23] This could well have signalled the downfall of Theosophy and its co-founder, since Madame Blavatsky was undoubtedly a fraudulent medium. Nevertheless, Theosophy was very successful in introducing significant ideas into the metaphysical arena. Several have persisted to the present day, greatly influencing the New Age movement.

A sympathetic statement published in an Australian religious newspaper in 1890 provides a summary of the early Theosophical views:

> The Theosophical Society, whose headquarters are New York and Madras, is now, it appears, a large body. Its aim is the foundation of a universal brotherhood, and the study specifically of the religions and science of the East. Theosophy presupposes that beneath all the creeds and religions there lies a *secret doctrine*, which has been corrupted and lost sight of amid the materialism and unspiritualness [sic] of the religionists and the world. To restore to men this hidden treasure, and unite them on the basis of a universal religion (or Divine Wisdom) is the object of the theosophist. There are also, it is asserted, certain *psychic powers* in human nature, which have been allowed, through non-cultivation, to die out in most people, or which, in the hands of the ignorant or unscrupulous, have been abused and perverted to the ends of sorcery and the black arts. These powers a section of theosophists seek to cultivate and to use for the good of their fellow-men. Mesmerism and hypnotism they affirm are only re-discoveries of certain natural powers, and anticipations of a power possessed by man far beyond what modern science even dreams of.[24]

Madame Blavatsky clearly considered herself a spokesperson for this ancient wisdom tradition, and seems to have regarded the Masters as members of an occult hierarchy ruling the world from the inner planes, assisting devotees in finding their spiritual return to the Godhead. Theosophy also drew attention to the psychic potential of human nature, and the New Age movement continues to be concerned with new paradigms of consciousness, and with the exploration of the psychic aspects of human nature.

The article mentions the fundamental Theosophical idea that spiritual truth is found only by embracing both religion and science. Indeed, although she was opposed to the evolutionary biological determinism of Charles Darwin, Madame Blavatsky believed that the truths of religion and science could be fused to produce a grand synthesis – this was developed in detail in her major work, *The Secret Doctrine*. The idea of integrating science and spirituality was also taken up by the New Age movement many decades later.

For many years the Theosophical Society has sought to explore and promote the study of comparative religion, and it can rightly be considered the first institutional supporter of Eastern spirituality in the West. The authority on Buddhism, Christmas Humphreys, wrote in 1977:

> The original objects of the Theosophical Society were not as now. At that time the main purpose was the study of spiritualistic phenomena, while the present first and most important object, 'to form a nucleus of the universal brotherhood of humanity', only appeared at the virtual refounding of the Society in India in 1879. [In its first object] it failed. It succeeded, nevertheless, in its second object, the study of comparative religion, and the present Western interest in the study of religions, in an attempt to find the spiritual truths at the heart of all of them, comes largely from the pioneer work of the Theosophical Society.[25]

01.10 Vedanta devotee Swami Vivekananda (1862–1902), who electrified audiences in the USA with his bold oratory.

VEDANTA

The Theosophists were not alone in stressing the universal aspects of the religious experience. This was also a theme of the Indian spiritual teacher, Vivekananda (1862–1902), who first visited the United States in 1893 as a delegate to the Parliament of Religions in Chicago.

Vivekananda was the leading disciple of the great Hindu mystic Ramakrishna (1836–86), who was widely regarded in India as a saint. Ramakrishna taught Vedanta, a philosophy that draws on the Vedas, the non-dualistic philosophy of Shankara, and the yoga of Patanjali. According to Vedanta, God is both transcendent and immanent. The transcendent aspect of God is Brahman – absolute existence, knowledge and bliss beyond space, time and form. The immanent aspect of God is Atman, who dwells within man as his real Self or soul. In truth, Brahman and Atman are one.

Vivekananda first met Ramakrishna in 1881, when he was only eighteen. Significantly, Ramakrishna was not only an exponent of Vedantist non-dualism but had also explored Christian and Islamic approaches to meditation and prayer, and he believed they were all paths to the same experience of God. He therefore impressed upon his young disciple that all the major religions of the world are essentially aspects of the same universal truth.[26] In his 1893 address, Vivekananda explained that every religion had its own appointed time and place, and yet all religions belonged to a universal and eternal tradition, and he did not believe religious unity would ever come about through the triumph of one religion over another.[27]

Despite this, Vivekananda was not inclined to support the cause of Theosophy, which he referred to as the 'Indian grafting of American Spiritualism – with only a few Sanskrit words taking the place of spiritualistic jargon'. Although he avoided direct public criticism of Theosophy during his two national tours of the United States – these tours extended from 1893 to 1895 and resumed when he visited America again in 1899 to 1900 – he clearly had little interest in the popular forms of occultism and psychic phenomena that had attracted many to Theosophy. 'We are fools indeed,' he told his audience, 'to give up God for legends of ghosts or flying hobgoblins.' He later wrote scornfully that 'the Hindus have enough of religious teaching and teachers amidst themselves…and they do not stand in need of dead ghosts of Russians and Americans.'[28]

As religious scholar Hal Bridges has noted, Vivekananda's national lecture tours 'electrified large audiences with his bold oratory'.[29] Soon after his first visit to the United States the Vedanta Society was established in New York, and by 1904 there were also branches in San Francisco and Los Angeles, and centres were set up in due course in several other American cities including Boston, St Louis, Chicago and Seattle.[30]

The psychologist and philosopher William James was greatly impressed by Vivekananda's presentation of Vedanta, and made frequent references to it in his ground-breaking work *The Varieties of Religious Experience* (1902). Vedanta also transformed the lives of the British intellectuals Aldous Huxley, Gerald Heard and Christopher Isherwood, who all made their mystical pilgrimage to the United States in the late 1930s. Many believe that it was Gerald Heard who changed Huxley from a writer of novels into a mystic,[31] and after moving to Los Angeles in 1937 both Heard and Huxley were attracted to the Vedanta teachings of Swami Prabhavananda, head of the local branch of the Ramakrishna Order. Heard and Huxley were also early visitors to the Esalen Institute when it was established in Big Sur, California, in the early 1960s.[32] In something of a departure from Vedantist tradition, Huxley would also become a pioneer of the American psychedelic revolution – an early advocate of the spiritual significance of mescaline with its potential to open the mystical 'doors of perception' (mescaline is the principal alkaloid constituent in the hallucinogenic peyote cactus).

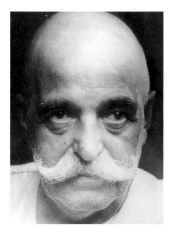

01.11 George Ivanovitch Gurdjieff (1872?–1949), instigator of the Fourth Way.

01.12 The Order of the Mevlevi, Dervish dancers, Konya, Turkey.

GURDJIEFF AND THE FOURTH WAY

George Ivanovitch Gurdjieff (1872?–1949) maintained that he was born in 1866, but according to his sister the year was 1877, and one of his biographers, J. G. Bennett, gave the year as 1872. It is generally agreed, nevertheless, that Gurdjieff was born in Alexandropol near the Russo-Turkish border. The son of a Greek father and an Armenian mother, he was brought up in a patriarchal society, and spent his early years in the village of Kars, where he would have been subject to Christian, Armenian, Assyrian, Islamic and Zoroastrian influences while he was growing up.

As a youth, Gurdjieff and a group of friends, who called themselves 'the Seekers of Truth', wandered through Central Asia and the Mediterranean, and also visited such distant places as Ethiopia, Mecca, the Gobi Desert and Tibet. In his first book, *The Herald of Coming Good*, published in 1934, he said that at this time he was driven by a yearning for 'secret knowledge'. In Central Asia Gurdjieff observed the dance practices of Sufi dervishes, and on visits to monasteries and lamasaries he paid close attention to the techniques of rhythmic breathing and

mental prayer that were part of the monks' religious practice. One of his many biographers, Louis Pauwels, says that he was influenced by the Vajrayana Buddhist tradition of Tibet, the 'Diamond Vehicle' school that developed out of Mahayana Buddhism. It fused elements of yoga with original Buddhist thought, and involved highly developed ritual practices.[33] Pauwels also said that Gurdjieff worked for a time as a tutor to the Dalai Lama.[34]

Having explored a whole range of transformative techniques and spiritual philosophies, Gurdjieff sifted out what he found useful, and began to hold study groups in St Petersburg and Moscow in 1914–15. It was here that he met Peter D. Ouspensky, a member of the Russian intelligentsia who became one of his leading disciples, and who later wrote of his encounter with Gurdjieff: 'I realized that I had met a completely new system of thought surpassing all I had known before. This system threw quite a new light on psychology and explained what I could not understand before in esoteric ideas.'[35] Ouspensky was a Theosophist, and, just before meeting Gurdjieff, had visited Adyar. Gurdjieff was opposed to Theosophists and occultists in general, regarding their beliefs and traditions as 'breeding grounds of delusion'. His approach was much more grounded and practical, although it did appear to draw on various mystical traditions and the sacred symbolism of numbers. Gurdjieff called his technique 'self-remembering', and said it would help people 'wake up' and develop spiritually. He never revealed the sources of his esoteric knowledge, but stated that his principal goal was to arouse humankind from its complacency and to help people become aware of their limitations. It was only through 'conscious labours and intentional suffering' that humanity could evolve.

The 1917 Russian Revolution caused Gurdjieff to move his study groups away from Moscow and St Petersburg, and with a small band of students, including Ouspensky and his wife, he travelled on foot across the mountains to Essentuki in the Caucasus. Within a few months, however, the war between the Red and White Russian Armies forced them to move to Tbilisi in Georgia. Here he established the Institute for the Harmonious Development of Man as a centre for his educational programme, but it was soon disbanded. Gurdjieff and his followers moved to Constantinople and then to Berlin, finally settling in France. In 1922 he acquired a large château in the Forest of Fontainebleau 65 kilometres (40 miles) outside

01.13 According to one of his biographers, Gurdjieff was influenced by the Tibetan Vajrayana Buddhist tradition. This 18th-century gilt bronze depicts Ghantapani holding the double-*vajra*.

01.14 Russian mathematician and Theosophist Peter D. Ouspensky (1878–1947), who became one of Gurdjieff's leading disciples. Ouspensky later rejected Gurdjieff's autocratic approach.

Paris. The Prieuré des Basses Loges, known simply as the Prieuré or Priory, became the new home of the Institute for the Harmonious Development of Man.

By this time Ouspensky had already left Constantinople for London. Although he admired Gurdjieff's teachings, he could no longer tolerate the Master's autocratic style. Nevertheless, he gave a series of lectures on the teachings in Britain, and encouraged those interested to go to the Priory and explore Gurdjieff's approach first hand. Another former Theosophist, A. P. Orage, did the same in New York.[36]

At his Institute, Gurdjieff formalized the activities that came to be known as 'the Work'. It was work of a very specific kind, and his followers soon found themselves engaged in hard physical labour in the house or gardens. Gurdjieff liked to keep his classes small and intimate, and conveyed the impression to his followers that they were partaking of something precious and elusive. He forbade them to talk about the Work to outsiders, and after meetings they were told to disperse quickly and quietly, like conspirators in a secret cabal. At night they were involved in sacred dances known as 'Movements', partly based on Gurdjieff's observation of Sufi dervishes in Central Asia, and intended to help his followers rid themselves of any conditioning and enhance self-awareness. Because 'self-remembering' involved cultivating a state of 'perpetual watchfulness and readiness' Gurdjieff sometimes went to the dormitory at four in the morning and clapped his hands to keep his followers 'alert'.

In 1924 Gurdjieff visited the United States for the first time, and a group of around forty of his followers gave demonstrations of the sacred Movements. Gurdjieff also provided displays of trick and genuine paranormal phenomena, and asked his audience to distinguish between the two. He made it clear that he was not engaging in acts of magic based on fear or exploitation – the only true magic involved what he called 'doing'. One of his favourite expressions was: 'Only he who can *be* can do.' His own particular form of magic was grounded in conscious self-transformation.

Gurdjieff felt that most human beings had almost limitless potential and yet suffered from a form of sleeping-sickness. He proclaimed : 'Man is a machine. All his deeds, actions, words, thoughts, feelings, convictions, opinions and habits are the result of external influences. Out of himself a man cannot produce a single thought, a single action.'[37] He thought that man was in prison: 'All you can wish for, if you are a sensible man, is to escape.'

Although Gurdjieff was capable of great kindness and warmth, and did not deny himself the comforts of tobacco, vodka and sex, there was a very confrontational side to him. He was resolute in destroying the masks behind which people hid: 'Beneath the exacting benevolence of Gurdjieff's gaze everyone was naked.'[38]

01.15 A performance of Gurdjieff's sacred dance movements (The Great Prayer), Sherbourne, England, 1973.

He also made people pay as much as they could afford when they came to the Priory because he subscribed to the view – later championed by American self-help organizations like Erhard Seminars Training (est) – that people only value what has cost them effort or sacrifice.

In 1933 Gurdjieff sold the Priory and moved to Paris, where he was based until his death in 1949. While still at the Priory, he had begun to draw his teachings together in a major work titled *All and Everything*, in which he sought to cover every aspect of human life. It reiterated his central message that man has a unique role in the cosmos, but is asleep, and only when he awakens into consciousness can his spiritual evolution begin. *All and Everything*, better known as *Beelzebub's Tales to his Grandson*, was published in 1950, a year after his death. It was soon followed by Ouspensky's *In Search of the Miraculous*, financed by English disciples who had joined the Paris group after the death of Ouspensky in 1947. The two works clearly complemented each other – the second helped clarify the first and 'opened up the teaching'. Gurdjieff's *Meetings with Remarkable Men*, which was intended as a sequel to *All and Everything*, was published in 1960, and a third, fragmentary work, *Life is Real Only Then, When 'I Am'*, was released in the early 1970s.

Gurdjieff's writing is often abstruse and complex, but certain main themes are clear. He taught that we are all capable of achieving the enlightened state he referred to as 'objective consciousness', but most of us do not know this because we are 'prisoners' in our everyday lives. He regarded the Work as a method of self-development that could help individuals liberate themselves from the heavy burden imposed by the universe itself. His view of the universe is reflected in his notion of good and evil, which is explained in Ouspensky's book *In Search of the Miraculous*:

> A permanent idea of good and evil can be formed in man only in connection with a permanent aim and permanent understanding. If a man understands that he is asleep and if he wishes to awake, then everything that helps him to awake will be *good* and everything that hinders him, everything that prolongs his sleep, will be *evil*.… But this is only so for those who want to awake.… Those who do not understand that they are asleep…cannot have understanding of good and evil.[39]

Gurdjieff also maintained that the Universe was governed by two cosmic laws – the Law of Three and the Law of Seven. The Law of Three was based on three forces: active, passive and neutral. These forces could be found everywhere in the universe, and nothing could occur without all three being present. Gurdjieff maintained that human beings have three bodies: carnal, emotional and spiritual. If people were prepared to work on themselves, they could raise themselves from being carnal to being truly spiritual.

Gurdjieff's Law of Seven, based on Pythagoras' theories of harmonics, purported to describe the succession of events in daily life. He associated it with what he called the Ray of Creation, linking this to seven notes of the musical scale and ascribing numerical values to each of the seven levels. The Law of Seven was reflected in the following cosmological structure:

	Musical Note	Numerical Value
Level of the Absolute	Do	1
Level of All Possible Systems of Worlds	Si or Ti	3
Level of our Milky Way	La	6
Level of our Sun	Sol	12
Level of Planets	Fa	24
Level of our Earth	Mi	48
Level of our Moon	Re	96

Gurdjieff taught that once the thread of occurrences (initiated by the Law of Three) had begun to take place in any given situation, the Law of Seven would begin to operate. He believed there is an orderly discontinuity in every progres-

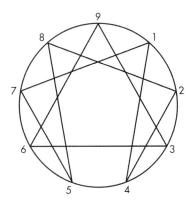

01.16 A Gurdjieff 'enneagram' encompassing the Law of Three and the Law of Seven.

sion of events. This is characterized by what he called the 'law of shock' where additional energetic input from living things would disturb an otherwise natural flow of events. To demonstrate this principle, he made use of a mystical diagram known as an enneagram, probably derived from the Sufi tradition, a circle whose circumference is divided by nine points, yielding an uneven six-sided figure and a triangle. The enneagram represents the whole universe and encompasses both the Law of Three and the Law of Seven. Man is created in an incomplete form, and has the potential to evolve to a higher octave. Points 3, 6 and 9 on the enneagram represent 'shock points' that allow this spiritual development to take place.[40]

Gurdjieff also believed that before the introduction of the Work there had been three fundamental approaches to spiritual enlightenment, each associated with three different types of man.

Instinctive man, primitive and sensual, and drawn to religious rites and ceremonies, is represented by the **Fakir**.

Emotional man, sentimental and drawn to religions involving faith and love, but also inclined to persecute heretics, is represented by the **Monk**.

Thinking man, intellectual and drawn to religions characterized by proofs and arguments, is represented by the **Yogi**.

Traditionally, if they are to attain enlightenment, the fakir, monk and yogi are all obliged to renounce the world and devote their entire energy and commitment to their own personal development. Also, in a very real sense, each has to 'die' to his past in order to achieve enlightenment in the future. Gurdjieff, however, proposed what he called the Fourth Way – the Way of the **Sly or Cunning Man** – which required that the spiritual seeker should be 'in the world but not of it'. In pursuing the Fourth Way, one could ground oneself in everyday experience, and there was no need to renounce one's human relationships in order to achieve a spiritual breakthrough. The Fourth Way also offered opportunities that were lacking in the other spiritual paths:

The fakir undergoes tremendous physical torture and reconditioning to suppress his body to his will, but has no outlet for the emotional or the intellectual. The monk possesses great faith and gives himself to his emotional commitment to God, but suffers pains of the body and intellectual starvation. The yogi studies and ponders the mysteries of life, but has no emotional or physical expression. But in the Fourth Way, people do not need to suffer physical, emotional or intellectual tortures, but merely start from their own life experiences. They work on themselves as they are, trying to harmonize all paths and using every cunning trick they know to keep themselves 'awake'.[41]

Gurdjieff's influence on the New Age movement has been considerable, and is reflected in what the American counterculture historian Theodore Roszak has called 'therapy by ordeal' – encounter groups, Gestalt therapy with its confrontational take-no-prisoners approach and other techniques of practical self-transformation that tend to focus primarily on the mechanistic aspects of human nature. These include Erhard Seminars Training (est), a training programme founded by Werner Erhard in California in 1971, which was designed to strip away the fictitious levels of the self to find out 'who one really is'. The Arica Institute, founded by Oscar Ichazo in New York in 1971, has also been strongly influenced by Gurdjieff.

It can be argued that Gurdjieff was one of the first gurus of spiritual self-help in the West. He used to say, 'Man must live till he dies', by which he meant that man should consciously labour and voluntarily suffer in order to achieve true spiritual growth – and he not only believed it, but he put it into practice. In many ways Gurdjieff was years ahead of his time.

2
Pioneers of the Psyche

At the heart of the New Age movement is the view that we must explore human consciousness if we are to gain insights into the nature of everyday reality. For this reason the New Age has drawn strongly on applied, experiential psychology as well as embracing a wide range of metaphysical and mystical beliefs. In order to understand contemporary New Age philosophies, therefore, it is necessary to consider the work of several pioneers of modern psychology, among them William James, Sigmund Freud, Carl Jung, Alfred Adler and Wilhelm Reich. Whether or not these towering figures of Western thought would have approved of the New Age movement is entirely another question. The fact is that their ideas have been absorbed into New Age beliefs, and have since acquired a separate momentum of their own.

COSMIC CONSCIOUSNESS

William James (1842–1910), the brother of the writer Henry James, helped to initiate the study of consciousness before the advent of Freudian psychoanalysis and the rise of the behaviourist school of psychology (which focuses on the observable behaviour patterns of human beings and animals). He taught anatomy, psychology and philosophy at Harvard University, and was interested in altered states of consciousness, from religious and drug-induced ecstasy through to mediumistic and psychic phenomena. His most influential publications include *The Principles of Psychology* (1890), *The Varieties of Religious Experience* (1902) and *Pragmatism* (1904).

James defined psychology in 1892 in a way that still sounds completely modern, referring to it simply as 'the description and explanation of states of consciousness'.[1] For him, individual consciousness was characterized by a process of continuous thought and everyday human awareness could be regarded as part of a much broader spectrum of universal consciousness. 'Our normal waking consciousness is but one special type of consciousness whilst all about it, parted from it by the filmiest of screens, there lie potential forms of consciousness entirely different.'[2] Influenced by Eastern mysticism, while also maintaining that he was not himself a mystic,[3] William James wrote that 'there is a continuum of

02.01 Self-portrait (*c.* 1865) of American psychologist and philosopher William James, who studied human consciousness before the advent of Freudian psychoanalysis.

cosmic consciousness, against which our individuality builds but accidental fences, and into which our several minds plunge as into a mother-sea or reservoir',[4] a view reminiscent of Vedanta. Indeed, William James was impressed by the published addresses of Swami Vivekananda, referring to them in *The Varieties of Religious Experience.*

James was especially interested in applying the systematic techniques of scientific observation to the visionary realm of the paranormal, and he was convinced that psychical research could bridge the gulf between 'impersonal science and personal reality'.[5] But he was also aware that such a marriage of ideas would require a major change of attitude among his scientific peers. His essay 'What Psychical Research Has Accomplished' (1897) drew a clear distinction between science and personal experience, and he noted that premonitions, apparitions, dreams and visions were highly significant for those who experienced them, yet these would not be investigated impartially because science itself remained 'callously indifferent to their experiences'.[6]

It is not only in relation to the visionary realms of the paranormal that there is a resonance between William James and mystical New Age thinking. As a pragmatist, he emphasized the importance of personal self-improvement, which is also a distinctive aspect of the New Age credo. He believed that all individuals had an innate ability to modify their behaviour, 'evolving' to new levels of personal attainment. He also felt that a positive attitude was vital for mental health – a viewpoint now considered axiomatic in holistic health practices – believing, like Sigmund Freud and Wilhelm Reich after him, that blocking emotional energy could result in illness.

James thought that exercising the will was vital for personal growth, and described the human will as 'the pivotal point from which meaningful action can occur'.[7] Will, as an expression of mental perception, enabled the human mind to 'engender truth upon reality' and could thereby have a meaningful impact on the world at large. For this reason, he believed that all human beings should learn to develop their willpower. 'Willing orients consciousness, so that a desired action can unfold of its own accord.'[8]

The emotional aspects of human consciousness, on the other hand, held a less exalted position in James's psychological schema. He thought it was important to keep a balance between expressing passionate feelings and retaining an almost clinical sense of detachment, and quoted Hannah Smith, who said of the emotions: 'They are not the indicators of your spiritual state but are merely the indicators of your temperament or of your present physical condition.'[9] He was well aware that emotional expressions could become excessive, or obsessive. An excess of love, for example, could manifest as possessiveness, an excess of loyalty could become fanaticism, an excess of concern could become sentimentality. Such apparent virtues, he believed, 'diminished' a person when expressed in an extreme form.

On this point James parted company from the more hedonistic aspects of the New Age movement – for example, Bhagwan Shree Rajneesh's ashram practices in Oregon during the 1980s – but he anticipated the New Age in several other ways. He distinguished three aspects of the self – the material (physical body/home/family) from the social (social roles and recognition) and the spiritual (inner being) – foreshadowing the emphasis in transpersonal psychology on the spiritual dimensions of human wellbeing. For William James the reality of the inner self was paramount, and the body was an expressive tool of the indwelling consciousness, rather than the source of stimulation itself.[10] He also supported a practice that New Age devotees would later call 'imaging' or 'creative visualization' – the technique of focusing on specific mental images in order to train and develop the will.

Twentieth-century scientific psychology was to become increasingly more reductionist and tried to explain the subtleties of human perception and brain function in terms of basic biological activity, but James believed that consciousness itself posed a mystery and that human consciousness provided a possible opening to broader and unfamiliar domains of existence and causality:

> The whole drift of my education goes to persuade me that the world of our present consciousness is only one of many worlds of consciousness that exist, and that those other worlds must contain experiences which have a meaning for our life also; and that although in the main their experiences and those of this world keep discrete, yet the two become continuous at certain points and higher energies filter in.[11]

FREUD: DREAMS AND THE UNCONSCIOUS

These days it has become rather fashionable to denigrate Sigmund Freud (1856–1939) for explaining the multi-faceted human personality primarily in sexual terms. While there is some truth in the assessment, and Freud always maintained his original position that sexuality in its various aspects is the central problem underlying psychological adjustment, his contribution to modern thought is much more far-reaching in its scope. He was the first person in the history of Western psychology to stress the importance of the unconscious mind, to systematize the study of dreams, and to distinguish certain elementary instincts. And while Freudian psychotherapy sometimes seems heavily laden with analytical concepts, Freud did not dwell on repressed sexuality and other aspects of neurosis for their own sake. In his view, the essential task of the therapist, in aiding the process of self-knowledge and personal growth, was to help the patient recover and reintegrate material from the unconscious mind and in so doing to counter psychosis and neurosis. Carl Jung said of Freud:

> His greatest achievement probably consisted in taking neurotic patients seriously and entering into their peculiar individual psychology. He had the courage to let the case material speak for itself, and in this way was able to penetrate into the real psychology of his patients.… By evaluating dreams as the most important source of information concerning the unconscious processes, he gave back to mankind a tool that had seemed irretrievably lost.'[12]

In Freudian terms, self-knowledge entails discovering who one truly is. Ilham Dilman, a noted interpreter of Freud, has observed that the process of Freudian psychotherapy involves 'not only the shedding of screens, but also the integration of what is old, and the assimilation of what is new.'[13] Like William James, Freud believed that the starting point in the study of psychology was consciousness itself, although in his view the conscious mind could only be regarded as a small part of the whole. Freud was especially interested in what he termed the 'pre-conscious' mind, which included the immediate memories readily accessible to consciousness, and the 'unconscious' mind, that vast pool of non-conscious material which included instincts and repressed memories.

At first, Freud considered physically gratifying sexual instincts and aggressive, destructive instincts the two main impulses of human life. He later changed his emphasis, contrasting life-supporting and life-denying instincts as the unresolved polarities in human nature. He described a conscious ego welling up from a formless, unorganized id – representing a kind of 'reservoir of energy for the whole personality'.[14] The life-instinct, or libido, he equated primarily with sexual energy: a support for the ego in its pursuit of pleasure and self-preservation. Freud also formulated his idea of the superego as a censor to the ego, inhibiting unwelcome thoughts and providing a sense of conscience.

According to Freud, the unconscious contents of the mind only remained unconscious at the expense of a considerable amount of libidinal energy, and the dramatic release of pent-up energies invariably provided a sense of 'explosive satisfaction'. This influenced not only Wilhelm Reich but also New Age bodywork practitioners for whom the body's musculature is a repository of tension and sexual repression. This insight also made possible the later rise of modern cathartic mind/body therapies like Bioenergetics, developed by Dr Alexander Lowen, in which individuals learn to move through their barriers of blocked emotion and are encouraged to release these pent-up energies in a supportive setting.[15]

Freud's opinion was that libidinal energy could be re-channelled from essentially sexual or aggressive goals towards artistic, intellectual or cultural pursuits. Nevertheless, he also believed that human beings are not the rational animals they think they are, but creatures driven by powerful emotional forces unconscious in origin, and he noted that the repression of these forces led to neurosis, suffering and pain. He believed in a world where, ideally, the rational ego could rise up and overcome the irrational id – he once famously declared, 'Where id is, there let ego be.'[16] He would allow no psychological accidents in human behaviour, believing that that our choice of friends, locations, favourite foods and recreational pastimes are all linked to unconscious memories and provide clues for our conscious lives. The essential task was to further self-knowledge by probing as far as possible into the unconscious mind, and Freud developed psychoanalysis specifically for this purpose: to 'liberate previously inaccessible unconscious materials so that they may be dealt with consciously'.[17]

02.02 Renowned psychoanalyst Sigmund Freud, who systematized the study of dreams. Photo taken in 1920.

In this way people could be freed from the suffering they perpetually bring upon themselves.

The related idea that we cause our own suffering, and, by extension, that we are primarily to blame for the diseases we inflict upon ourselves, is also very much a New Age belief. Blending Freud's basic concept with the Hindu teaching of karma, it has become fashionable in New Age circles to say that we all 'create our own reality' and that we should then 'take the responsibility' to liberate ourselves from the shortcomings we have unconsciously chosen. Admittedly, this is Freud simplified to the point of cliché, but it nevertheless allows us to see how the New Age movement draws on psychological concepts and adapts them to its own ends.

The practical goal of psychoanalysis is to strengthen the ego and to eliminate the unconscious blocks that cause self-destructive behaviour. The Freudian idea of personal growth is to reclaim one's life-energy from the grips of the unconscious. As Ilham Dilman puts it, 'A neurotic who has been cured has really become a different person, although at bottom of course he remains the same – that is, he has become his best self, what he would have been under the most favourable conditions.' The analyst aims to bring about the change by 'making conscious the unconscious, removing repressions [and] filling in the gaps in memory'.[18]

Dreams, in Freud's view, provided 'the royal road to a knowledge of the unconscious'. His most enduring work, *The Interpretation of Dreams*, was published in 1900, and it was this book that first drew Carl Jung into Freud's circle. It also made a strong impression on Alfred Adler, Otto Rank and Ernest Jones, all of whom were early members of Freud's psychoanalytic movement. Freud originally believed that dreams were a garbled expression of mental events, but, after formulating the concept of the id in 1897, he came to the view that we dream because the id yearns for self-expression. Sleep relaxes the ego's censoring control of the unconscious, making way for fantasies and wish-fulfilments. For Freud, all dreams – even nightmares or anxiety dreams – represented attempts to fulfil wishes, and these wish-fulfilments could stem as much from early childhood as from the day's events.

Freud also noted that in neurotic behaviour sexuality was invariably associated with repressed or suppressed wishes, and these patterns could be uncovered through dream analysis, or, as he termed it, 'dream-work'. He therefore developed the technique of talking his patients through their dreams, listening to their own 'free association' of ideas and memories, and then scrutinizing the dream reports in detail. He thought that dreams help the psyche to protect and satisfy itself, channelling unfulfilled desires through to awareness without arousing the resting physical body. Dreams allowed the dreamer to overstep the boundaries of conventional morality, but this in turn was a key to understanding their role: dreams were able to help release tension because the id made no distinction between the resolution of needs in the physical world or the dream-world.

Although dreams often appeared jumbled and distorted, Freud showed that they could be unravelled and decoded. He was inclined to look for recurring motifs in dream – long stiff objects were associated with the penis, hair-cutting with castration, boxes and chests with the womb, walking up and down steps with coitus, and so on – and for him dreams were symbolic expressions of sex-wishes.[19] It was here that he later parted company with Carl Jung. Nevertheless, Freud was the first to undertake the enormous task of unravelling the contents of the unconscious mind, and it is this more than anything that aligns him with the spirit of the New Age. And it is clear that his contribution to our understanding of the inner world of the psyche derived substantially from his evaluation of dreams. As Freud wrote in 1900:

Dreams are not to be likened to the unregulated sounds that rise from a musical instrument struck by the blow of some external force instead of a player's hand; they are not meaningless; they are not absurd; they do not imply that one portion of our store of ideas is asleep while another portion is beginning to wake. On the contrary, they are psychical phenomena of complete validity – fulfilment of wishes; they can be inserted into the chain of intelligible waking mental acts; they are constructed by a highly complicated activity of the mind.[20]

02.03 According to Freud, dreams were constructed by a 'highly complicated activity of the mind'. Grandville, *First Dream: Crime and Expiation*, woodcut, Paris, 1847.

ARCHETYPES AND THE COLLECTIVE UNCONSCIOUS

For a time Freud saw Carl Jung (1875–1961) as his chosen successor and protégé in the psychoanalytic movement. Unlike Freud, however, Jung was deeply interested in psychical research and the paranormal, and this finally became the major bone of contention between them. In his memoir, *Memories, Dreams, Reflections* (1961), Jung provides a fascinating account of his discussions with Freud:

It interested me to hear Freud's views on precognition and on parapsychology in general. When I visited him in Vienna in 1909 I asked him what he thought of these matters. Because of his materialistic prejudice, he rejected this entire complex of questions as nonsensical, and did so in terms of so shallow a positivism that I had difficulty in checking the sharp retort on the tip of my tongue. It was some years before he recognized the seriousness of parapsychology and acknowledged the factuality of 'occult' phenomena.[21]

02.04 Sigmund Freud and some of his colleagues in the psychoanalytic movement. Top row (l to r) A. A. Brill, Ernest Jones, Sandor Ferenczi. Seated (l to r) Sigmund Freud, Stanley Hall, Carl Gustav Jung. Clark University, Worcester, Massachusetts, USA, 1909. The Clark Conference introduced psychoanalysis to the American psychiatric community.

Jung soon discovered the depth of Freud's commitment to the sexual paradigm and his antipathy to metaphysical interpretations of the unconscious mind:

> I can still recall vividly how Freud said to me, 'My dear Jung, promise me never to abandon the sexual theory. That is the most essential thing of all. You see, we must make a dogma of it, an unshakeable bulwark.' … In some astonishment I asked him, 'A bulwark – against what?' To which he replied, 'Against the black tide of mud' – and here he hesitated for a moment, then added – 'of occultism'. … It was the words 'bulwark' and 'dogma' that alarmed me…that no longer had anything to do with scientific judgement; only with a personal power drive. This was the thing that struck at the heart of our friendship. I knew that I would never be able to accept such an attitude. What Freud seemed to mean by 'occultism' was virtually everything that philosophy and religion, including the rising contemporary science of parapsychology, had learned about the psyche.'[22]

Jung had originally accepted the Freudian concept of the personal unconscious, but he soon arrived at the idea of a 'collective' unconscious whose contents far exceeded the individual psyche. He also found himself increasingly dissatisfied with Freud's model of sexual repression and made the final split with him in 1912 following the publication of *Symbols of Transformation*, in which he rejected the concept of the sexual libido.

Jung viewed the unconscious mind as a repository containing much more imagery than the repressions of the individual. He also began to move away from Freud's technique of dream analysis, relying less and less on 'free association'.

Gradually Jung came to believe that Freud's method of allowing a patient to discuss dreams at random could lead away from the dream itself. For Jung each dream was complete and was expressing 'something specific that the unconscious was trying to say'. Whereas Freud tended to uncover sexual motifs in dreams, Jung regarded each dream as conveying its own message based on a specific context and situation, and he was much less interested in attempting to identify such motifs as the penis or the breast.

> A man may dream of inserting a key in a lock, of wielding a heavy stick, or of breaking down a door with a battering ram. Each of these can be regarded as a sexual allegory. But the fact that his unconscious, for its own purposes, has chosen one of these specific images – it may be the key, the stick or the battering ram – is also of major significance. The real task is to understand why the key has been preferred to the stick or the stick to the ram. And sometimes this might even lead one to discover that it is not the sexual act at all that is represented but some quite different psychological point.[23]

At the same time it was important to recognize that dreams were not random occurrences. Each dream was 'a specific expression of the unconscious' and arose because the unconscious was trying to address aspects of the personality that were fundamentally unbalanced. Nevertheless, Jung's clinical observations led him to believe that there were also certain dream-motifs of a religious or mythic nature that did not belong to the individual psyche. It was the study of these mythic motifs that gave rise to his concept of the 'collective unconscious'.

> There are many symbols that are not individual but collective in their nature and origin. These are chiefly religious images; their origin is so far buried in the mystery of the past that they seem to have no human source. But they are, in fact, 'collective representations' emanating from primeval dreams and creative fantasies. As such, these images are involuntary spontaneous manifestations and by no means intentional inventions.[24]

02.05 Carl Jung's discovery of 'mythic' motifs in the human psyche led him to formulate the concept of the collective unconscious. Here Hercules (Herakles) battles the Hydra of Lerna in an archetypal encounter. Attic black-figure Greek vase, 500–490 BCE.

Jung noted that while 'collective' symbols could manifest in individual dreams, the symbols themselves appeared to be based on 'the constantly repeated experiences of humanity' – recurrent and universal experiences embedded in the psychic patterns of the human species. He called these primordial images 'archetypes', and in 'Two Essays on Analytical Psychology' (1928), he gave an example of how an archetype is formed – the apparent daily movement of the sun has been translated into the myth of the sun hero in all its countless modifications.[25]

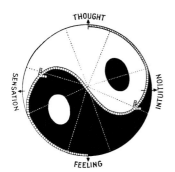

02.07 Jung employed symbols like the Taoist *yin-yang* circle to represent the dynamics of the psyche.

02.08 One of Jung's female patients produced this mandala. Jung believed it represented the archetype of the 'self'. From C. G. Jung and R. Wilhelm, *The Secret of the Golden Flower*, 1931.

02.06 C. G. Jung at his home in Bollingen, Switzerland.

'The archetypes,' he said, 'are always there and they produce certain processes in the unconscious one could best compare with myths. That's the origin of mythology. Mythology is a dramatization of a series of images that formulate the life of the archetypes.'[26] For Jung, myths were also an expression of the divine life of humanity. 'It is not we who invent myth, rather, it speaks to us as a Word of God.'[27] The archetypes had 'a kind of primeval force' that could reveal itself in religious visions and other transcendental experiences.[28] They also appeared to have their own independent existence in the psyche so that individuals who had personal encounters with them readily believed that the voice of the Divine had communicated with them directly.[29]

Jung now considered the deepest regions of the psyche to be profoundly spiritual, whereas Freud's concept of the id suggested formlessness or chaos. Jung began to explore what he believed to be the major structures of the personality. These included the persona, the person we present to the world; the ego, which includes all the conscious contents of personal experience; the characteristics of the opposite gender (the anima for men and the animus for women); and the 'shadow', a composite accumulation of repressed memories that could appear in dreams and nightmares. Jung argued that much of the fear associated with the shadow would disappear if the individual was willing to acknowledge it and draw its psychic energy into conscious awareness. Confronting the repressed aspects of the psyche remains an important dimension of Jungian psychotherapy.

Jung regarded all these aspects of the personality as archetypes in their own right, but one of the most significant was the archetype of the 'self', frequently represented by the circle or mandala. According to Jung, the 'conscious and unconscious [were] not necessarily in opposition to one another, but [complemented] one another to form a totality, which is the self'.[30] The aim of all individual self-development was therefore towards wholeness of being. Self-realization, which Jung referred to as 'individuation', simply meant 'becoming oneself' in a true and total sense.

Jung's influence on New Age thinking has been enormous – greater, perhaps, than many people realize. Jung treated dreams as direct communications from the psyche, and we find the principle of listening to the inner voice not only in New Age dream workshops, but also underlying the resurgence of inner-directed growth and visualization techniques in general. He believed that spontaneous manifestations of the psyche were highly important, and this is reflected in the free-form sketch-drawings of psychic and spiritual states that feature so prominently in many New Age workshops. And while some Jungian scholars, such as David Tacey, have portrayed contemporary New Age devotees as narcissistic hedonists unwilling to encounter the 'shadow',[31] Jung's insights on this have percolated through to the New Age movement through works by such bestselling authors as Robert A. Johnson, Shakti Gawain and Susan Jeffers.[32]

Jung's idea of the collective unconscious has encouraged many to search in myths, fables and legends for insights into the human condition, and has also led to the connection of cycles of symbolic rebirth, found in many of the world's major religions, with the process of personal individuation. Jung's focus is undoubtedly on individual transformation, and this reinforces a commonly held New Age perception that one must work on oneself first before extending the process of self-development to include others, otherwise it is simply a matter of the blind leading the blind. In the final analysis, Jung is respected by the New Age movement because he is saying that we hold our spiritual destinies in our own hands.

Jung's belief that we are all connected to the universal realm of sacred archetypes has led many to ask whether Jung was himself a mystic or a prophet of *gnosis*. He had his own response to this question. Although he found himself addressing matters of the spirit throughout his professional life, Jung continued to regard himself as an empirical scientist rather than a metaphysician: 'I am a researcher and not a prophet,' he wrote to one of his many correspondents. 'What matters to me is what can be verified by experience. But I am not interested at all in what can be speculated about experience without any proof.'[33] Elsewhere, in an essay titled 'Spirit and Life' (1928), Jung says of himself: 'Not being a philosopher, but an empiricist, I am inclined in all difficult questions to let experience decide.'[34] Nevertheless, Jung sometimes acted like a spiritual prophet. During an interview for the BBC in 1959, Jung was asked by John Freeman whether he believed in God. Jung replied that he didn't believe, he *knew* – a response clearly based on spiritual experience rather than on faith. Jung later elaborated on this point in a letter to Valentine Brooke: 'When I say that I don't need to believe in God because I "know", I mean I know of the existence of God-images in general and in particular. I know it is a matter of universal experience and, in so far as I am no exception, I know that I have such experience also, which I call God.'[35]

If Jung says he knows God, does this make him a Gnostic? After all, the word *gnosis* itself refers to a personal knowledge of the sacred and transcendent. Jung's approach to personal spiritual experience has led Jungian scholar Robert A. Segal to the conclusion that even if Jung is not a Gnostic in the classical and historical sense – that is, he did not reject the physical world as the evil creation of a misguided demiurge – he nevertheless emerges as a type of 'contemporary' Gnostic:

Like ancient Gnostics, Jung seeks reconnection with the lost essence of human
nature and treats reconnection as tantamount to salvation. For Jung, as for ancient

Gnostics, reconnection is a lifelong process and typically requires the guidance of one who has already undertaken it – the therapist functioning as the Gnostic revealer. Knowledge for both Jung and ancient Gnostics is the key to the effort, and knowledge for both means self-knowledge. In these respects Jung can legitimately be typed a Gnostic. He is, however a contemporary Gnostic because the rediscovered essence is entirely human, not divine, and lies entirely within oneself, not within divinity as well.[36]

The Reverend Don Cupitt, theologian and Chaplain of Emmanuel College, Cambridge, has a more direct way of explaining Jung's relationship with the realm of the Spirit. In the Jungian approach, says Cupitt, 'the real encounter with God is the encounter with your own unconscious. Religious experience is the psyche's own struggle towards integration.'[37]

ADLER AND LIFE-GOALS

02.09 Alfred Adler, founder of the Association for Individual Psychology. Adler emphasized self-improvement and 'life-goals'.

Alfred Adler (1870–1937) was born in Vienna and studied medicine at the University of Vienna, graduating in 1895. One of the first four members of Freud's circle, he was recommended by Freud as the first president of the Viennese Psychoanalytic Society. By the following year, he had developed views that Freud found unacceptable, and he resigned his position. Adler then founded the Association for Individual Psychology, which achieved widespread recognition in Europe, but he was forced to flee the rise of Nazism, emigrating to the United States in 1932.

Adler's formulation of Individual Psychology, like Jung's concept of individuation, has had a major impact on humanistic psychology, and this in turn has influenced the New Age movement. His thinking, reinforced by tragedies and struggles in his own life, focused strongly on the idea of self-improvement. He thought that all healthy, motivated individuals should develop their own capacities and potential. 'The striving for perfection is innate, in the sense that it is part of life.'[38] Adler took up Darwin's thesis of the adaptation of living forms to the environment, and said that 'life-goals' should be a focus for individual achievement in overcoming life's obstacles. Life-goals, he believed, generally served as a defence against feelings of impotence, as a bridge from the unsatisfying present to a bright, powerful and fulfilling future.[39]

Adler emphasized individualism even more than Jung, ascribing to each human being such qualities as uniqueness, genuine awareness and an ability to take control of one's own life – aspects he felt Freud had not put to the fore. He was convinced, in fact, that we can mould our own personalities, a belief that has continued, in force, in the New Age. 'Every individual', he said, 'represents both a unity of personality and the individual fashioning of that unity. The individual is thus both the picture and the artist. He is the artist of his own personality.'[40] For him, all human behaviour was ultimately social – one had to develop a sense of fellowship within the community, a feeling of kinship which would ultimately embrace all humanity. Adler moved the emphasis from individual self-growth towards contributing to the community:

> Psychological growth is primarily a matter of moving from a self-centred attitude and the goal of personal superiority to an attitude of constructive mastery of the environment and socially useful development. Constructive striving for superiority plus strong social interest and co-operation are the basic traits of the healthy individual.[41]

Two philosophers who influenced Adler also held views that presaged New Age thought. The first was Hans Vaihinger who subscribed to the interesting view that people are more affected by their future expectations in life than they are by past experiences – a completely different slant from Freud's. He saw human behaviour as a fiction based on personal conceptualizations of the world. This coloured Adler's concept of life-goals, and is also reflected in the New Age dictum that the way we see ourselves has an effect on the person we finally become: ultimately our thoughts create our reality.

The second was Jan Smuts, the distinguished statesman and field-marshal who was twice Premier of the Union of South Africa between 1919 and 1948. He was deeply interested in science and philosophy and he and Adler corresponded. In his book *Holism and Evolution* (1926), Smuts took the unorthodox scientific view that there is a tendency in Nature to produce wholes that cannot be explained in terms of the sum of their parts. He thought there was always an impulse towards greater organization in Nature, and within all individuals an innate movement towards wholeness. Adler made holism an integral part of his Individual Psychology, defining the self as the personality viewed as an integrated whole. He wrote: 'The foremost task of Individual Psychology is to prove this unity in each individual – in his thinking, feeling, acting; in his so-called conscious and unconscious – in every expression of his personality.'[42]

REICH AND SEXUAL ENERGY

Among the other pioneers of psychology who have influenced the New Age, Wilhelm Reich (1897–1957) must be acknowledged. His concepts of sexual energy and body armouring continue to influence contemporary holistic body-work practices, and Reich himself represents a tangible link between the early

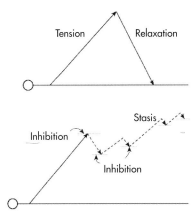

02.10 Wilhelm Reich explored the relationship between sexual energy, human behaviour and health. Photo taken in his laboratory in Rangeley, Maine, late 1940s.

02.11 Sketch diagrams by Reich showing the relationship between tension and relaxation (above) and inhibition and stasis (below).

days of Freudian psychoanalysis and the body/mind frameworks adopted by the New Age.

Reich studied medicine at the University of Vienna, qualified in 1922, and then went to work with Sigmund Freud. As with Jung and Adler before him, Reich's views soon began to diverge from Freud's. Moreover, Freud refused to give Reich personal analysis and did not share his strong Marxist leanings. Nevertheless, a strongly Freudian flavour characterizes much of Reich's thinking on sexual energy, although he developed his theories in relation to the body rather than the mind.

Reich believed in the concept of 'bioenergy flow' through the body and considered that repression of the emotions and sexual instincts could lead to 'blockages' resulting in rigid patterns of behaviour (character armour) and the tightening of specific muscle groups (body armour). As such blockages increased, the energy flow in the organism was impeded, and in chronic instances led to a marked deterioration of health. For Reich, as for Freud, sexual energy was the very essence of human existence. The climax of orgasm was a completely satisfying release from tension in which sexual energy was discharged in an act of physical love. Reich later drew up his formula of 'biological tension and charge' which involved four stages:

mechanical tension
bioenergetic charge
bioenergetic discharge
relaxation

He noted, too, that the full orgasm had an almost transcendent quality, involving loss of ego and a profound sense of peace. By contrast, people who felt guilty in sexual expression worked against the current of bioenergy, or 'orgone energy' as he called it, and produced frustrations and emotions that were subsequently repressed. This brought with it the neurotic, negative behaviour that Reich termed 'character armouring'. Sexual energy produced an effect on the autonomic nervous system, which controls the involuntary functions of the body, such as peristaltic action and the heartbeat. While a healthy organism normally exhibited patterns of contraction and expansion – a rhythm of life – in the case of an 'armoured' organism there was a permanent state of contraction. Reich was appalled by the fact that mass neurosis appeared to be the norm in Western society, derived primarily, he thought, from defences against the free flow of sexual energy.

Reich's therapy is a dismantling of layers of pent-up emotion. He divided the body into seven zones at right-angles to the spine, and centred in the eyes, mouth, neck, chest, diaphragm, abdomen and pelvis (including the legs). Reich believed that orgone energy was bound up in chronic muscular spasms and that it was necessary to free this energy progressively. Reichian 'bodywork' therapy entails dissolving the armour, beginning with the eyes and working down the body. Several methods are used:

Deep breathing
Breathing conforms to patterns proposed by the therapist. The patient may feel the stream of bioenergy in the form of prickling or tingling sensations.

Deep massage
Pressure is applied to muscle spasms. Sometimes such areas of tension are pinched to loosen them up.

Facial expressions
The patient 'makes faces' expressing certain emotions while retaining eye-contact with the therapist and maintaining certain patterns of breathing.

Chest-work
The therapist pushes down on the chest while the patient exhales or screams. Such bodywork is designed to remove blockages to breathing.

Convulsive reflex-work
Convulsions break down armouring. The therapist may work with the disruptive effects of coughing and yawning.

Stress positions
Stress positions may be maintained to produce an effect of bodily irritation. This may lead in turn to tremors which similarly break down the body armour.

Active movements
The therapist may encourage the patient to kick and stamp and move parts of the body vigorously as a 'loosening up' exercise.

In general, Reichian therapy penetrates from the outer, accessible layers of armouring through to the deeper levels. Reichian therapists believe it is important that such probing occurs at a pace that the patient can handle. Different effects are noted in each of the body segments:

The eyes
The eyes may appear dull and lifeless. The patient is encouraged to roll them from side to side and perhaps open them wide, as if in a state of sudden amazement.

The mouth
This area includes the muscles of the chin, throat and back of the head. The patient may be asked to cry, shout or suck, or move the lips in various ways, in order to loosen up the muscles concerned.

The neck
Screaming and yelling may be used intentionally to free up tensions.

The chest
Any armouring in this region will show up when the patient breathes or laughs. Inhibition of breathing is a means of suppressing the emotions and may require the use of special gestures involving the arms and hands.

The diaphragm
Armouring tends to reveal itself via body posture in this segment. The spine may curve forward, constricting outward breath. Such armouring is loosened with breathing exercises and the so-called 'gag reflex'.

The abdomen
This segment includes the back and abdominal muscles which are often tense if a person is defensive. Armouring is loosened up in these muscle regions.

The pelvis and lower limbs
With strong armouring the pelvis is pulled back and may stick out, revealing signs of deep-seated repressed anxiety. There is also a tightening of the pelvis, inhibiting sexual expression and pleasure. The patient may be asked to strike the couch with the pelvis region or kick the feet until a sense of freedom in this region develops.

Reichian therapy seeks to do for the body what Freudian psychoanalysis seeks to do for the mind. Reich's approach has been a major influence on New Age body-work therapies, including Bioenergetics, Rolfing and the Feldenkrais method of Awareness Through Movement – all therapies that have played a distinctive role in the personal growth movement pioneered by Esalen Institute and other experiential holistic health centres. Reichian therapy provides further evidence of the way in which the work first undertaken by Freud and his former associates continues to flow through to the New Age movement.

3

Towards the Transpersonal

While Wilhelm Reich's contribution to bodywork provides a link between the early schools of psychology and the rise of the personal growth movement, another development in psychology also had a major role to play. This was the emergence of the 'humanistic' school and its offshoot, transpersonal psychology.

Transpersonal psychology is sometimes referred to as the 'fourth force' following Freudian psychoanalysis, behaviourism (which concentrates on 'conditioned responses') and humanistic psychology. As its name suggests, transpersonal psychology refers to states of being beyond the ego. It seeks to broaden the traditional scope of psychological enquiry, taking in such studies as the nature of holistic wellbeing, peak religious and mystical experiences, the experiential psychotherapies, and the wisdom traditions of East and West. Humanistic and transpersonal psychology both emerged as a response to the reductionist and mechanistic approach of behaviourism.

The literal meaning of the term psychology is the study of the *psyche* – that is to say the study of mind, consciousness or 'soul'. In the early years of the twentieth-century, however, American and European psychologists wanted to be seen as truly scientific, and increasingly attempted to measure, validate and objectify. As a consequence, the discipline of psychology began to turn away from the intangibles of human experience, such as emotions, feelings, intuition and aesthetic values – intangibles that William James had been willing to explore – and there was more emphasis on the aspects of human behaviour that could be measured.

The pioneering American behaviourist John B. Watson focused on objectivity in the study of psychology. He denied that consciousness actually existed and claimed that all forms of learning were dependent on the external environment. He also believed that all aspects of human activity were conditioned, regardless of genetic make-up. He defined psychology as follows:

Psychology as the behaviourist views it is a purely objective branch of natural science. Its theoretical goal is the prediction and control of behaviour. Introspection forms no essential part of its methods.... The behaviourist, in his efforts to get a unitary scheme of animal response, recognizes no dividing line between man and brute.[1]

The behaviourist approach was consolidated by the Russian physiologist Ivan Pavlov's work on controlling behaviour and conditioning, and by the American psychologist B. F. Skinner's concepts relating to conditioning and reinforcement as part of learning theory. Skinner rejected the concept of the 'personality', arguing that this was simply a collection of behaviour patterns, as were the emotions and intellect. He did not think that the notion of the 'self' was essential in analysing behaviour, and believed that any idea of self-knowledge was a convenient fiction. 'There is no place in the scientific position', Skinner wrote in 1974, 'for a self as a true originator or initiator of action.'[2]

With the development of phenomenology (a philosophy that allowed that it was as legitimate to draw data from the imagination as from the objective world),[3] and the rise of transpersonal research and the experiential psychotherapies in the 1970s, however, Skinner's approach began to look less and less complete. The Californian-inspired personal growth movement – sometimes referred to in the late 1960s and early 1970s as the Human Potential Movement – can be seen in part as a response to the limitations of behaviourism. The movement consisted substantially of people intent on uncovering the motivating forces that reflected and influenced human behaviour – habitual patterns, fears, intuitions, repressions – and how these interactions worked. Personal growth seemed then, as it

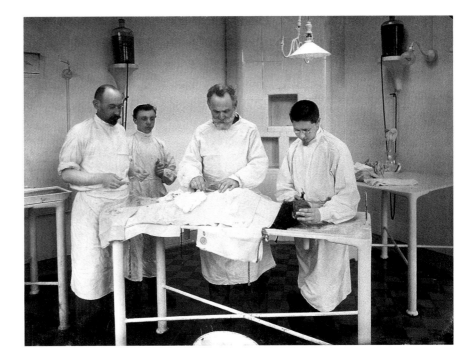

03.01 Russian physiologist Ivan Pavlov consolidated the behaviourist approach to scientific methodology. Here he is seen operating on a dog in the Imperial Institute of Experimental Medicine, St Petersburg, 1902.

does now, to be very much about understanding inner states of being as well as modifying outer forms of behaviour.

HUMANISTIC PSYCHOLOGY

Humanistic and transpersonal psychology owe their development to Abraham Maslow (1908–70) and Anthony J. Sutich (1907–76). Their interest in creative and spiritual values as part of the definition of a human being led to a psychological approach that has continued to thrive on a more popular level in the New Age movement.

Abraham Maslow was born in New York in 1908, the son of Jewish immigrants from the Russian city of Kiev, and received his PhD in 1934 at the University of Wisconsin. He returned to New York to study at Columbia University, and then joined the psychology faculty at Brooklyn College. Maslow had been taught by several distinguished psychotherapists, including Erich Fromm, who sought to combine Freudian and Marxist frameworks; Alfred Adler; and neo-Freudian psychiatrist Karen Horney, a well known advocate of self-analysis (who was a key mentor during the 1930s and '40s). He was also strongly influenced by Max Wertheimer, a founder of Gestalt psychology, and later he had contact with Viktor Frankl, author of *Man's Search for Meaning* (1963), and psychologist Rollo May. In 1952 Maslow moved to the newly established Brandeis University as chairman of the first psychology department, and stayed at Brandeis until 1968. Maslow spent the last two years of his life in the Bay Area of California as a Fellow of the W. P. Laughlin Foundation, which specialized in developing humanistic approaches to business management and organization.

By the time he joined the faculty at Brandeis University, Maslow was strongly opposed to the behaviourist frameworks that dominated most American psychology departments in the 1950s. In 1954 Maslow began to draw up a mailing list of other psychologists around the country who shared his own personal interests and were concerned with such issues as creativity, love, self-actualization and personal growth. Three years later the list still held fewer than a hundred and twenty-five names.

Maslow drew on cultural anthropology and neuropsychiatry, but he was also influenced by Gestalt psychology (the underlying principle of which is that an analysis of parts does not lead to an understanding of the whole), and he was similarly strongly holistic in his approach. Like Jung and Adler before him, he stressed that the human organism should be viewed in terms of its total potential. He developed his 'hierarchy of needs', which included physiological considerations like hunger and sleep; safety (stability and order); belonging and love (family and friendship); and esteem (self-respect and recognition). This hierarchy culmi-

03.02 Abraham Maslow regarded creativity and spiritual values as important dimensions.

03.03 Diagram of Maslow's 'hierarchy of needs'.

SELF-ACTUALIZATION
Pursue Inner Talent
Creativity Fulfilment

SELF-ESTEEM
Achievement Mastery
Recognition Respect

BELONGING-LOVE
Friends Family
Spouse Lover

SAFETY
Security Stability
Freedom from Fear

PHYSIOLOGICAL
Food Water
Shelter Warmth

nated in the need for self-actualization, or, as he defined it, 'the full use and exploitation of talents, capacities [and] potentialities'.[4] He was also very interested in the types of people capable of self-actualization, and found that they tended to be spontaneous and independent, given to deep relationships, democratically inclined, creative, and able to rise above cultural limitations. He also found that self-actualizers were capable of having mystical or peak experiences.

Maslow's particular research focus was to evaluate people who seemed healthy and creative. He felt that unhealthy, psychologically unbalanced or mal-adjusted people did not provide adequate research data relating to the true nature of human potential in terms of personal growth; on the other hand, self-actualization had everything to do with it. Maslow thought it was vital to transcend the distorting images we have of ourselves and overcome the defence mechanisms that hide the real person inside. No one could 'choose wisely for a life unless he dares to listen to himself, his own self, at each moment in life.'[5]

The other key figure in the emergence of humanistic and transpersonal psychology was Anthony Sutich. He was not an academic in the strict sense of the word and he came to think of himself as a 'maverick psychotherapist'. He brought with him, however, a profound interest in spiritual and mystical concerns.

Sutich had developed progressive rheumatoid arthritis following an accident when he was twelve. By the time he was eighteen he was totally physically disabled, and his formal education had already finished three years earlier. The remainder of his life was spent for the most part on a gurney – a four-wheeled stretcher fitted with a telephone, reading stand and other devices. Despite this setback, Sutich continued to function very effectively. He talked to nursing staff about their personal problems, and soon acquired a reputation as a trusted friend and counsellor. For many years people came to him in hospital seeking advice, and in 1938 he was asked to become a group counsellor for the Palo Alto Society for the Blind. In 1941 he began a full-time private practice in both individual and group counselling.

Sutich also became involved in political and social issues related to the labour movement and worked as a Serbo-Croat translator for the State Department during World War II. He had a long-standing interest in both Western and Eastern religion – especially the latter. He read widely in the fields of Yoga, Vedanta, Theosophy and Christian Science, and was interested in psychedelic and mystical states of consciousness. As he wrote in a dissertation presented shortly before his death, 'I myself had had a mystical experience, or something like one, several times, with and without psychedelic substances, as early as 1935.'[6]

Sutich was already familiar with the spiritual philosophies of Ramakrishna and Vivekananda, and was able to travel in his especially adjusted car to seminars on psychology and mysticism. He was especially impressed by Ashokananda of the San Francisco Vedanta Society, who lectured on 'the strong case for the value and validity of scientific investigation directed toward the inner realm of human potentialities, especially the spiritual potential'.[7] In the summer of 1948 he attended a series of lectures by Krishnamurti at Ojai, California, but found the Indian thinker's 'vague generalities' about 'Reality' disappointing. 'He struck me as a cold, detached, rather negative person', wrote Sutich later. 'It was his lack of warmth and humorless manner that made me feel that something was lacking in Eastern mysticism.'[8]

Reading Akhilananda's *Hindu Psychology: Its Meaning for the West* (1946), however, rekindled his interest in mysticism, while at the same time he began to feel increasingly alienated by the rising wave of behaviourist psychology at nearby Stanford University. He would often test the attitudes and expressions of his clients, and he began to think very much in terms of their 'psychological growth'. Few of his colleagues used terms like this in their practices.

Sutich was particularly keen on group therapy which emphasized spiritual as well as emotional development and he was delighted when he heard about Maslow's work. He decided to write to Maslow in November 1948:

> I understand that you have recently been working on something that has been vaguely described to me as the 'extremely well-adjusted personality'; alternatively, the 'super-normal personality'. The reference to your work came up as a result of my exploratory and experimental counselling work on what I call the 'growth-centred attitude' ('growth-conscious' or 'growth-minded') as the 'core' of a 'full-valued personality'.[9]

Maslow did not reply directly, but in March 1949 he visited Berkeley and one of Sutich's clients arranged for the two to meet. It was a friendly meeting, and on Maslow's recommendation Sutich submitted an article to the *Journal of Psychology* entitled 'The growth-experience and growth-centred attitude', which was accepted for publication. Between 1949 and 1957 Sutich had little further contact with Maslow, but he did attend a lecture at Stanford University where he noted that there was strong opposition from Ernest Hilgard's behaviourist Department of Psychology to Maslow's idea of self-actualization.

In 1952 Sutich met the expatriate British writer Alan Watts, and this once again renewed his interest in mysticism and psychotherapy.

> The more I talked with him, the more I read about mysticism. In addition to Watts' books I read everything in mysticism I could get hold of. This carried me into the

03.04 'The spirit of Zen is everywhere'. The circle represents the totality of the universe and its ultimate void. Zen Buddhist calligraphy image, *Circle*, by Zen Master Sengai.

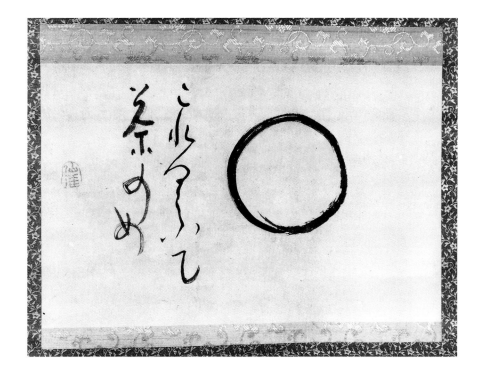

works of Sri Aurobindo (1948), Besant (1897), Blavatsky (1927), the *Bhagavad Gita* (Isherwood, 1947), Muller (1899), the *Upanishads* (Radhakrishnan, 1953) and a variety of books dealing with yoga.'[10]

Sutich began to help Watts with various counselling techniques, and was very interested when Watts said he intended combining these methods with Zen Buddhism. Watts felt he could apply 'non-directive counselling', the main idea being 'to help those who run into certain kinds of paradoxes or contradictions'. Sutich and Watts also discussed the idea of *satori* – the Zen experience of sudden enlightenment – in some detail.

Zen Buddhism had first arrived in the USA in 1930 with the foundation of the First Zen Institute of America, followed in 1931 with a Zen centre in Los Angeles. Alan Watts had already published *The Spirit of Zen* in Britain in 1936 – a popularization of the works of Buddhist scholar Daisetz T. Suzuki, who was a professor of religion at Columbia University, New York from 1951 to 1957, and whose books would become very influential in the USA in the 1950s and 1960s.[11]

Sutich took an interest in Maslow's list of psychologists who shared his views on peak experiences and self-actualization, and later reflected upon it as the very basis of the new humanistic psychology. 'The mailing list,' he commented, 'was like the Committee on Correspondence that played such an important part in the history of the American Revolution.'[12] He noticed, however, that even though the mailing list was growing, no substantial inroads were being made against the behaviourists, who still dominated the academic journals. Maslow, who had recently had an article on peak experiences turned down by the *Psychology Review*, urged Sutich to start a new journal on all the aspects of human potential that were being ignored by mainstream psychology. It was proposed to call it *The Journal of Ortho-Psychology* (from the Greek *ortho*, 'to grow straight'), and Maslow suggested the following statement of purpose:

> The *Journal of Ortho-Psychology* is being founded by a group of psychologists who are interested in those human capacities and potentialities that have no systematic place either in positivistic or behaviouristic theory or in classical psychoanalytic theory, e.g. creativeness, love, self-actualization, 'higher' values, ego-transcendence, objectivity, autonomy, responsibility, psychological health, etc. This approach to psychology can also be characterized by the writings of Goldstein, Fromm, Horney, Rogers, Maslow, Allport, Angyal, Buhler, Moustakas, etc. As well as by certain aspects of the writings of Jung, Adler and the psychoanalytic ego-psychologists. While the point of view of this 'Third Force' in psychology has not yet been synthesized, unified or systematized, nor is it yet as comprehensive as the Freudian or Behaviouristic systems, it is our feeling that this can come to pass, and probably soon will....[13]

At this time Maslow numbered among his sympathizers not only the distinguished figures listed above but also Rollo May and Gardner Murphy, both noted psychologists. Articles for the new journal began to arrive from March 1958, and then social philosopher Lewis Mumford, and Erich Fromm joined the Board of Editors. There were difficulties with the title, however, because it clashed with *The American Journal of Orthopsychiatry*. In December 1959 Maslow's son-in-law, Stephen Cohen, proposed that the journal should be renamed *The Journal of Humanistic Psychology*. Soon afterwards, the American Association of Humanistic Psychology and the journal were established under the auspices of Brandeis University.

In 1962, Maslow wrote to Sutich about an exciting new contact he had made. Fellow Stanford psychology graduates Michael Murphy and his friend Richard Price had established a centre called the Esalen Institute in Big Sur, California, south of Monterey. 'They are planning a conference centre there devoted, among other topics, to just the things you are interested in'; he added: 'By the way, I suggested you as a teacher to them.'[14] Murphy invited Sutich down as a guest once things were established. 'We are planning seminars and conferences for next fall and beyond and so are gathering ideas,' wrote Murphy. 'I have written to several people already, asking them to suggest ideas and people who would be good

03.05 *Dragon's Tail*, a fractal geometry image from the Mandelbrot set. These mathematically generated images extend into infinity and evoke a sense of timeless wonder and spiritual awakening.

leaders. One interest we hope to develop is the inter-disciplinary approach to human nature – getting people together who usually don't get together.'[15]

BEGINNINGS OF THE TRANSPERSONAL MOVEMENT

In one of his information newsletters circulated at Esalen Institute in May 1965, Michael Murphy posed a question that would become central to the transpersonal perspective as a whole: 'What is the fundamental growth process,' he asked, 'which takes the human organism beyond its present situation into the yet unrealized potential of its particular future?'[16]

In January 1966 a seminar on humanistic theology was held at Esalen, attended by a number of Jesuit theologians as well as leading humanists, among them psychologist James Fadiman, Stanford engineering professor Willis Harman and, of course, Anthony Sutich. One of the lecturers at the seminar asked the Jesuits whether they had ever had a mystical experience and whether it was Church policy to encourage attainment of that experience. To both questions the answer was 'No', and Sutich recalled that he was very surprised.[17]

Shortly after this seminar, Sutich attended two further meetings at Big Sur – on the limitations of humanistic psychology. He began to feel that the original idea of self-actualization was no longer comprehensive enough, and he expressed these views in a letter to Maslow in August 1966, noting that a humanistic therapist could hardly avoid the issue of 'ultimate goals' and mystical experiences. Accordingly, the therapist should also be able to help his client develop techniques for awakening these faculties. 'Esalen and other places and processes', he added hopefully, 'may become at least the American equivalent of Zen monasteries. The residential program that has just begun at Esalen may be a more concrete example of what may develop eventually throughout the country.'[18]

Increasingly, Sutich felt inclined to blend mysticism and humanistic psychology. He even proposed a new term, 'humanisticism', but Maslow pointed out that the British biologist Julian Huxley was already using a comparable expression, 'trans-humanistic', with the same idea in mind. Ever keen on new publications, Sutich suggested to Maslow in February 1967 that a new journal should be founded: a *Journal of Transhumanism* or *Transhumanistic Psychology*. Sutich also wrote to Julian Huxley requesting a detailed definition of the new term.

Meanwhile on 14 September 1967, in an address to the San Francisco Unitarian Church entitled 'The Farther Reaches of Human Nature', Maslow made the first reference to what he called the new 'Fourth Force', a school of psychology dedicated to the transformation of human life. Fond of delineating specific objectives, Sutich proposed to Maslow a more complete definition of the new school:

Transhumanistic (or Fourth Force) Psychology is the title given to an emerging force in the psychology field by a group of psychologists and professional men and women from other fields who are interested in those ultimate human capacities and potentialities and their actualization that have no systematic place in either the First Force (classical psychoanalytical theory), Second Force (positivistic or behaviouristic theory), or Third Force (humanistic psychology which deals with such concepts as creativity, love, growth, basic need-gratification, psychological health, self-actualization, etc.). The emerging 'Fourth Force' is specifically concerned with the study, understanding, and responsible implementation of such states as being, becoming, self-actualization, expression and actualization of meta-needs (individual and 'species-wide'), ultimate values, self-transcendence, unitive consciousness, peak experiences, ecstasy, mystical experience, awe, wonder, ultimate meaning, transformation of the self, spirit, species-wide transformation, oneness, cosmic awareness, maximal sensory responsiveness, cosmic play, individual and species-wide synergy, optimal or maximal relevant interpersonal encounter, realization, and expression of transpersonal and transcendental potentialities, and related concepts, experiences and activities.[19]

It was certainly a complex and long-winded definition, but Sutich was not without a sense of humour, and, as a playful aside to his statement – which surely must rank as one of the earliest descriptions of what later became the New Age – he added, 'How's that for a nice ride on "Astro-Bike" or perhaps better still, "Inner Space Bike"!'

In November 1967 Maslow wrote suggesting that the word 'transpersonal' might be the best expression of all. 'The more I think of it, the more this word says what we are all trying to say, that is, beyond individuality, beyond the development of the individual person into something which is more inclusive than the individual person, or which is bigger than he is.'[20] The term 'transpersonal' had already been used by Czech psychiatrist Dr Stanislav Grof – later to become scholar-in-residence at Esalen Institute – during a lecture in Berkeley two months earlier, and this finally carried the day. It was generally agreed that it was the most appropriate term for describing a psychology dedicated primarily to 'the advancement of mankind'.

There was now a sense that something really exciting was about to unfold – a study of the depths of human nature, the possibility of a new scientific synthesis of knowledge relating to relationships, self-realization and transcendental potentialities. As Maslow's biographer, Edward Hoffman, has observed, 'soon terms like *peak-experience* and *self-actualization* began to penetrate the popular vocabulary and help shape the zeitgeist of 1960s America'.[21] And the following decade indeed saw the full flowering of what became known as the Human Potential Movement – a significant precursor of the New Age – coinciding especially with the increasing influence of Esalen Institute in Big Sur and the rapid development of personal growth centres around the United States. There could be no doubt about it, a new era was beginning.

4
Esalen, Gestalt and Encounter

04.01 The Lodge at Esalen Institute, Big Sur, California.

04.02 The Big House at Esalen. In the early days Hunter S. Thompson took up residence here.

North of San Simeon, the Californian coastline becomes increasingly craggy and precipitous. Highway 1 soon transforms into a narrow, winding road with spectacular cliff-edges falling away to the left and the sudden and dramatic Santa Lucia mountains rising up on the right. Much of the terrain is rugged and severe, although wildflowers and lichen flash colour here and there, and there are pockets of beautiful greenery – regal cypresses growing on impossible ledges, above sharp rock spurs jutting out above the crashing sea.

Big Sur is only superficially tamed by human presence. Highway 1, completed in 1937, even now is often blocked by falls of stone or pockets of fog which roll in from the ocean. It is a route that dictates its own pace, and drivers wind carefully round the seemingly endless successions of hairpin bends, ever aware of the precarious balance between human life, cliff-edge and ocean.

The Spanish called this region after the river El Rio Grande de Sur, and the jagged, weaving coastline extends for some eighty kilometres (fifty miles), almost as far north as Carmel and Monterey. The town of Big Sur itself is still only a small settlement, famous mostly for its Nepenthe Inn, a vegetarian restaurant with impressive wooden sculptures and a wonderful view to the south. One of Big Sur's most famous residents was the controversial novelist Henry Miller, who first visited in 1944 and lived as a recluse in the region for over twenty years.

Esalen Institute, once known as Slate's Hot Springs, is located between Big Sur township and the charming hamlet of Lucia. It, too, rests on the cliff-edge. A place of considerable natural beauty, it is now part of local folklore, and has had much to do with the rise of the new consciousness. The land was acquired in 1910 by Henry Murphy, a doctor from Salinas, and he built the Big House as a holiday home. By the late 1950s, however, the grounds had fallen into disrepair, and Slate's Hot Springs was visited mostly by Henry Miller and his circle of bohemian friends. Old Dr Murphy had long since died and the Big House was being maintained by a young macho writer named Hunter S. Thompson. Nothing much was happening except occasional brawls among the locals.

In 1962, however, Dr Murphy's son Michael and Zen Buddhist enthusiast Richard Price drove down to the property to have a look at it. They came up with

04.03 The spectacular rugged coastline of Big Sur, California.

an idea that was to have far-reaching consequences – Big Sur Hot Springs, as it was now called, could be a meeting place for different spiritual traditions and for the exploration of consciousness. Philosophers, writers and mystics could impart their knowledge and share their experiences. It might become a very special place. The spirit of Esalen was born, although the Springs were still known by their old name for three more years. The Lodge, a meeting room up the hill from the Big House, became the centre for seminars, and early visitors associated with the Institute included Alan Watts, Aldous Huxley, Vedanta enthusiast Gerald Heard, writer Ken Kesey, folksinger Joan Baez, parapsychologist J. B. Rhine, shamanic practitioner Carlos Castaneda, Nobel Prize winning chemist Linus Pauling, Christian theologian Paul Tillich and Abraham Maslow. By the second half of the 1960s Esalen's famous visitors included the Indian musician, sarod player Ali Akbar Khan, environmentalist Buckminster Fuller and bodywork pioneer Ida Rolf. Esalen soon acquired a reputation as an idyllic therapeutic hideaway – a place to enjoy weekend seminars and workshops, and discover your inner being. It was a place to get in touch with your feelings, awaken your senses, reach out to your partner and enjoy the communal experience of bathing and massage on the cliff-edge above the Pacific Ocean.

04.04 Michael Murphy and Richard Price, co-founders of Esalen Institute.

GESTALT THERAPY

Not everyone at Esalen was mystical, however. A notable exception was Fritz Perls, the distinguished founder of Gestalt therapy. Arguably the most important single influence in the early years of Esalen, Perls took up residence in a two-bedroom stone house built especially for him on the property. As Edward Hoffman notes, Perls was a controversial figure at Esalen: 'Unquestionably a brilliant and masterful therapist, Perls was nevertheless well known among the Esalen community as an aged womanizer with a vulgar tongue and enormous ego. With his large, unkempt beard and predilection for jumpsuits, Perls strolled around Esalen as if he owned it.'[1] He despised what he called the 'woolly-headed' spiritual aspect of the personal growth movement and endeavoured to bring his own, much more confronting and sometimes brutal style of therapy to the fore.

While Gestalt therapy was particular to Fritz Perls, Gestalt psychology itself was much older – the movement dating back to a paper published by Max Wertheimer in 1912. The German word *Gestalt* refers to a pattern of parts making up a whole, and the underlying principle of Gestalt psychology is that an analysis of parts does not lead to an understanding of the whole – parts by themselves have no meaning. Building on the pioneering work of Wertheimer and also Wolfgang Kohler and Kurt Koffka, Perls maintained that Gestalt theory could be applied to the personality and to basic human needs: 'Every organ, the senses, movements, thoughts, subordinate to [an] emerging need and are quick to change loyalty and function as soon as that need is satisfied and then retreat into the background.… All the parts of the organism identify themselves temporarily with the emergent gestalt.'[2]

Born in Berlin in 1893, Perls had struggled through his school years, but went on to obtain his MD in psychiatry. He then moved to Vienna where he met Wilhelm Reich, and returned to Germany in 1936 to deliver a paper at a psycho-analytic congress attended by the founding father himself, Sigmund Freud. Perls came to the view quite early in his professional career that Freud's theory that sex and destructiveness were the twin motivating forces of human existence was incomplete. He rejected the idea of rigidly classifying instincts and analysing a patient's past, and chose to concentrate instead on the here-and-now. For people to be whole, or balanced, they had to recognize bodily yearnings and impulses instead of disguising them. In fact, life was a series of gestalts that emerged one after the other – a variety of needs requiring satisfaction. Perls developed Gestalt therapy to allow people to recognize their projections and disguises as real feel-ings, and subsequently to be able to fulfil themselves.

After breaking with the psychoanalytic movement, Fritz Perls emigrated to the United States in 1946 and established the New York Institute for Gestalt Therapy in 1952. He moved to California in 1959. His friend, fellow psychologist Wilson Van Dusen, explains how, at the time, his views were revolutionary:

> We were all basically retrospective, strongly retrospective, in both our analysis and therapies. We wouldn't conceive of understanding a patient without an extensive history. And for a man just to walk into a room and describe people's behaviour so accurately added a whole new dimension. This is where I considered Fritz very great. His incomparable capacity to observe.[3]

Fritz Perls had been strongly influenced by Reich's idea that the body reflected internal psychological processes. The person here and now showed every-thing through his or her being and behaviour – there was no need to delve into analysis. 'Nothing is ever really repressed,' he once commented, 'All relevant gestalten are emerging, they are on the surface, they are obvious like the emperor's nakedness.'[4]

As a therapist, Perls was often extremely curt and blunt, cutting through the niceties of social interaction to the person behind the image. At Esalen he would give demonstrations of Gestalt therapy before over a hundred people, inviting members of the audience to participate with him in role-play. He had two chairs beside him on the dais. One was the 'hot seat' from which the participant engaged in dialogue with Perls. The other chair was there to help the person switch roles and enact different parts, engaging in the self-questioning process. Frequently volunteers revealed their weaknesses and limitations during these sessions, but there was, after all, a lesson to be learnt.

Perls was very wary of the 'fun generation' who came to Esalen just for entertainment, and his dialogues with these people were always brutally honest. For some these were moments of revelation and awe, for others quite shattering experiences. His publisher, Arthur Ceppos, recalls: 'I think that Fritz's greatest contribution was his horror at how ridiculous man permits himself to become; and by becoming aware of how ridiculous he is, he can emerge into an identity that is no longer ridiculous, but is relatively free. This is the whole secret behind Fritz's hot seat. He would show people how they made fools of themselves.'[5]

Perls believed, like the Existentialists, that each person lived in his or her own universe and had to take the responsibility for his or her own behaviour and growth. The well-known Gestalt therapy prayer, which was often displayed as a poster at this time, reads as follows:

> *I do my thing, and you do your thing,*
> *I am not in this world to live up to your expectations*
> *And you are not in this world to live up to mine.*
> *You are you and I am I,*
> *And if by chance we find each other, it's beautiful.*
> *If not, it can't be helped.*[6]

Self-awareness and honesty were crucial to Perls's concept of Gestalt therapy: the essential point was to be aware of what you are experiencing, how you experience your existence *now*. Perls would urge people to pay particular attention to the ways in which they sabotaged their own attempts at sustained awareness, for these were ways in which they habitually prevented themselves from fully contacting the world and their own experiences.

Extending his scope from here-and-now interactions through dialogue and self-recognition, Perls also placed considerable emphasis on dreams. Dreams presented messages that could help people understand the unfinished situations they were still carrying around. In *Gestalt Therapy Verbatim* he wrote:

In Gestalt therapy we don't interpret dreams. We do something more interesting with them. Instead of analyzing and further cutting up the dream, we want to bring it back to life. And the way to bring it back to life is to re-live the dream as if it were happening now. Instead of telling the dream as if it were a story in the past, act it out in the present, so that it becomes a part of yourself, so that you are really involved.[7]

Perls suggested that dreams be written down with their various details as completely as possible. Then a dialogue or encounter between the different com-

04.05 T'ai Chi at Esalen looking out at the Pacific Ocean. Gia-fu Feng taught T'ai Chi here in the 1960s.

ponent parts or figures could be held. As the encounter process continued, a new integration could be reached. Perls described the dream, in fact, as 'an excellent opportunity to find the holes in the personality…if you understand the meaning of each time you identify with some bit of a dream, each time you translate an *it* into an *I*, you increase in vitality and in your potential'.

At Esalen, Perls worked alongside notable figures like Bernard Gunther, who taught massage and sensory awakening, Gia-fu Feng, who instructed in T'ai Chi, and George Leonard, who held seminars on inter-racial issues, but Perls remained the 'star attraction' for several years. Then, in the late 1960s, a major rival emerged who would increasingly take much of the limelight.

ENCOUNTER THERAPY

Will Schutz was a social psychologist who had graduated with a PhD from UCLA in 1951, worked at the University of Chicago, and later taught at Harvard and Berkeley. Like Perls, he advocated a way of liberating people from their social conditioning and false self-images, but whereas Perls relied mainly on acute personal observation and direct verbal interchange with his clients, Schutz used a method called 'open encounter'. He was building on an approach already developed by Carl Rogers and other American social scientists.

Modern encounter therapy derives substantially from a training programme developed for community leaders in Connecticut in 1946. A feature of this was regular feedback between trainers and participants to enhance the experience of all involved. Trainers from the Connecticut groups helped establish National Training Laboratories in 1947 to assist government and industry in assessing the efficiency of personnel. NTL established a system of providing direct personal feedback through what became known as training groups, or T-groups. Schutz was thoroughly conversant with group therapy and the T-group techniques when he arrived at Esalen in 1967.

In the classic encounter groups there were usually between ten and fifteen people who sat in a circle on the floor. Often there was no specified leader. An encounter session could last for a few hours or extend into days and even weeks. People taking part in an encounter group would try to 'reach' and perceive each

04.06 An encounter session in progress.

04.07 Encounter therapist Carl Rogers with a group in the Huxley Room, Esalen.

other in real ways and experience genuine inner feelings. Such therapy depended, of course, on developing honest relationships with the others involved, and expressing such feelings verbally or physically.

In the technique adopted by Carl Rogers, members of the encounter group initially interacted loosely, waiting for information on what to expect and how to act. A sense of frustration could develop as the group came to realize that it had to determine its own direction. Members often resisted expressing themselves personally, but then eased out of this by discussing past events and situations. Rogers discovered that it was quite common for the first exchanges to be negative ('I find you don't appeal to me'; 'Your manner of talking irritates me'; 'You are very superficial'), but this was because deep positive feelings were harder to express. Usually, providing the group passed through this phase without fragmenting, personally meaningful material began to come through and a sense of trust emerged. As sensitive and important recollections rose to the surface, the members of the group responded by seeking to help other members of the group who had deep inner problems.

An admirer of Rogers, Schutz's particular aim in group therapy was to help people feel good about themselves. In fact, he published a bestselling book *Joy: Expanding Human Awareness* in 1967, soon after his arrival at Esalen. He explained that the attainment of joy was at the very core of his method: 'Joy is the feeling that comes from the fulfilment of one's potential. Fulfilment brings to an individual the feeling that he can cope with his environment; the sense of confidence in himself as a significant, competent, lovable person who is capable of handling situations as they arise, able to use fully his own capacities, and free to express his feelings.'[8]

04.08 Will Schutz at Esalen. Schutz soon emerged as a potential rival to Fritz Perls.

At first Perls welcomed Schutz's presence at Esalen. He had solid academic credentials and was not a dreamy mystic like so many other visitors to the Institute. Perls may also have thought of Schutz as a potential convert to Gestalt therapy. But it soon became clear that he was intent on developing his own reputation. His book brought considerable publicity to Esalen, and when *Time* magazine published a largely favourable article on Esalen in 1967, there was no mention of either Perls or Gestalt therapy. Perls felt slighted and now began describing Schutz's open encounter sessions as insubstantial distractions – good fun perhaps, but not to be taken seriously.

Schutz continued to hold successful seminars at Esalen, although in due course he began to attract critics besides Fritz Perls. Several mainstream psychotherapists working in the United States voiced the opinion that it was unwise to encourage the sort of encounter sessions Schutz was holding. With no scope for further follow-up, the therapist in charge could hardly assume responsibility for what might happen later to participants. Schutz responded by stressing that anyone could do whatever they were willing to take responsibility for, and this included any clients wishing to involve themselves in encounter therapy. Obviously, open encounter was a risk-taking exercise, since there was always the possibility that damaging material could come to the surface during a session. But he pointed out that Esalen's main aim was to help already comparatively well balanced individuals with their self-actualization, rather than providing care for people who were mentally ill. Everyone coming to Esalen, said Schutz, had to take the responsibility for what they experienced there. It was up to them to respond to the challenge of self-transformation.

PSYCHEDELICS AND SUICIDES

During the late 1960s the range of seminars offered at Esalen grew rapidly – from some 20 programme options in 1965 to around 120 in 1968. The exciting expansion of activities, however, was not without its human casualties and part of the problem was related to casual experimentation with mind-altering drugs.

The attitude to psychedelics at Esalen in the early years had always been comparatively relaxed. In his 1962 book *The Joyous Cosmology*, Alan Watts had described his aesthetic and mystical experiences with psilocybin and LSD (lysergic acid diethylamide).[9] Aldous Huxley, like Watts an early visitor to Big Sur, had similarly related his wondrous encounter with mescaline in *The Doors of Perception* (1954). Michael Murphy had experimented with peyote in the Big House at Esalen in the early 1960s and around the same time Carlos Castaneda

04.09 *Mescalito*, the flowering peyote cactus (*Lophophora williamsii*) from which the psychedelic alkaloid mescaline is extracted.

had talked on the shamanic use of psychedelics during a celebrated visit to Esalen. Seminars on the relationship between drugs and mystical experiences were held at Esalen from time to time, but they were intended as theoretical seminars, not experiential workshops. It became necessary to include a note in Esalen brochures stating that no drugs would be used in such sessions.

The first death associated with Esalen, however, was drug-related. Lois Delattre was a member of the first residential programme at Esalen and later went to work in Esalen's San Francisco office. Like many others in the personal growth movement at that time she had experimented with LSD, but she also wanted to explore the effects of the so-called 'love drug', MDA, an amphetamine derivative of iso-saffrole which heightened sensory awareness and was said to produce states of emotional openness.[10] Delattre took MDA with three friends. She soon became very introspective and withdrew to lie down. For a while she seemed to be breathing deeply, as if in a trance, but her companions later found her dead. Her death caused a distinct sense of panic at Esalen. Even though it was not directly attributable to an Institute programme, it highlighted what no one had yet seriously considered – that seeking heightened consciousness could have fatal results.

There followed two deaths at Esalen that were not drug-related. Marcia Price had attended Fritz Perls's Gestalt therapy workshops, and was employed in the Esalen office. She was also involved sexually with Perls. The news that Price had shot herself devastated members of the residential programme at Esalen, and had a profoundly sobering effect. It was later revealed that Perls had mocked her suicide threats during a Gestalt therapy session. Then a young woman named Judith Gold drowned herself in the Esalen baths, early in 1969. Gold, too, had threatened suicide while sitting in the 'hot seat' and had been savagely mocked by Perls. He was not conciliatory after these deaths, maintaining that people who were potential suicides should be treated just like anyone else. If you were threatening to kill yourself, Perls would tell you to go right ahead and do it. The mood at Esalen now changed dramatically, and Perls's relationship with Murphy began to sour.

Perls himself became increasingly disturbed by the escalating street violence in California, and also felt that the political ascendancy of Ronald Reagan as Governor of California and the resurgence of George Wallace and Richard Nixon heralded a new right-wing direction in the United States which reminded him of events in Nazi Germany. With this dwelling heavily on his mind, and colleagues on all sides accusing him of paranoia, Perls decided to leave Esalen in 1969. He went to Canada, where he had a number of students, and bought a motel alongside Lake Cowichan on Vancouver Island. He named his new establishment the Gestalt Institute of British Columbia, but died six months later in March 1970.

The dramatic years of Fritz Perls at Esalen provided ample demonstration

04.10 A sunset party at Esalen in the late 1960s.

that the brutal stripping away of personal defence mechanisms could have tragic consequences – a potent lesson for the personal growth movement. At the end of it all, Will Schutz's more optimistic mode of encounter therapy seemed more compatible with the Esalen style, and Schutz outlasted Fritz Perls by several years, continuing with his open encounter sessions at Esalen Institute until 1973, before deciding to leave and head north to San Francisco.

Today the range of experiential workshops offered at Esalen is enormous. Visitors come to learn techniques of T'ai Chi, massage, Zen, hypnosis, dance, shamanism, Taoism, 'creative sexuality' and Feldenkrais body awareness, or to attend lectures on quantum physics, Gnosticism, Tibetan Buddhism, deep ecology or feminist spirituality. The range is diverse and ever-changing, but Esalen is much less controversial than it used to be. The general public now has a much greater familiarity with mysticism, mind and body therapies, and the philosophy of 'health for the whole person'. It took some time, however, for these holistic frameworks to emerge. In the late 1960s the full impact of the psychedelic years was yet to come, and important lessons were learned as the youth culture began to pursue its often reckless exploration of drug-induced altered states of consciousness.

5
The Psychedelic Years

For many people the psychedelic era is epitomized by the so-called 'Summer of Love' in 1966–67, which shrouded San Francisco's Haight-Ashbury district in a haze of drug-induced joy-consciousness. It was at this time that the media first began to draw attention to the emergent counterculture – that rapidly increasing group of mostly well educated, young middle-class Americans who were rebelling against the materialism of the 'American Dream', against the war in Vietnam, and against the rising levels of violence in cities at home.

The controversy surrounding psychedelic mind-altering drugs and the quest for spiritual transcendence had, however, already surfaced several years before the Summer of Love. The issue of psychedelics and mystical enlightenment was already a hot topic of interest at Esalen, and had also been raised by Aldous Huxley and Alan Watts. Not surprisingly, some of the earliest debates concerning the relationship between psychedelics and mystical consciousness focused on what was 'authentic' and what was 'artificial' in the pursuit of 'chemical ecstasy'.

THE DOORS OF PERCEPTION AND INFINITY

The debate over 'drugs and mysticism' had been triggered initially by the publication in 1954 of Aldous Huxley's *The Doors of Perception*. Huxley had taken his title from William Blake's 'if the doors of perception were cleansed, everything would appear to man as it is, infinite'. Huxley's book later inspired the rock singer Jim Morrison to name his band The Doors by way of tribute.

Huxley related how in May 1953 he had swallowed four-tenths of a gram of mescaline dissolved in a glass of water and sat down to wait for results. Mescaline brought revelation: his 'I' became 'Not-Self' and the everyday objects around him – flowers, books and furniture – seemed to radiate jewel-like colours and profound significance. Here, he felt, was 'contemplation at its height'. Huxley later conceded that mescaline could plunge some people into hell rather than lifting them into heaven, but on balance he decided that it could certainly serve as a catalyst to mystical awareness – especially for rational or 'verbal' intellectuals like himself who felt 'compelled to take an occasional trip through some chemical Door in the Wall into the world of transcendental experience'. Later, in 1958, in

05.01 *A Gathering of the Tribes for a Human Be-In*, poster by graphic artist Stanley Mouse for the festival in Golden Gate Park, San Francisco, 14 January 1967.

05.02 Aldous Huxley in California. Huxley was an early visitor to Esalen.

The Saturday Evening Post, Huxley emphasized the mystical relevance of both mescaline and LSD. Referring specifically to LSD, he noted, 'It lowers the barrier between conscious and subconscious and permits the patient to look more deeply and understandingly into the recesses of his own mind. The deepening of self-knowledge takes place against a background of visionary and even mystical experience.'[1]

Huxley's views on LSD were subsequently endorsed by Alan Watts in his book *The Joyous Cosmology*, published in 1962. Referring both to LSD in particular and to psychedelics in general, Watts wrote:

> These drugs… provide the raw materials of wisdom, and are useful to the extent that the individual can integrate what they reveal into the whole pattern of his behaviour and the whole system of his knowledge… the hours of heightened perception are wasted unless occupied with sustained reflection or meditation upon whatever themes may be suggested.[2]

05.03 Counterculture guru Alan Watts photographed at Esalen wearing traditional Zen Buddhist robes.

05.04 A disciple of Zen Buddhism practising *zazen* – Zen meditation – in Japan.

Watts had emigrated to the United States in 1936 – a year before Huxley – and was best known for his writings on Zen Buddhism. After switching his allegiance to Christianity, Watts was ordained as an Anglican priest in 1944, and then served as the Episcopal chaplain at Northwestern University for six years. He then renounced Christianity as his spiritual path, and accepted an offer to teach at the School of Asian Studies in San Francisco. Retaining his interest in Zen Buddhism and Taoism, Watts now sought to reconcile these Eastern philosophies with the West Coast counterculture, in which the 'Beats' actively divorced themselves from a society devoted to making money and mixed Zen in with their poetry, painting and jazz so that it became part of the bohemian way of life.

Watts began experimenting with LSD, and from this time onwards his lifestyle blended free love, mysticism and psychedelics. He had arrived at the view that Christianity did not trust humanity's natural urges – that it was always down-playing the flesh in favour of the spirit – and that it had inherited this dualism from the ancient Greeks:

> It has often been said that the human being is a combination of angel and animal, a spirit imprisoned in flesh, a descent of divinity into materiality, charged with the duty of transforming the gross elements of the lower world into the image of God. … Not to cherish both the angel and the animal, both the spirit and the flesh, is to renounce the whole interest and greatness of being human.[3]

Watts had been deeply interested for many years in the way in which Zen Buddhism could help alienated and lonely people find spiritual 'release'. He was a friend of the Beat poet Gary Snyder, who had spent over a decade in Zen temples in Kyoto, and knew a number of the other Beats – including Jack Kerouac, Lawrence Ferlinghetti and Allen Ginsberg – all of whom were already familiar with Zen Buddhism and the concept of *satori*, or direct enlightenment. Watts personally felt that the Zen style adopted by the Beats was not authentic, and pre-ferred Chinese Taoist forms of Zen, but together with Snyder and Kerouac he denounced bourgeois suburban values and took up residence on an old ferry boat called *Vallejo*, moored in Sausalito.

A skilled teacher and radio broadcaster, Watts soon became a frequent visitor on college campuses across the country. In 1961 he addressed students and academics at Columbia, Cornell, Chicago, Harvard and Yale Medical School, and also held seminars on the *Vallejo*. He would address all the current issues of the day – sexuality, sensuality, mind-expanding drugs, food and popular lifestyles – everything that at the time was considered risqué in conventional middle-class society. Watts had taken LSD on several occasions and believed, like Aldous Huxley, that

psychedelics could be used as spiritual sacraments rather than for recreational 'kicks'. Similarly, Snyder believed that Zen meditators who had previously experienced LSD would find it easier to practise *zazen* in their journey towards *dhyana*, or ultimate enlightenment.

There were, however, other prominent voices in the debate over drugs and mysticism. They included a small group of radical psychologists working at Harvard University, who had already attracted national attention for their views on psychedelics and personal transformation.

THE HARVARD TRIUMVIRATE

Ralph Metzner, Richard Alpert and Timothy Leary all had distinguished academic backgrounds. German-born Metzner graduated from Oxford University in 1958 and received a doctorate in clinical psychology from Harvard University in 1962. The following year he became a post-doctoral fellow at Harvard Medical School, specializing in psychopharmacology. Richard Alpert – later known as Baba Ram Dass – had taken his doctorate at Stanford University. In 1953 he became an assistant professor at Harvard University, and in 1956 he was appointed co-director of the Harvard Psychedelic Drug Research Project. And Timothy Leary, who would later become famous for his psychedelic dictum 'Turn On, Tune In and Drop Out', had a similarly impeccable academic background. He obtained his MA at Washington State University in 1946, and his PhD from the University of California in 1950 for his thesis 'The Social Dimensions of Personality'. He published a conventional textbook, *The Interpersonal Diagnosis of Personality* in 1957, and was appointed to the Harvard Center for Personality Research in 1960. As it transpired, this triumvirate of PhDs – Metzner, Alpert and Leary – were poised to become pioneers of the psychedelic revolution.

During Leary's summer vacation in 1960, in the first year of his new position at Harvard, he took his two children down to Cuernavaca in Mexico. As Leary later related in his autobiography, *Flashbacks*, 'In the days of Montezuma this town, called "horn-of-the-cow", was the home of soothsayers, wise men and magicians. Cuernavaca lies south of a line of volcanic peaks, Popo, Ixtacihuatl, and Toluca. On the slopes of the volcanoes grow the sacred mushrooms of Mexico, divinatory fungi, *teonanacatl*, flesh of the gods.'[4] In Cuernavaca Leary would experience the flesh of the gods for the first time and it would change his life forever.

Among the guests who called on the Learys at their holiday villa was Gerhart Braun, an anthropologist from the University of Mexico. Braun had studied Aztec culture, had translated various Nahuatl texts and was intrigued by the references he had found in their literature to sacred mushrooms known locally as *hongos*.

05.05 Hieronymus Bosch, *Garden of Earthly Delights*, (detail from central panel), *c*.1500–16. Timothy Leary believed Bosch belonged to the ancient and honorable fellowship of 'early trippers'.

Leary asked if he could find some. A week later, Braun phoned to say that he had obtained several from a *curandera*, or folk healer, in the village of San Pedro near Toluca. He came round with some friends, spread the mushrooms out in two bowls, and said to Leary that everyone should take six. It was generally agreed that they tasted a lot worse than they looked, but expectations were high.

The *hongos* made Leary slightly nauseous at first, and his face began to tingle. Soon his vision was awash with hallucinatory impressions and, like Aldous Huxley who had charted this strange terrain many years earlier, he began to discover a profound richness in the kaleidoscopic imagery unfolding before his eyes:

Mosaics flaming colour Muzo emerald, Burma Rubies Ceylon Sapphire,
Mosaics lighted from within, glowing, moving, changing, Hundred reptiles, jewel
encrusted.[5]

Leary now began to ponder the nature of his own life-force, his bloodstream, his pulsing arteries. The organic basis of all creativity overwhelmed him. His body contained a myriad universes; his cell tissue seemed to hold the secret of life and energy. Leary was perceiving the motions of the universe at the atomic and sub-atomic levels. Finite imagery had been left far behind. He was witnessing the tides and motions of energy and form in their most profoundly elementary and essential phases of manifestation. And, surprising though it must have seemed, the experience was quintessentially religious: 'I came back a changed man,' Leary later recalled. 'You are never the same after you have had that one flash glimpse down the cellular time tunnel. You are never the same after you have had the veil drawn.'[6]

It was this initiatory experience that led Leary and his friends towards a systematic exploration of inner space. It seemed to him at that time that a new chapter in the development of human thought was opening: the search for the very source of mystical awareness. There had been visionaries before, but they had all been isolated individuals. Now a movement could get under way. The earlier mystics and seers were forerunners and could act as guides:

We did sense that we were not alone. The quest for internal freedom, for the elixir of life, for the draught of immortal revelation was not new. We were part of an ancient and honorable fellowship which had pursued this journey since the dawn of recorded history. We began to read the accounts of early trippers – Dante, Hesse, Rene Daumal, Tolkien, Homer, Blake, George Fox, Swedenborg, Bosch, and the explorers from the Orient – Tantrics, Sufis, Bauls, Gnostics, Hermetics, Sivits, Saddhus… no, we were not alone.[7]

05.06 Timothy Leary at the Human Be-In Festival in Golden Gate Park, San Francisco, 1967, wearing flowers in his hair.

During the autumn and winter of 1960, Leary spent most of his spare time studying the hallucinogenic qualities of psychotropic mushrooms. By day he continued to deliver lectures on clinical psychology at the Harvard Graduate School. One of his students was Ralph Metzner – a man who seemed to Leary at the time to be rather academic and 'ivory-towerish' in his attitudes but who was nevertheless brilliant at his work. Metzner said he wanted to experiment with psilocybin, a psychedelic synthesized from the mushroom *Psilocybe mexicana*, and was keen to evaluate its effect on prison inmates. He thought that it could provide them with an experience to change the pattern of their lives. Of course, there was no way in which they could predict the outcome, or the reaction of either inmates or wardens, but it might lead to new methods of integration and rehabilitation.

At first the series of psychedelic prison sessions weren't entirely successful. Leary on one occasion found himself looking at one of the inmates, a Polish embezzler, with acute distrust. Someone put on a jazz record, alleviating the tension, and everyone relaxed. The mood ebbed and flowed. As Leary later wrote: 'There were high points and low points, ecstasies and terror.' There were more sessions. Some of the convicts were able to leave on parole. Mild-mannered and changed men, they were sometimes, on Leary's admission, unable to cope with society's pressures, but the prison and its psychiatric unit had become, in certain measure, a 'spiritual centre'. It felt like a step towards a new understanding.

The prison sessions inspired Leary towards a sense of brotherhood. He had been able to communicate with men of a quite different background. The psilocybin had unshackled the psychiatric doctor–inmate–warden roles and they were 'all men at one… all two-billion year-old seed centres pulsing together'. But the effect was not enduring. 'As time slowly froze,' noted Leary, 'we were reborn in the old costumes and picked up the tired games. We weren't yet ready to act on our revelation.'

It took an eccentric Englishman, Michael Hollingshead, to point out the next stage. Hollingshead was a yoga practitioner and fiction writer whose novels were semi-autobiographical. He also had a strong interest in psychedelics. Furthermore, he had taken LSD – the most potent of all hallucinogens in terms of dose and quantity – and he urged Leary to do so. At first Leary refrained. After all, LSD was a chemical that had been synthesized in a laboratory, whereas the mushrooms had a natural and cultural origin – the Aztecs regarded them as holy. Hollingshead insisted that LSD was of overwhelming 'religious' significance and would make the mushrooms pale into insignificance, and Leary was eventually won over. With a group of friends, he and Hollingshead consumed a dose in November 1961.

Once again Leary found himself caught up in an eddy of transforming shapes and forms. As he reflected on these visionary sequences he thought of his role as father of his children. Had he been living a sham existence based merely on a routine form of parental devotion? Suddenly he seemed to be surrounded with death and falsity. Amid all this confusion, what could be said to be real? Leary considered the structures and patterns of society: the cultivation of crops, the growth of cities, the nature of invasions, migrations, moral codes and laws – but eventually these too seemed illusory and insubstantial as a basis for being. They were merely constructs and episodes of man; they did not identify his origins.

Leary now found himself falling inwards, beyond structure, into a swirling vortex of energy: '…nothing existed except whirring vibrations, and each illusory form was simply a different frequency.' His perception had been reduced to a primal level, but then, as the effects of the psychedelic began to wear off, he experienced a terrible sense of loss. He had entered the heart of an energy vortex. 'Why had we lost it?' he asked himself. 'Why were we being reborn?... in these silly leather bodies with these trivial little cheese-board minds?' Leary had reached a level of consciousness which for the first time had seemed to define a sense of reality and being-ness. He had never reached this level before. He had never been to the core. Why couldn't it be more accessible?

He continued to try out other hallucinogens as a means of entry to these states of self-realization. With his colleague Richard Alpert, he took DMT (dimethyltryptamine, similar in its effects to LSD, but lasting only thirty minutes or so), and discussed these experiences with Alan Watts, who described them as like 'being fired out of the muzzle of an atomic cannon'.[8] He also had lengthy discussions with William Burroughs who had chronicled his personal experiences in the South American jungle with the shamanic potion known as *yage*, or *ayahuasca*. Burroughs had begun to wonder whether the visions of the mystics and seers of the past had a biochemical origin. Had he entered the same 'psychic spaces' as Jacob Boehme, William Blake and St John of the Cross before him? Leary, meanwhile, received some insights into these matters from an unexpected source.

THE GOOD FRIDAY EXPERIMENT

As with the prison experiments suggested by Ralph Metzner, the new development owed its impetus to the enthusiasm of a Harvard student. This time it was Walter Pahnke, young and eager, with a medical degree and a divinity qualification already under his belt. Pahnke was undertaking PhD studies in the philosophy of religion, and wanted to pin down the visionary experience within experimental parameters. Twenty theological students could be assembled in a church setting. Some were to be given psilocybin while others were to be the 'control group'. There would be organ music, prayers and a sermon – all the normal things in a Protestant service – and it would be interesting to see whether anyone found their consciousness expanding in a transcendental, mystical direction.

Leary thought the suggestion was outrageous, but Pahnke persisted. He had a medical degree, after all, and would undertake psychiatric interviews to screen out 'pre-psychotics' beforehand. The volunteers would be carefully chosen and the experiment would proceed in the respectable presence of Dean Howard Thurman of the Boston University chapel and Dr Walter Huston Clark, a visiting theological scholar.

Pahnke suggested using as his framework a list of common mystical attributes that had been drawn up by W. T. Stace (1886–1967), a leading scholar in the field of comparative religion.[9] These attributes, or qualities, fell under nine headings which represented the most commonly reported aspects of mystical experience. Stace's defining attributes, as applied by Pahnke, were as follows:[10]

Unity

The mystic experiences a profound sense of 'one-ness' both within his or her own being, and also in the external world.

Transcendence of time and space

The mystical experience is not contained within three-dimensional space. It is often described as 'eternal' and 'infinite'.

Deeply felt positive mood

Feelings of joy, blessedness and peace impart to the person the sense that the mystical experience has been of incalculable value.

The sense of sacredness

Profound sense of awe. Something is experienced that can be 'profaned'.

Objectivity and reality

Knowledge and illumination come together: the experience seems to be overwhelmingly authoritative. No 'proof' is necessary, 'ultimate reality carries its own sense of certainty.'

Paradoxicality

Following the illumination, rational interpretations seem to be logically contradictory. There is a feeling of an all-encompassing Unity devoid of specific attributes.

Alleged ineffability

Words fail adequately to express the mystical experience.

Transiency

Mystical consciousness is not sustained indefinitely; it is more of a 'peak experience'.

Persisting positive changes in attitude and behaviour

Lasting psychological changes are experienced that affect the quality of one's interaction with others, and with life itself. The mystical experience itself is held in awe, and one is more at peace with oneself than before.

Walter Pahnke's session, known as the 'Good Friday Experiment', took place on Good Friday 1962 in the chapel at Boston University. Ten theological students were given psilocybin, ten nicotinic acid, a vitamin that causes transient feelings of warmth and tingling in the skin. They all participated in a two-and-a-half-hour religious service of organ music, four solos, readings, prayers and personal meditation. During the weeks before the experiment, care had been taken to reduce fear and maximize expectancy, and during the experimental session itself participants did not know whether they had taken the psilocybin or the placebo.

Pahnke collected data for up to six months afterwards, and each student prepared an account of his own personal experiences. Pahnke's statistics, condensed into percentages, are admittedly clinical but they do make interesting reading.

These are the recorded experiences of those who had taken psilocybin:

inner unity	70 per cent
external unity	38 per cent
transcended time and space	84 per cent
deeply felt positive mood	57 per cent
feeling of sacredness	53 per cent
sense of objectivity and reality	63 per cent
element of paradoxicality	61 per cent
ineffability	66 per cent
transiency	79 per cent
substantial changes in psychological attitudes	50 per cent

The control group for the most part had less intense religious experiences:

feeling of love (positive mood)	33 per cent
unity	7 per cent
time and space	6 per cent
positive mood	23 per cent
sacredness	28 per cent
objectivity and reality	18 per cent
paradoxicality	13 per cent
ineffability	18 per cent
transiency	8 per cent
psychological changes	8 per cent

Pahnke's experiment did not in itself prove that a person taking psychedelic substances would necessarily have a mystical experience, and it is clear that this is not the case. But the session did seem to show the value of hallucinogens in intensifying what would normally be a mild and rare religious experience. Within a religious setting it was therefore not surprising that any expansion of consciousness would tend to be mystical. The Good Friday Experiment helped consolidate Leary's belief that 'set' (mental attitude) and 'setting' (the chosen supportive environment) were important factors in the outcome of a psychedelic session: 'Our studies, naturalistic and experimental…demonstrate that if the expectation, preparation and setting are spiritual, an intense mystical or revelatory experience can be expected in from 40 to 90 per cent of subjects.'[11]

As Leary noted, when a human being ascends to the lofty heights of enhanced spiritual consciousness during a mystical illumination, the personality undergoes a dramatic process of transformation. The capacity for visionary insight reveals the limitations of all ego-based human frameworks – jealousies, fears, guilt, insecurities and so on – as if from a new vantage point. On returning to everyday awareness the person who has had this peak experience may find he or she is able to bring some of this unifying spiritual knowledge back into normal consciousness, assimilating it and perhaps remoulding the previous, more limited personality. It was meaningful, therefore, to regard mystical illumination as a type of rebirth. Not only did one change, but the more negative, or non-integrated, aspects of one's being were subsumed by a more positive and integrated perspective.

This, at least, was the apparent promise of psychedelically assisted mystical illumination. On a more mundane level, however, Leary's excursions from normality into altered states of consciousness were leading to a political showdown at Harvard University. Media reports of the controversial drug experiments conducted at the Center for Personality Research had enraged Professor Herbert Kelman, a fellow psychologist on the faculty. They had also infuriated Professor Brendan Maher, who dismissed Leary's findings, and believed psilocybin and LSD were dangerous drugs that should only be administered by physicians in a medical setting.

The campus debate was highlighted in the media, and came to the notice of the Massachusetts State Narcotics Bureau. After several police investigations and considerable departmental wrangling, Timothy Leary and Richard Alpert were dismissed from Harvard University in May 1963. It was the first time in three hundred years that faculty members had been asked to leave because of controversy surrounding new research.

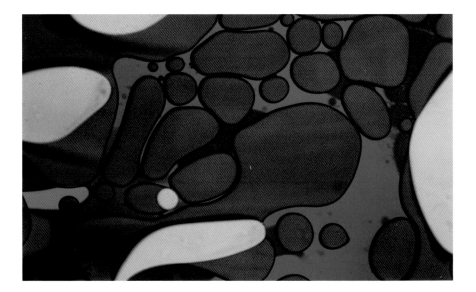

05.07 Detail from the Sensory Daze Lightshow.

05.08 LSD blotting paper – favourite fare in the 1960s – showing the image of Ganesh, the elephant-headed Hindu god of wisdom, literature and worldly success.

05.09 Female flower of *Cannabis sativa*, the source for marijuana. During the late 1960s marijuana became part of the anti-war protest.

THE SUMMER OF LOVE

Less than three years later, recreational drug use in the counterculture in both Britain and the USA was widespread. In San Francisco, the centre of the Summer of Love in 1966/67, LSD was readily available to 'acid trippers' in such forms as White Lightning or Orange Sunshine; marijuana was commonplace and smoked openly in the streets; and 'hash cookies' were favourite fare at parties.

In political terms the 1960s were tumultuous years, dominated by the war in Vietnam. Between 1961 and 1963 President Kennedy committed 16,000 military personnel to the campaign. At the end of 1965, after President Johnson had ordered the bombing of North Vietnam, this number had escalated to 200,000, and in early 1968 exceeded 500,000. The anti-war movement had been steadily building in the United States since October 1964, when vigils began on a weekly basis in Times Square. Soon opposition to the war began to spill over on university campuses. In May 1965 the Interreligious Committee on Vietnam, which included Martin Luther King and Daniel Corrigan, the Episcopal bishop of New York, sponsored a vigil at the Pentagon to protest against the human tragedy of Vietnam, and on 2 November 1965 American Quaker Norman Morrison doused himself with kerosene and burned to death in front of the Pentagon, emulating the suffering of napalm victims in North Vietnam. In the same year an apocalyptic message entered popular music for the first time with the release of Barry McGuire's chart-topping protest song *Eve of Destruction*, suggesting that the Vietnam conflict was bringing the world to the brink of catastrophe.

The anti-war movement also mobilized a powerful response in Europe. In March 1968 hundreds of anti-Vietnam-war demonstrators attempted to storm the American Embassy in London's Grosvenor Square, and in the following October a massive anti-war march was staged in central London on such a scale that shops and banks were boarded up and newspaper offices placed under extra guard.

Psychedelics, and marijuana in particular, had already become part of the international anti-war protest. In Berlin in 1968 a popular slogan appeared everywhere: 'A gun in your right hand – a joint in your left.' And as Felix Scorpio reported in the British radical newspaper *IT* (formerly *International Times*) in April 1969: 'Of course, the real change in the scene here has been the dope revolution.... Berlin is alive with heads dropping acid and STP in cinemas, parks, buses, and this too is a kind of revolution, and an interesting antithesis to America, where pot came first and politics followed.'

The response of the hippies to the conflict engulfing mainstream Western society was everywhere essentially a message of peace. Hippies wore flowers in their hair, and although some projected an idyllic sense of innocence regained,

05.10 Jerry Garcia (top of the steps, on the left) lead singer with The Grateful Dead and other 'family' members outside their house at 710 Ashbury Street, San Francisco, c.1966–67

05.11 Hippies in the Haight-Ashbury district of San Francisco.

many were also determined to overthrow cultural and social norms through displays of bizarre behaviour. This was a time of handpainted, multicoloured Volkswagen vans, exotic and unconventional clothes, patchouli incense, politically driven itinerant folksingers, and innovative rock groups. In the USA Fritz Perls was proclaiming a message of personal liberation at Esalen, and so were street banners in San Francisco: 'The time has come to be free. BE FREE. Do your thing. Be what you are. Do it NOW.'[12]

The Psychedelic Shop, run by Jay and Ron Thelin, opened at 1535 Haight Street, San Francisco, on New Year's Day 1966. It sold all manner of books, records and psychedelic posters while also reserving a third of its floor space for a 'calm centre', where hippies could come to meditate or sleep. The Print Mint sold old movie posters, doubled as a community centre where people could leave messages for each other, and was invariably populated by wandering musicians and appreciative hippies. Nearby were eateries like Tracy's and the psychedelically decorated Drog Store Café. Gonzo journalist Hunter S. Thompson provides us with a tantalizing description of everyday life at the Drog Store:

The best show on Haight Street is usually on the sidewalk in front of the Drog Store, a new coffee bar at the corner of Masonic Street. The Drog Store features an all-hippie revue that runs day and night. The acts change sporadically, but nobody cares. There will always be at least one man with long hair and sunglasses playing a wooden pipe of some kind. He will be wearing a Dracula cape, a long Buddhist robe, or a Sioux Indian costume. There will also be a hairy blond fellow wearing a Black Bart cowboy hat and spangled jacket that originally belonged to a drum major in the 1949 Rose Bowl parade. He will be playing the bongo drums. Next to the drummer will be a dazed-looking girl wearing a blouse (but no bra) and a plastic mini-skirt, slapping her thighs to the rhythm of it all.[13]

The Haight-Ashbury district was served by a newspaper called *The Oracle*, which was hawked in the streets and distributed through various 'alternative' outlets around the Haight. Printed in different coloured inks that fused together in rainbow patterns, *The Oracle* kept residents up-to-date with what was happening in the local community, as well as publishing controversial articles on such diverse topics as the horrors of prisoner-of-war camps and the joys of masturbation.

Joyce Ann Francisco, who sold advertising for *The Oracle*, told *Time* reporter Judson Gooding that she loved being a hippie. 'Human beings need total freedom', she said enthusiastically, 'That's where God is at. We need to shed hypocrisy, dishonesty, phoniness, and go back to the purity of our childhood values.' She also endorsed the casual, hedonistic approach to drugs in the Haight-Ashbury subculture. 'Whatever turns me on is a sacrament – LSD, sex, my bells, my colours. This is the holy communion.… When I find myself becoming confused, I drop out and take a dose of acid. It's a short-cut to reality – throws you right into it.'[14]

The Haight-Ashbury soon came to be known as the Hashbury, and it had its own heroes. One of these was novelist Richard Brautigan, who later became fashionable as the author of the avant-garde *Trout Fishing in America* and *In Watermelon Sugar*. Brautigan liked to parade in the streets carrying a large mirror and calling out, 'Know thyself!' to the surprised visitors and tourists who saw their own reflections in his mirror. Other notables on the local scene included psychedelic artist Michael Bowen, who later helped create the Love Pageant Rally; the Diggers (named after the British radicals of the 1640s), who fed hundreds of hungry passers-by free of charge at the Panhandle; poets Allen Ginsberg and Michael McClure; Jerry Garcia, the lead singer with The Grateful Dead, and poster artists Stanley Mouse, Alton Kelley and Wilfried Satty. Local entrepreneur Bill Graham staged many of the early acid-rock concerts at San Francisco's Fillmore Auditorium, including performances by Janis Joplin and Grace Slick – making him a special figure in the counterculture – and there were dramatic

05.12 Novelist Richard Brautigan.

05.13 Ken Kesey and the Merry Pranksters in their handpainted 1939 International Harvester bus, Aspen Meadows, New Mexico, 1968. The bus was called 'Further'.

impromptu street theatre performances by the Mime Troupe who were dedicated to 'undermining society'. Hippie poet Lenore Kandel gained notoriety overnight for her collection of rapturous, sexually explicit poems, *The Love Book*, and biochemist Augustus Stanley Owsley III was already famous for producing the best 'acid' (LSD) in the country.

One of the most respected psychedelic pioneers in the Bay Area was Ken Kesey, who had studied at the University of Oregon, and went on to Stanford in 1958 after winning a literary competition. There he completed *One Flew Over the Cuckoo's Nest*, a work that provides profound insights into the oppression and loss of freedom experienced by psychiatric patients. One of Kesey's fellow graduate students, Vik Lovell, suggested that Kesey participate in a CIA-funded research study involving mind-altering drugs. Kesey and Lovell were paid $75 a night by the CIA to take psilocybin and LSD under clinical conditions, and this, predictably, earned them hero status in the Hashbury counterculture. Kesey dedicated *One Flew Over the Cuckoo's Nest* in this way: 'To Vik Lovell – who told me there were no dragons, then led me to their lairs.'[15]

Kesey also gathered around him a group of musicians, jugglers, magicians and

05.14 An enthusiastic crowd gathering for the Love Pageant Rally at Panhandle Park, San Francisco, 6 October 1966 – the day that LSD was banned in California.

clowns known as the Merry Pranksters. The idea was to mount spontaneous recreational 'acid-happenings', any place, any time. The Pranksters had a 1939 International Harvester bus that had been handpainted in bright psychedelic colours. Wherever the Pranksters travelled, performed and handed out 'acid' to onlookers, their presence was guaranteed to make an impact.[16]

It was a crazy, wild and happy time and for a while it must have seemed it could go on forever. Kesey himself said the main idea was 'to be peaceful without being stupid, to be interested without being compulsive, to be happy without being hysterical.'[17] But then came the announcement that on 6 October 1966 the State of California would ban the use of LSD, a date many in the Hashbury would come to associate with the symbolism of 666 – the mark of the Beast in the Book of Revelation. Accordingly, Michael Bowen and the Psychedelic Rangers declared that on the same day there would also be a Love Pageant Rally at Panhandle Park between Masonic Avenue and Ashbury Street. The 'protest' invitation sent by the Rangers to Mayor John F. Shelley provides a clear indication of the schism that was now rapidly developing between the psychedelic generation and mainstream 'straight' society:

Sir,

Opposition to an unjust law creates futility for citizens who are its victims and increases the hostility between the governed and the governors. In the case of the LSD prohibition, the State has entered directly into the sacrosanct, personal psyches of its citizens. Our Love Pageant Rally is intended to overcome the paranoia and separation with which the State wishes to divide and silence the increasing revolutionary sense of Californians. Similar rallies will be held in communities such as ours all over the country and in Europe. You are invited to attend and address our rally. Thankyou.

Sincerely yours,

Citizens for the Love Pageant Rally of October 6, 1966[18]

The rally began, as promised, on the morning of 6 October, as employees of *The Oracle* and the Psychedelic Shop, intent on 'turning on' Mayor Shelley, led a delegation to City Hall, laden with flowers and morning glory seeds. Later, as crowds steadily gathered, the back of a truck became an impromptu stage for The Grateful Dead, Janis Joplin, and Big Brother and the Holding Company. It was a joyous time, 'a hell of a gathering', with three thousand people really enjoying themselves. One observer was moved to say: 'It's just being. Humans being. Being together.' 'Yes', agreed Michael Bowen, 'It's a Human Be-In.'

The term 'Be-In' soon became popular with the street culture of the time. But Bowen didn't want things to stop there, and after meeting with Allen Cohen, editor of *The Oracle*, it was agreed that there should be a much bigger love-rally in San Francisco – a rally that would be remembered for years to come. On 14 January 1967, in the afternoon. there was to be a 'Gathering of the Tribes for a Human Be-In at the Polo Fields in Golden Gate Park'. In a press-release issued two days before it was announced that:

Berkeley political activists and the love generation of the Haight-Ashbury will join together with members of the new nation who will be coming from every state in the nation, every tribe of the young (the emerging soul of the nation) to powwow, celebrate and prophesy the epoch of liberation, love, peace, compassion and unity of mankind. The night of bruted fear of the American eagle-breast-body is over. Hang your fear at the door and join the future. If you do not believe, please wipe your eyes and see.[19]

Another press-release provided details:

Twenty to fifty thousand people are expected to gather for a joyful powwow and

Peace Dance to be celebrated with leaders, guides and heroes of our generation. Timothy Leary will make his first Bay Area Public appearance; Allen Ginsberg will chant and read with Gary Snyder. Michael McClure and Lenore Kandel, Dick Alpert, Jerry Rubin, Dick Gregory and Jack Weinberg will speak. Music will be played by all the Bay Area rock bands, including The Grateful Dead, Big Brother and the Holding Company, Quicksilver Messenger Service, and many others. Everyone is invited to bring costumes, blankets, bells, flags, symbols, cymbals, drums, beads, feathers, flowers.[20]

This time a crowd of around ten thousand people came together in a rapturous union of love and activism. It was clearly an auspicious day, for astrologer Ambrose Hollingsworth had calculated that it marked a time when the population of the earth numbered the same as the total number of dead in the whole of human history.

Luckily 14 January was a crisp winter day. The sun was streaming down as thousands of flower-wearing hippies waved colourful banners, burned incense, smoked marijuana and shared food. There were laughing children, frolicking animals, Hare Krishnas beating on drums, and a procession of guest speakers and musicians. Jefferson Airplane and Quicksilver Messenger Service played their rock songs to an enthusiastic audience. Near the grandstands a group of white and African-American musicians played guitars and flutes together. Members of the Hell's Angels motorcycle gang also came to watch, clad in black leather, mixing in among the incense and the flowers. Amazingly, there were no fights, and the crowd was extraordinarily well behaved all afternoon. Psychedelic guru Dr Timothy Leary declared, 'Whatever you do is beautiful,' and poet Allen Ginsberg chanted, 'We are one! We are all one!' As the sun set across the park there was a feeling of deep and pervasive peace.

The gathering was proclaimed a great success, and afterwards Michael Bowen and Allen Ginsberg were ecstatic – they felt it was the birth of a new era, a new-found harmony of consciousness. For others it seemed almost like Eden regained, lost innocence rediscovered. But the question on everyone's lips was: 'Would it last? Would the Summer of Love simply prove ephemeral? Would the joy-consciousness endure? Would psychedelics transform the nation?' As it turned out, the hippie phenomenon of Haight-Ashbury would not last long. Within a year the Psychedelic Shop had closed down, Michael Bowen had moved to Mexico to paint, *The Oracle's* editor, Allen Cohen, had moved to Northern California to write, and there was a general dispersal of local energy.

It would be a mistake to identify the impact of 'hippie consciousness' simply with what happened in San Francisco during the Summer of Love. In many ways

05.15 Poet Allen Ginsberg at the
Human Be-In Festival in
Golden Gate Park, San
Francisco, 1967: 'We are one!
We are all one!'

this particular manifestation of psychedelic culture was just the most visible expression of a much wider phenomenon that had now begun to filter across the whole country, and was already established in parts of the UK. There were hippies all over the United States – in Boston, Seattle, Detroit, New Orleans, Austin, and New York. In June 1967 a gathering of hippies met in Greenwich Village's Washington Square Park to assist the cause of dog owners protesting against the leash laws. Here, revelling in playful paradox, they chanted, 'What is dog spelled backwards?' And in Stone Place Mall in Dallas, around a hundred 'flower children' assembled to protest against a proposed ban against large public gatherings. There were also small hippie communities springing up all around the country, such as the group who lived in a cluster of geodesic domes constructed from old automobile tops at 'Drop City' near Trinidad, Colorado, and the hippies at Morning Star Ranch near Sebastopol, north of San Francisco.

In one of the most symbolic occurrences of the psychedelic period, in October 1967, Abbie Hoffman, Jerry Rubin and a large group of counterculture devotees organized the National Mobilization demonstration at the Pentagon in Washington, D.C. An underground publication, *The East Village Other*, called for the presence at this event of 'mystics, saints, artists, holymen, astrologers, witches, sorcerers, warlocks, druids, hippies, priests, shamen, ministers, rabbis, troubadours, prophets, minstrels, bards [and] roadmen' in a magical ceremony which would attempt to levitate the Pentagon. This was a period of quasi-surreal political activity in which a group of hippies formed the Youth International Party and the so-called 'yippies' (a term adopted in 1967 and derived from the initials of the Youth International Party) emerged as the result of 'cross-fertilization of the hippie and New Left philosophies'.[21] And even though the levitation did not occur, this very public magical ceremony would nevertheless come to symbolize, in the popular mythology of the day, the encounter between the cosmological forces of love and magic on the one hand, and the symbolic military might of the Pentagon on the other – a clear distinction between the country's rulers, with their symbols of external political strength, and the youth-culture with its internal vitality and magic.

Maps for Inner Space

Leary, Metzner and Alpert had been deeply interested in the transformative potential of psychedelics long before the Harvard dismissal in May 1963, and they had already discussed the idea of developing some sort of guiding framework for their mystical ventures. It seemed appropriate that they should now venture towards the East – the direction of the rising Sun – for their inspiration. Looking for insights into the nature of mystical and visionary experiences, they decided to explore Tibetan Buddhism, choosing as a key work the ancient *Bardo Thodol*, or *Tibetan Book of the Dead*, which had been compiled and edited by the American Buddhist scholar W. Y. Evans-Wentz.[1] Aldous Huxley, who was also a practising Buddhist, prized this text and had alluded to it in *The Doors of Perception*.

Traditionally Tibetan priests read passages from this text to those approaching death, but Leary believed it was also extremely relevant to the living – sooner or later everyone has to face the inevitability of death. The book described a series of post-mortem events – the so-called *Bardo* visions experienced between incarnations – and Leary believed that these descriptions could also be used as a guide to mind-expansion. The *Bardo* levels of consciousness were psychic realms that could be explored long before the final post-mortem separation of mind and body.

THE TIBETAN BOOK OF THE DEAD

The *Bardo Thodol* begins with the loftiest mystical experience of all: the Clear Light of Illumination experienced as the beholder loses his own ego in surrendering to the Void. This is a state of supreme transcendence, of Unity with All. It is a state of sublime Liberation from the constrictions of the sensory world. According to the *Bardo Thodol*, if this state of consciousness cannot be sustained, a realm of awareness known as the Secondary Clear Light arises in its place. At this level the beholder is swept up in a state of ecstasy which Leary calls *wave energy flow*: 'The individual becomes aware that he is part of and surrounded by a charged field of energy, which seems almost electrical.' If he rides with the flow he may find he can sustain this sublime level of consciousness. Should he attempt to control it, this in itself represents an act of ego, which in turn reflects duality –

06.01 19th-century Thangka painting of the *Bardo* realms, showing the principal deities mentioned in the *Tibetan Book of the Dead*.

a state of consciousness where he is aware of himself as separate and distinct from the immediate surroundings. In such a dualistic state, the flow of energy associated with the experience of Unity begins to ebb away and the individual falls into lower levels of the mind referred to as the *Chonyid Bardo*, or karmic hallucinatory stages.

In the second *Bardo*, writes Leary:

> …strange sounds, weird sights and disturbed visions may occur. These can awe, frighten and terrify unless one is prepared…any and every shape – human, divine, diabolic, heroic, evil, animal, thing – which the human brain conjured up or the past life recalls, can present itself to consciousness; shapes and forms and sounds whirling by endlessly. The underlying solution – repeated again and again – is to recognize that your brain is producing the visions. They do not exist. Nothing exists except as your consciousness gives it life.[2]

It is in this phase that Tibetan Buddhists believe they encounter the Seven Peaceful Deities and the Seven Visions of the Wrathful Deities – counterpart of the Western Heaven and Hell. These deities incorporate fifty-eight embodiments of the human personality couched within traditional, culturally delineated forms. Evans-Wentz describes these deities as follows:

> The chief deities themselves are the embodiments of universal divine forces, with which the deceased is inseparably related, for through him, as being the microcosm of the macrocosm, penetrate all impulses and forces, good and bad alike. Samanta-Bhadra, the All-Good, thus personifies Reality, the Primordial Clear Light of the Unborn, Unshaped *Dharma-Kaya*. Vairochana is the Originator of all phenomena, the Cause of all Causes. As the Universal Father, Vairochana manifests or spreads forth as seed, or semen, all things; his *shakti*, the Mother of Great Space, is the Universal Womb into which the seed falls and evolves as the world systems. Vajra-Sattva symbolises Immutability. Ratna-Sambhava is the Beautifier, the Source of all Beauty in the Universe. Amitabha is Infinite Compassion and Love Divine, the *Christos*. Amogha-Siddhi is the personification of Almighty Power or Omnipotence. And the minor deities, heroes, *dakinis* (or 'fairies'), goddesses, lords of death, *rakshasas*, demons, spirits and all others, correspond to definite human thoughts, passions and impulses, high and low, human and sub-human and super-human, in karmic form, as they take shape from the seeds of thought forming in the percipient's consciousness content.[3]

The third phase, or *Sidpa Bardo*, is the period of 're-entry' – the descent from the transcendental heights of spiritual awareness through to the familiar context of the everyday environment. Mahayana Buddhist tradition maintains that a person who brings full knowledge of spiritual Unity through into incarnation can rightly be considered an avatar, or saint. Such people are rare indeed, and most human beings function on a far less exalted level where there is a vast spectrum of dualistic states of awareness, from greater-than-normal human perception through to the lowest forms of animal consciousness re-awakened in man.

The *Tibetan Book of the Dead* warns against being trapped or seduced by the apparent reality of the visionary images encountered in the *Bardo* states. For this reason it is important during the 're-entry' phase to focus the will as much as possible on spiritual values rather than on symbols of the ego. If this does not happen, one may find oneself enmeshed in 'Judgment' visions resulting from karma associated with the personality, debased sexual fantasies or other projections of the psyche.

To summarize the essential teaching of the *Bardo Thodol*: the Great Liberation is achieved by ego-loss, or 'the death of the ego'; this state of spiritual self-realization is reached in the first *Bardo* of the Clear Light or by transcending the images of deities that arise in the second *Bardo*. Below these levels the ego gains more and more strength, and seeks 'rebirth' in the world of the senses where it is able to assert itself once more as dominant. Most of us, says Leary, are doomed to return to normality after our encounter with the realms of Spirit, but training for these levels provides greater familiarity with the most sacred dimensions of the psyche. It is inevitable that each of us will one day have to make the choice for spiritual Liberation.

The *Bardo Thodol* was the ideal map of inner space that Leary, Metzner and Alpert had been looking for. It seemed to provide one of the best available frameworks for exploring the heights of mystical perception as well as the 'rebirth', or return-phase of coming back to waking reality. *The Psychedelic Experience*, published in New York in 1964, was therefore based almost entirely on the *Bardo* sequences in the *Tibetan Book of the Dead*. It became a classic in the literature of altered states of consciousness, and remained an essential guide for the wisdom-seeking hippie counterculture through the rest of the decade.

The trauma of Alpert and Leary's dismissal from Harvard led to a temporary parting of the ways. The third member of the triumvirate, Ralph Metzner, later collaborated with Leary in creating the International Foundation for Internal Freedom and the Castalia Foundation. He also edited *The Psychedelic Review* for several years, and went on to produce a number of notable books, including *The Ecstatic Adventure*, *Maps of Consciousness* and *The Unfolding Self*. He is

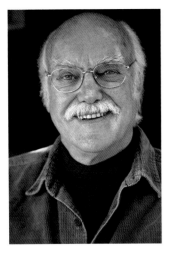

06.02 Recent photograph of Ralph Metzner.

06.03 Ram Dass (aka Richard Alpert). Both Metzner and Dass were members of the Harvard Triumvirate.

06.04 A mid-career photograph of Timothy Leary. During the 1980s Leary embraced cyberspace technology and was a frequent guest on the American campus circuit.

now Professor of Psychology at the California Institute of Integral Studies in San Francisco.

Richard Alpert went to India in 1967, initially to discover what the holy men of the East could make of LSD. A Californian named Bhagwan Dass took Alpert into the foothills of the Himalayas, and Alpert showed his sacrament to Dass's guru, Neem Karoli Baba, known to his followers as Maharaj-ji. The holy man consumed Alpert's entire stock – 900 micrograms – and was apparently totally unaffected. Alpert was told that the sage operated in a mental space called *sahaj samadhi* which was not dependent on sources of stimulation from the bio-physical level. Alpert realized that he had found a higher source of spiritual authority than he had anticipated. The Maharaj-ji allowed him to stay, providing him with a teacher, and the former Harvard professor took the name Baba Ram Dass. Ram Dass now says that 'the only thing you have to offer to another human being, ever, is your own state of being'. He remains a Westerner, if only by heritage, and for over thirty years has spent much of his time communicating the spiritual truths of Eastern mysticism to Western audiences. A stroke, however, has confined him to a wheelchair and is likely to curtail his public appearances. Ram Dass's most famous book is *Be Here Now* (1971), which has sold over two million copies. His other books include *Doing Your Own Being, The Only Dance There Is* (1974), *Grist for the Mill* (co-written with Stephen Levine) and *Still Here* (2000), full of insights on ageing, changing and dying.

Leary became a scapegoat for the widespread political distrust of psychedelics. For many years after his dismissal from Harvard he lived the life of a jail escapee and hunted man because of an initial charge of possessing under an ounce of marijuana. In his later years Leary returned to a state of comparative normality. Following the successful publication of his autobiography *Flashbacks* in 1983, Leary spent much of his time working as a talk-show host and as a lecturer on the American campus circuit. He also became passionately interested in cyberspace technology, and towards the end of his life advocated what he called 'designer death' – the act of consciously planning one's personal transition through death. Leary died in 1996.

Metzner, Alpert and Leary were not alone as psychedelic pioneers of inner space. During the 1970s Dr John C. Lilly and Dr Stanislav Grof also gained increasing recognition for their innovative exploration of psychedelic states of consciousness. Both believed the psychedelic experience had important therapeutic and transformative possibilities, and both also had a significant influence on the personal growth movement in the years ahead – Lilly as the inventor of the float-tank used for sensory isolation and meditation, and Grof as a pioneer of holotropic breath therapy, a variant on the holistic therapy known as rebirthing.

Born in 1915, Lilly graduated from the California Institute of Technology and received his doctorate in medicine from the University of Pennsylvania in 1942. He worked extensively in various research fields, including biophysics, neurophysiology, electronics and neuroanatomy. He became known for his study of dolphin-human relationships, and published two books, *Man and Dolphin* and *The Mind of the Dolphin*, before his acute awareness of the sensitivity and intelligence of dolphins aroused his ethical objections to further clinical research. He then adopted the position that it is preferable for a scientist to act as his own guinea-pig rather than inflict his research on his subjects.

Lilly switched his research to the study of human consciousness, using his own experiences as the focus of his enquiry. He decided to test the idea that a person remains awake because he is bombarded with sensory stimuli. While working for the National Institute of Mental Health in Bethesda, Maryland, he developed the first prototype of the float-tank, an environment of solitude, isolation and confinement where sensory input was minimized as far as possible. Wearing a special latex rubber mask fitted with a breathing apparatus, Lilly floated naked in quiet solitude and darkness in seawater heated to a constant 33.8°C (93°F), the temperature at which one is neither hot nor cold when resting. In the darkness Lilly felt as if he were floating in a gravity-free dimension. He discovered that the brain compensates for the reduction of sensory stimulation by producing a marked degree of heightened inner awareness. 'I went through dream-like states, trance-like states, mystical states,' he wrote later. 'In all of those states I was totally intact.' At all times he remained simultaneously aware of his floating body and the nature of the experiment.[4]

This experiment was Lilly's first scientific contact with mystical reality. It seemed to him that under these conditions the brain, or 'bio-computer', released a particular 'programme' of sensory experiences, directly related to the individual's concepts and beliefs; that is to say, he would only perceive things within the grasp of the imagination. Someone with a narrow conceptual framework would find himself in a barren, constricting 'space' when his mind-contents were revealed, but Lilly found that sensory deprivation states could also offer tremendous freedom. External reality had been shut out. He could programme a mental journey to any place that his imagination could create – his choice of programme could take him to various specific 'spaces', or to states of consciousness representing various levels of transcendence.

During the early 1960s Lilly also took LSD for the first time, and he found that this enabled him to enter mystical dimensions. Raised as a devout Roman Catholic, he believed that at death the pure soul winged its way to God. Now, years later, while listening to Beethoven's Ninth Symphony under hallucinatory influence, Lilly found himself experiencing a similar 'flight of the soul'. He saw angelic beings and an aged patriarchal God seated on a throne. The programmed learning from his youth had been re-activated by the LSD. 'Later,' wrote Lilly, 'I was to realize that the limits of one's belief set the limits of the experience.'

Sometimes on his inner journeys Lilly contacted entities he called his 'two guides'. He resists describing these beings, however, beyond indicating that they represented a particular type of direction and knowledge applicable only to his own wanderings on the inner planes. On occasion they appeared to epitomize his higher self talking down to the more constricted everyday personality, showing the way towards more integrated being. At other times they took the form of 'karmic' conscience, reminding Lilly that he had commitments to his friends and family, and could not become an 'inner-plane drop-out' without dire consequences.

As he explored the different states of inner space, Lilly also began to look for what he called a 'safe place', a point of reference. Lilly's was the dark and silent void of the water tank – 'absolute zero point' – a place 'out of the body, out of the universe as we know it.' Before him lay endless planes of possibilities barred only by the limits of the imagination.

On one occasion Lilly found himself in a space which he called the 'cosmic computer'. It seemed to him that he was a very small and insignificant part of someone else's macro-computer, in rather the same way that the Argentinian writer Jorge Luis Borges had described individuals being 'dreamed' into reality by the power of another person's imagination. Lilly sensed tremendous waves of energy, of the same intensity as those described in the Tibetan *Bardo* of the Secondary Clear Light. There was no sense of wellbeing in this experience and he found himself overwhelmed with terror, swept up in a whirlpool of meaningless energy – a loveless cosmic dance with 'no human value'.

Afterwards Lilly thought over his ideas about the origin of the physical universe, which had been formulated during his scientific training. There had been no room here for mystical trance elements, or doctrines of 'love' and 'meaning'. His negative *Bardo* visions showed that a new programme was necessary. He had failed to acknowledge the energies of the Godhead working through him.

Later Lilly had discussions with Alan Watts about Eastern mysticism. At Esalen he talked over the merits of Gestalt therapy with Fritz Perls and Ida Rolf, and here, too, he met Ram Dass, the former Richard Alpert, who had recently returned from India. Ram Dass introduced him to the *sutras* of Patanjali – a classic text on yoga – and Lilly came to realize that if he wished to find Union with the Infinity of the Void he would have to stand back from both the programmer

and the programme. He would have to see his results and frameworks in a new light, for the twofold division of seer and seen could no longer apply in a state of Unity Consciousness. He later wrote, 'Beyond transcendence is an infinite variety of unknowns.… Beyond these unknowns, now unknown, is *full complete Truth*.' For Lilly, this meant that even when we hold to a set of beliefs, they must always remain open-ended, for they cannot hope to encompass the Transcendent Unknown and contain it within finite expressions and concepts.

Lilly was later closely involved with Oscar Ichazo, a Bolivian spiritual teacher who headed a group of dedicated spiritual seekers in Arica, a town on the Pacific coast of Chile. With Ichazo he discussed the concept of 'negative spaces' and the 'burning of karma'. A high degree of concentration was called for: negative qualities were mentally 'seized' and ruthlessly exhumed in transcendentally negative spaces where they could not exert any further influence on one's state of being. Never again would they register on one's personal map of inner consciousness.

Oscar Ichazo's system was based partly on the teachings of George Gurdjieff, whose method was to push his followers physically to the edge of their endurance. Only through this effort, Gurdjieff argued, could one overcome the slavery of robot-like existence that most people confuse with real life. Like Gurdjieff, Ichazo emphasized the need for authentic spiritual awakening, and he claimed in an interview in *Psychology Today* that one of his major aims was to destroy ego-dominated thoughts.[5] He said that when the ego, or a society of egos, reaps the full hell it has sown in its search for false security and status, it comes to a point of collapse and rebirth. The collapse comes at the moment when the ego games are completely exposed and understood: illusion is shattered, subjectivity is destroyed, karma is burned. For Ichazo, the decline of society also brought with it the first moment of enlightenment – its roles and 'programmes' were suspended. The only thing left was the *first Satori*, the *first enlightenment*.

Lilly had come to Ichazo for an alternative to the contemporary scientific frameworks, and it was he who provided Lilly with a structure of the positive and negative states of consciousness from Satori through to anti-Satori. Following Gurdjieff's system, Ichazo had identified nine states of consciousness, beginning with the highest state – assigned a 'vibrational' number of 3 – through to successive states, identified symbolically by doubling the number of the previous state:

3   6   12   24   48   96   192   384   768

The last of these in the Ichazo model was considered to be a type of hell state.

Lilly now redesigned the scale, assigning positive and negative values to states on either side of what he called 'the middle of the range', or 'normal reality' (state

06.05 During his sensory isolation experiments with LSD John Lilly encountered angelic beings and saw God seated on a throne – images that reflected his traditional Roman Catholic upbringing. From the 15th-century German illuminated manuscript *The Bomberg Apocalypse.*

48). This made the nine-level spectrum of consciousness look quite different:

$$+3 \quad +6 \quad +12 \quad +24 \quad +48 \quad \text{and} \quad -48 \quad -24 \quad -12 \quad -6 \quad -3$$

Lilly's sequence identified the highest state of awareness as +3 and the lowest as -3. In the composite framework presented in Lilly's book *The Center of the Cyclone*, he identifies these states as follows (I have presented them in a simplified form here):

	State of Consciousness	Description
+3	*Dharma-Megha/Samadhi* Classical *Satori*	Death of the ego. Fusion with the Universal Mind. Union with the Godhead.
+6	*Sasmita-nir bija* Buddha Consciousness	A point source of consciousness, energy, light and love. Communication at the level of essence.
+12	*Sananda* Christ Consciousness	A state of cosmic love and divine grace. Highest state of bodily awareness.
+24	*Vicara* Basic *Satori*	Control of the human biocomputer. Ability to act knowledgeably and freely.
+48	*Vitarka*	Normal human consciousness.
-48		Openness to new ideas.
-24		Pain, guilt and fear.
-12		Extremely negative bodily state. Consciousness dominated by pain.
-6		A purgatory-like situation. A sense of meaningless is prominent.
-3		The 'quintessence of evil, the deepest hell of which one can conceive'.[6]

In a memoir published in 1990, entitled *John Lilly, So Far…*, Lilly mentions that, while his initial relationship with Ichazo was one of 'immediate rapport', they soon came to a major hurdle over the issue of ego. Ichazo's philosophy focused on reducing ego, while, as Lilly himself expresses it, his role 'wasn't to get rid of ego but rather to spend as much time as possible near the top end of the scale.'[7] Lilly became gradually disenchanted by what he perceived as Ichazo's unwillingness to entertain any belief systems other than those which he had developed through the Gurdjieff work. Lilly acknowledged that his six-month stay in Arica had helped him find his own centre – 'the eye of his storm of Being' – but by the end of 1970 their paths were diverging. Intent on pursuing complete freedom of spiritual belief, Lilly realized he could not confine himself to the restrictions of spiritual organizations – even those based on the work of Gurdjieff and the Arica mystery school teachings. In the later years of his life, he chose to go his own way, maintaining that there were few answers he took for granted. He had instead begun looking for 'a few good questions' – new scientific ideas to stretch his mind.[8] Lilly died in 2001.

HOLOTROPIC BREATH THERAPY

06.06 Transpersonal psychiatrist Dr Stanislav Grof – a pioneer of LSD psychotherapy and holotropic breath therapy, *c.* 1988.

As with Dr John Lilly, Dr Stanislav Grof became involved in the personal growth movement following years of research into psychedelics and altered states of consciousness. Born in Prague in 1931, Grof studied medicine and received his PhD from the Czechoslovakian Academy of Science. In 1954 he began research into the psychotherapeutic uses of LSD, a controversial line of enquiry which he continued after emigrating to the United States in 1967. He worked in Baltimore at the Maryland Psychiatric Research Center and became an assistant professor at Johns Hopkins University. One of his particular fields of interest was research into the use of psychedelics for easing the pain of terminal cancer patients. He also conducted studies with depressed and alcoholic patients, schizophrenics, narcotic drug addicts and people suffering from psychosomatic illnesses. He soon discovered that his research was leading him into deeper levels of consciousness than expected. Reflecting on this during an interview in 1984, he explained how he was increasingly drawn towards a transpersonal view of the human psyche:

> I was brought up and educated as a Freudian analyst and so when we started doing the LSD work I expected that we would mostly be working with biographical material. I was looking for a tool that would somehow bring out the unconscious material much faster, so that it would deepen and intensify psychoanalysis. To my surprise people would not stay in the biographical domain which, according to Western psychology, is considered to be the only domain available – memories from

childhood and the individual unconscious. Without any programming, and actually against my will, my subjects started moving into realms that hadn't been chartered in psychoanalysis at all. The first encounter was powerful – death and birth. People started having sequences of dying and feeling reborn, frequently with details from their biological birth. But this experience of death then reversed and became like a gateway into the transcendental, the archetypal – the transpersonal as we call it now. All this material emerged as a great surprise for me.[9]

As a result of his LSD research, Grof began to develop a model of the human mind which could accommodate these new elements. In this model there are basically four levels in the psychedelic encounter with the mind. The first of these, experienced at the most superficial level, involves sensory and aesthetic phenomena – for example, visionary episodes characterized by vibrant colours, geometric patterns, and experiences of beautiful natural vistas and exquisite architectural forms. There is also an increased awareness of sounds – humming, chimes and so on.

The next level Grof refers to as the 'biographical' level, and its content includes important memories, emotional problems, repressed material and unresolved conflicts from one's present life. Basically, this is the realm of the individual unconscious, associated with areas of the personality accessible in familiar states of awareness – the unconscious mind as conceived by Freud. Grof coined the term 'COEX System' to describe a 'specific constellation of memories consisting of condensed experiences (and related fantasies) from different life periods of the individual', and he recognized early on that these COEX patterns in individual patients could be triggered into conscious awareness using LSD in a therapeutically controlled environment.[10] On the basis of the data he was uncovering, however, Grof felt obliged to move beyond Freud's model of the mind, because he came to believe that restricting his framework of the unconscious to 'biographical' or ego-based elements was no longer tenable.

Grof's third level of consciousness encompasses realms of awareness 'characterized by a degree of experiential intensity that transcends anything that is usually conceived to be the limit for the individual human being'. This might involve a 'deep, overwhelming confrontation with the existential realities of death and dying, pain and suffering, birth and agony' but could also open the individual to profound religious and spiritual experiences.[11] Grof calls these levels of awareness – which relate closely to the process of birth and the intra-uterine experience – Basic Perinatal Matrices, and he identifies four of them (BPM 1–4). He believes that each of these four matrices can be linked to different types of religious or spiritual experience:

06.07 Cosmic unity in the womb – BPM 1.

06.08 Hell states and 'lurking evil' – BPM 2.

06.09 The struggles continue but transcendence is possible – BPM 3.

06.10 The spiritual experience of death and rebirth – BPM 4.

BPM 1 is associated with the intra-uterine bond of the foetus to the mother, a type of 'symbiotic unity' reflected in the mystical experience as feelings of cosmic unity, tranquillity, bliss and transcendence of time and space – they are often what Grof calls 'good womb' experiences. Grof correlates BPM 1 with Maslow's 'peak experiences' and has described them as 'an important gateway to a variety of transpersonal experiences'.[12]

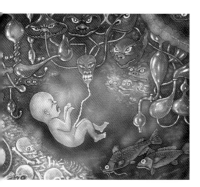

BPM 2 is related to the first clinical stage of biological delivery, characterized by muscular uterine contractions while the cervix is closed. This is experienced as a feeling of 'no exit', of cosmic engulfment, or being trapped in a torturous domain. Understandably, it is often a terrifying time for the subject, who feels overwhelmed by increasing levels of anxiety, unseen sources of danger and sometimes a strong sense of lurking evil. Grof correlates this level with Hell states and the 'expulsion from Paradise'.[13] Examples of this type of experience include Prometheus chained to a rock and tortured by an eagle who feeds on his liver, Christ's visions in the Garden of Gethsemane, and the Dark Night of the Soul as described by St John of the Cross.

BPM 3 is associated in the birth process with the second stage of delivery, when the cervix is dilated. Here, although the uterine contractions are still continuing, the open cervix offers the prospects of survival through the struggle along the birth canal. Grof associates this, in the LSD experience, with death-rebirth struggles, and says that at this time the individual can still have frightening encounters with repulsive materials – faeces, blood and urine, and so on. But there is also the sense of impending release – the distinct impression that transcendence is possible. Grof believes that this level sometimes produces visions associated with bloody sacrifice – mythic images of Moloch, Astarte, Kali, or Aztec/Mayan ceremonies – but he also associates BPM 3 with 'the transcending aspects of the crucifixion and of Christ's suffering, as well as the positive aspects of the Last Judgment'.[14]

BPM 4 is associated with the spiritual experience of death and rebirth and, according to Grof, is linked in the birth process with the actual birth of the individual. LSD subjects entering this phase report visions of vivid white or golden light, the universe is perceived as indescribably beautiful and radiant, and those experiencing it feel cleansed and purged, as if they have entered a state of spiritual redemption or salvation. Grof associates this state mythically with the rebirth of Osiris – the ancient Egyptian god who was brought back to life by Isis after being murdered and dismembered by Set – and also with the resurrected Christ, who is crucified on the cross but triumphs over death.[15]

Grof does not believe that the correlations between the birth process and the levels of consciousness accessed through LSD are coincidental. Sometimes individuals appear to relive their actual birth experiences and even seem to tap into the thought processes of their mothers. He also maintains that his LSD research confirms the presence of Jungian archetypes in the collective unconscious – that it is no longer appropriate to consider such a concept as simply theoretical:

> LSD subjects frequently report that in their transpersonal sessions they have had a vivid and authentic sense of confrontation or identification with archetypes representing generalized biological, psychological or social types and roles; these can reflect various levels of abstraction and different degrees of generalization. The Old Wise Man, Good Samaritan, Conqueror, Martyr, Fugitive, Outcast, Tyrant, Fool or Hermit are examples of the more specialized archetypal images. The most general archetypes always have strong elements of numinosity, as exemplified by the Great Mother, Terrible Mother, Father, Child-King, Great Hermaphrodite, Animus and Anima, or Cosmic Man. Frequently transpersonal experiences of this kind have concrete cultural characteristics and take the forms of specific deities, demons, demi-gods and heroes.… Quite common also are experiences with spirits of deceased human beings and suprahuman spiritual entities.[16]

Significant and powerful though they are, Grof does not regard perinatal and archetypal experiences as the most profound or transcendent levels of human awareness. In his view, it is possible to extend still further along the spectrum of consciousness – from the four perinatal levels to an experience of the complete transcendence of human individuality. Here, he writes, 'we begin to free ourselves from the preconception that consciousness is something created within the human brain. Transpersonal consciousness is infinite, rather than finite, stretching beyond the limits of time and space.'[17] For Grof, consciousness would seem to be an innate characteristic of the natural universe:

> Mind and consciousness might not be exclusive privileges of the human species but [may] permeate all of Nature, existing in the most elemental to the most complex forms. Struggle as we might, we seem unable to free ourselves from preconceptions imposed on us by our culture and by what we believe to be common sense. However, if we are to maintain these illusions it becomes necessary to ignore a vast body of observations and information coming from modern consciousness research and from a variety of other scientific disciplines. From all these sources comes evidence strongly suggesting that the universe and the human psyche have no boundaries or limits. Each of us is connected with, and is an expression of, all of existence.[18]

When research into the medical and therapeutic possibilities of LSD became politically untenable in the mid-1970s, Grof was forced to explore other techniques of achieving transpersonal states. Gradually he moved towards what he now calls holotropic breath therapy, a technique that resembles the more widely known 'rebirthing'. The latter was developed by Leonard Orr in California during the early 1970s, and both rebirthing and holotropic breath therapy derive substantially from *Pranayama* – the Indian Yoga of breath – which employs a connected breathing rhythm to produce an altered state of consciousness. In both therapies the subject lies horizontally in a comfortable position with a facilitator, or helper, sitting nearby to assist in any experiential crisis. The session begins as the subject engages in rhythmic in-and-out breathing, with no pauses in between. As Orr has written: 'You merge with your breath, flowing, glowing, soaring, relaxing profoundly, your mind melting into your spirit, surging, awakening your inner being and the quiet sounds of your soul.'

In holotropic breath therapy, however, the technique is more intense and the results more sudden and dramatic. The breathing is accompanied by recorded music which is chosen to reflect different phases of the cathartic process. As Grof explains: 'The music is the vehicle itself, so at the beginning we start with some very activating, powerful music. Then, maybe an hour into the session, we move into a kind of culminating, "breakthrough" type of music – for example using the sounds of bells or similar, very powerful, transcendental sounds.'[19] His musical selections include African tribal rhythms, Sufi chants, Indian ragas, Japanese flutes and various forms of ambient music.

The hyperventilation employed in the holotropic approach actually reduces the amount of oxygen transmitted to the cortex of the brain, producing a natural 'high'. The technique simulates the experience of mystics who live in high altitudes where the air is more rarefied, and is therefore ideal, as Grof himself says casually, for those who can't make the trip to the Himalayas. More importantly, Grof has found that holotropic breathing, like LSD psychotherapy, can resolve profound emotional problems associated with the birth process, and can also take subjects into the furthest transpersonal realms. A significant finding of Grof's more recent work is that his original model of consciousness remains basically unchanged: the same transpersonal levels of awareness can be accessed either through such psychedelics as LSD or through non-drug, altered-state modalities like holotropic breathwork. The human mind and the universe are as they are. Different modalities and techniques may be used to explore what remains, essentially, the same terrain.

7

The Holistic Perspective

07.01 18th-century Chinese acupuncture chart showing the points for controlling diseases of the heart and sexual organs.

The 1960s psychedelic consciousness brought in its train a widespread awareness that inner states of being were vitally important in any definition of human-ness.[1] This, of course, was a central tenet of both humanistic and transpersonal psychology, but it now began to influence concepts of health and medical care as well. On the American west coast especially, the pioneering work of Abraham Maslow on 'self-actualization' was beginning to lead to a broader understanding of what it meant to be a healthy individual. According to Maslow's holistic model, individuals could increasingly assume responsibility for their own health and gradually lessen their dependency on doctors by adopting preventive healthcare measures and early intervention approaches to illness.

THE TOTAL HUMAN BEING

A characteristic definition, epitomizing the new ideas, appeared in *Dimensions of Humanistic Medicine*, published in San Francisco in 1975. Here the authors described human healthcare in a way that acknowledged the *total* human being both in physical and spiritual terms:

> A person is more than his body. Every human being is a holistic, interdependent relationship of body, emotions, mind and spirit. The clinical process which causes the patient to consult the medical profession is best understood as this whole and dynamic relationship. The maintenance of continued health depends on the harmony of this whole.[2]

The idea of tapping one's own self-healing powers, of regarding the challenge of overcoming disease as a learning experience, and of becoming more self-reliant, were all perceptions that had spilled over from the earlier years of Maslow, Sutich and Esalen. In more traditional styles of Western medical practice, patients were generally seen as dependent on the doctor and illness was considered a complaint to be eliminated, but the new focus was now on helping the patient to become more knowledgeable about his or her condition and to participate in the healing process, providing the patient with insights and opportunities for self-discovery.

The old concept was that health could be defined as the absence of disease, and that in addressing states of illness one should pay attention primarily to the specific symptoms, or body parts, that had 'gone wrong'. Now, however, the emphasis was being placed on health as a positive and natural state of human wellbeing – the whole person, and not just the symptom or organ, was the subject of the medical enquiry.

The new public awareness of the relationship between diet, exercise and health was beginning to show up in the US National Center for Health Statistics, particularly in relation to the incidence of stroke. Between 1962 and 1973 the average figure of 102.1 deaths per thousand had been reasonably constant, but by 1976 it had dropped to 88.2. A major reason for this marked improvement were the 'advances in lowering blood pressure, a reduction in fat intake by many citizens…[and] more vigorous exercise programs', as well as the development of coronary care units and better emergency care in many hospitals.[3]

Among those who were drawn to the holistic model of preventive healthcare there was also an increasing recognition that the frame of reference should not be physical alone but should also encompass mental and emotional aspects of health, and could even include such areas as spiritual values, the search for personal meaning, and the integrative elements of religious beliefs. At the same time, in the holistic paradigm there was a shift away from curative medicine towards the prevention of illness. This brought with it the long overdue acceptance that sensible nutrition, regular exercise, personal preventive health-care and other self-help measures were all vital in avoiding illness. In a 1977 speech outlining his commitment to a comprehensive national health programme, newly elected US President Jimmy Carter placed a clear focus on prevention, alternatives to expensive therapies and community-based health institutions.

It's time for us to get back to the basics and the basic need of any health-care system is to care about people and to prevent disease and injury before they happen. Prevention is both cheaper and simpler than cure. But we have stressed the latter – cure – and we have ignored, to an increasing degree, the former – prevention. Our traditional self-reliance, our emphasis on family and community health, our concern about prevention of disease, regular check-ups, early diagnosis, and early treatment has been almost forgotten by many in the onrush of technology and increasing specialization.[4]

As Schutz, Maslow and Perls had already been emphasizing, it was a matter of taking substantial responsibility for your own healthcare. And where treatments *were* required from a doctor, it was preferable that they were intended not just to repress isolated symptoms but to help restore balance to the organism as a whole. Most importantly, the new holistic health paradigm also acknowledged the potential value of many natural remedies, which could complement, and in some instances replace, expensive synthetic medicines, whenever they were appropriate. The holistic counterculture now brought to the fore the remarkable capacity of the human organism to rectify imbalance and initiate processes of self-healing. Meditation and yoga could be used to help reduce stress, and naturopathy, acupuncture, shiatsu, homeopathy and other 'natural' therapies, all of which stimulated healing processes from within the organism itself, were preferred to conventional medical treatments. This brought in its wake the belief that healing should be as non-intrusive as possible, and that synthetic chemicals and other 'unnatural' agents were to be totally avoided, or used only as a last resort.[5]

Perhaps the most far-reaching implication of the holistic health perspective was that mind, body and spirit were regarded as interrelated, and healthcare was being called upon to address all these aspects as one. This idea tended towards mysticism, and still attracts widespread resistance among many conventional Western doctors. Indeed, the whole issue of the interrelatedness of mind and body – quite apart from spirit – has only recently begun to gain momentum in orthodox medical circles. From a medical viewpoint it has been clinically difficult to identify specific links between mind (*psyche*) and body (*soma*) in causing disease even though many individual doctors have believed for some time that such connections do indeed exist.

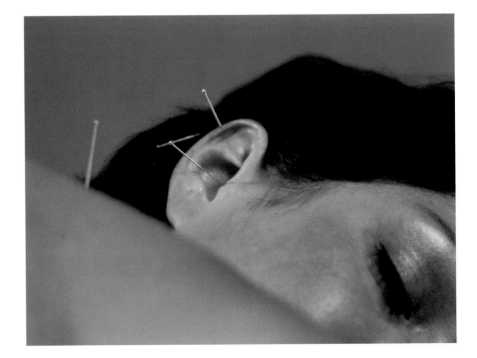

07.02 Modern acupuncture
using fine stainless steel needles.

07.03 Yoga on the beach.

PSYCHOSOMATIC ASPECTS OF DISEASE

Hans Selye, Emeritus Professor at the University of Montreal, President of the International Institute of Stress and a pioneering figure in the holistic health movement, had long regarded stress as an important factor in causing illness, but underlined that stress could not be equated simply with intensity of lifestyle. Stress, he believed, was best thought of as deriving from the perception of events in our lives and was therefore a reflection of our ability to deal with the demands of those events. Stress could be measured by general irritability, depression, high blood pressure, impulsive and aggressive behaviour, inability to concentrate, emotional tension, sexual problems, insomnia, migraine headaches and a variety of other symptoms. Selye noted that people react differently to the demands made upon them. We learn to adapt to pressures, but stress arises when the process of coping starts to fail. We all have to develop daily priorities for regaining equilibrium – by slowing down or altering our pace of life, and so on, otherwise we risk a breakdown of health – beginning with relatively minor conditions like skin complaints and intestinal upsets, but leading perhaps to more serious illnesses.[6]

07.04 Canadian stress expert Dr Hans Selye in a meeting with graduate students.

Many studies have since been made to determine whether stress is related to the incidence of cancer and heart attacks, and researchers have also wondered whether certain personality types are more susceptible than others to outbreaks of ill-health. In 1974 the Californian cardiologists Dr Ray Rosenman and Dr Meyer Friedman published a highly influential book which described how a behavioural pattern known as 'Type A' correlated with the likelihood of heart disease.[7] The Type A person was typically extremely competitive and aggressive, was inclined to schedule more and more activities into less and less time, was usually in too much of a hurry to derive any sense of beauty from the environment, did not delegate tasks easily, exhibited explosive speech patterns, had trouble sitting and doing nothing, and was given to lip-clicking, head nodding, fist-clenching and other related traits. In a business setting the typical Type A person could

07.05 Psychotherapist Dr Lawrence Le Shan, a leading advocate of the health benefits of meditation in the 1970s.

appear to be productive and full of confidence, but underneath felt inferior and was prone to failure. By contrast, the Type B person was calmer, had more inner composure, and was less demonstrative in his actions. He could be as self-motivated as Type A, but his behaviour was not as competitive or aggressive.

A similar relationship was seen between psychological factors, stress and the outbreak of cancer. Dr Lawrence Le Shan, a research psychotherapist based in New York, was a leading advocate of meditation and holistic health during the 1970s. After studying 250 cancer patients and administering personality tests, Le Shan compared them with 150 non-cancer subjects. He came to the following conclusions:

77 per cent of cancer subjects but only 14 per cent of healthy subjects showed extreme tension over the loss of a close relative or friend.

64 per cent of cancer subjects as opposed to 32 per cent non-cancer subjects showed signs of being unable adequately to express anger, resentment and aggression towards other people, but bottled up their feelings instead.

69 per cent of cancer patients had low personal esteem and feelings of culpability while only 34 per cent of the control group showed this characteristic.

Typically, cancer patients had experienced a major emotional trauma 6–18 months before the development of the disease.[8]

Dr Carl Simonton, a physician from the University of Oregon specializing in the holistic treatment of cancer, extended the Friedman and Rosenman hypothesis with his view that there was also a 'cancer' personality. He described it as tending to resentment, self-pity, low self-esteem and difficulties in sustaining long-term relationships.[9] He also placed great emphasis on Professor Selye's discovery that chronic stress suppresses the immune system, which provides the mechanism for destroying or keeping at bay the cancerous cells in the body. Dr Simonton summarized his conclusions during the 'May Lectures' in London in 1974:

All human beings have cancer cells within them. The problem is not the cancer cells but the breakdown of the body's ability to deal with them and rid itself of disease. I see cancer, therefore, as having much in common with diseases like tuberculosis, the common cold and so forth. We are continually exposed to many dangerous agents both from within and without, but it is only when we become susceptible to them that the disease actually develops.'[10]

07.06 Dr Carl Simonton, a pioneer in the use of visualization and relaxation to treat cancer, Zuma Beach, Malibu, 1999.

One of Simonton's most distinctive techniques, introduced as an adjunct to orthodox radiation therapy, was the use of visualization and relaxation to help his patients concentrate on their cancerous growths. He asked his patients, three times a day, every day, to visualize their medical treatment and the body's white blood cells acting positively and victoriously over the disease. He discovered that those with a positive attitude towards their disease had a much more favourable clinical response to treatment than those with a negative attitude. And it was Dr Simonton's visualization for health that would be taken up in earnest by the New Age movement.

While many orthodox doctors continue to be wary of psychosomatic treatments and do not rush to acknowledge that meditation and visualization can produce clinical effects, a relatively new discipline, psychoneuroimmunology (PNI) has gone a long way towards endorsing the holistic health perspective. Since the 1980s PNI researchers have been involved in investigating how the brain interacts with the body's immune cells – how it sends signals along the nerves to prime the body to fight disease. Because these neural pathways can be triggered by thoughts and emotions, such research has been useful for discovering how holistic therapies like visualization and meditation are in fact working with something physiologically real. It would seem that the brain and immune system constitute a closed circuit and that there is a two-way interaction between them that monitors the presence of intrusive bacteria, viruses and tumours in the body.[11]

Neuropharmacologist Dr Candace Pert, a research Professor in the Department of Physiology and Biophysics at the Georgetown University Medical Center in Washington, D.C., and author of *Molecules of Emotion* (1997) – a popular book among many New Age readers – believes the mind is not confined to the brain. In fact, she says we can regard the mind as being present in every cell of the body.[12] Each cell in the human organism has intelligence and each has receptors that can send and receive information.

Pert's scientific concern is with neuropeptides, small protein-like chemicals, similar to morphine, made in the brain, that operate like 'biochemical units of emotion', producing marked changes in mood. It also appears that neuropeptides can connect with macrophages, the cells that help destroy infection and disease. The interaction of these two classes of chemicals in the body appears to offer a scientific explanation for a phenomenon most of us acknowledge intuitively – that our moods and state of mind can affect our state of health. For example, it may be the sheer emotional power of optimism and positive thinking that helps some people recover from seemingly terminal illnesses – the positive attitude itself helps to keep the immune system fighting. As PNI researcher Professor Ed

07.07 Neuropeptides, small protein-like chemicals in the brain that connect with macrophages, the cells that help destroy infection and disease.

07.08 Dr Candace Pert, author of *Molecules of Emotion*. According to Dr Pert every cell in the body has intelligence and receptors that send and receive information.

Blalock, of the University of Texas has observed: 'Your classical sensory systems recognize things you can see, taste, touch, smell and hear. Bacteria and viruses have none of these qualities, so how are you going to know they are there unless the immune system lets your brain in on the secret? The immune system may be the sixth sense we've been seeking all these years.'[13]

THE PROPHETS OF SELF-HELP

An awareness of psychosomatic factors in health is one thing, the exploration of 'personal growth' and 'human potential' quite another. As the widespread interest in holistic health gathered momentum during the 1970s, the body-mind-spirit paradigm soon began to acquire a particular viewpoint that would lead the youthful wisdom seekers of the Leary generation in an entirely new direction. It was based on *personal motivation* – on the idea, central to the American dream, that we all have the potential to achieve wealth, success and happiness if we have the drive and vision to bring it about. The United States had long had its share of popular writers of the 'you-too-can-be-a-success' school, most of whom were self-taught and self-educated. Introducing the elements of 'self-help' and 'success' to the holistic concept of inner balance and wellbeing was decisive in the birthing of what has now become known as the New Age movement.

WORLD'S HIGHEST STANDARD OF LIVING

There's no way like the American Way

The use of this Poster Panel donated by Foster and Kleiser Company

07.09 Chasing the American dream of health, wealth and prosperity: a billboard on Highway 99 in California, erected to foster optimism and confidence during the Depression.

One of these early motivational writers was William H. Danforth, founder of the Ralston Purina Company, whose book *I Dare You!* ran through many editions in the 1950s. A chapter in this book, entitled 'You can be bigger than you are', epitomized his approach and his potent message that everyone could transform themselves into happier, more prosperous individuals.

A similar work was Napoleon Hill's *Think and Grow Rich* (1950), which announced to the reader that it would 'help you to negotiate your way through life with harmony and understanding [since] you are the master of your fate and the captain of your soul'. Hill was aware that success depended on positive motivation, and this, in turn, was based on positive thoughts. He believed that to implant the concept of achievement in the mind was a necessary precondition for success. The individual, he argued, should 'feed his subconscious mind on thoughts of a creative nature', and visualize himself on the road to success. He advocated a form of self-hypnosis, which he called 'auto-suggestion', as a way of doing this. Hill's approach is mirrored in the New Age notion of 'prosperity and abundance consciousness', where devotees visualize their future wealth and happiness, bolstering it all the time with affirmations intended to guarantee a successful outcome. Interestingly Hill anticipated the New Age in other ways. He maintained that to contact the Infinite Intelligence in the Universe, one's mind would have to operate with the highest 'vibrations', transcending the barriers of ordinary perception to look beyond to richer horizons.

Also in this style, but rather more sophisticated, was the bestseller *Psycho-Cybernetics* (1960) by Maxwell Maltz, a plastic surgeon. He had noticed that modifying his patients' features often led to positive changes in personality, and he postulated that one could similarly visualize a more positive internal self-image to effect constructive change in one's life. The term 'cybernetics' (from the Greek for 'steersman') had been coined in 1947 by mathematician Norbert Wiener and the physicist Arturo Rosenblueth, and was defined as the 'science of control and communication in the animal and the machine'. Wiener and Rosenblueth were aware that biological organisms seemed to have sensors that measured deviations from set goals, and provided 'feedback' to enable such behaviour to be corrected. Basically, Maltz believed that the visualization of the internal self-image could help provide a base for the personality and behaviour, and that, as long as the self-image was positively reinforced, there were no limits to individual accomplishment. In this way, as one hears so often in the New Age today, people could readily learn to 'create their own reality' through a process of transforming the self.

For Maltz, however, 'positive thinking' by itself wasn't enough – the self-image had to be positive as well. A person endeavouring to think positively with a negative self-image could hardly hope to be successful; the two dimensions of the personality would simply fight against each other. He also noted that a person harbouring resentment, for example, was effectively allowing others to determine how he should feel or act by fixating on past events. This was completely inconsistent with a striving for a positive future of success and self-fulfilment. Guilt was also a matter of living in the past by trying to atone in the present for some previous 'wrong'. He argued that no one could change the past, so guilt was hardly warranted. The appropriate task, emotionally, was to respond to the present situation.

He believed that physical relaxation, imagination and hypnosis were the most important ways to change the self-image from negative to positive. 'The proper use of the imagination can be equivalent to the beginning of a goal and a belief in this goal. And if this belief is strong enough we hypnotize ourselves with it… all our habits, good and bad, are daily forms of self-hypnosis. Belief is a form of creative hypnotism.'[14]

The New Age counterpart of Maxwell Maltz is Shakti Gawain, author of *Creative Visualization* (1978) and *Living in the Light* (1986) – works now regarded as New Age classics. In the first of these books Gawain provided exercises, meditations and affirmations to assist readers in visualizing health, prosperity, loving relationships and 'the fulfilment of desires'. In an interview in 1988 with New Age newspaper, *LA Resources*, she said that creative visualization is a technique 'of being able to imagine having what you want in your life so that you can create the internal experience of having your life be the way you want it to be.… Creating that internal experience seems to open us up to creating it externally as well.'[15]

With the publication of her second book, *Living in the Light*, Gawain moved towards recognition of an internal guiding intelligence accessed by following one's deep intuitions. During her interview, she mentioned that this heightened awareness provided her with a higher quality of life: 'Moving with the energy of life and with the energy of the universe in a really spontaneous way is just the most exciting and wonderful way to live.' Clearly, her view of visualization and intuition had taken her beyond the more specifically goal-oriented concepts of Hill and Maltz, and she now also acknowledged Carl Jung's idea of confronting the 'shadow', even maintaining that facing one's darker side was a vital part of the process of planetary transformation:

> To 'live in the light' you really have to be willing to go into what you feel is the darkness. You have to face your shadow self and bring that into the light. I believe that as we are doing that individually we are also doing that on a worldwide level. The world is going through a lot of darkness, upheaval and pain, but we are becoming conscious of the things which we have repressed in the past – the things we have not been willing to deal with. Just as each of us are doing that in our own lives, it's happening on a mass consciousness level too. I feel that if we keep having the courage, those of us who are willing to really face ourselves and really do delve into ourselves and really start living in accordance with our own inner truths to the best of our abilities, we will see that reflected in the world around us. We're just going to keep seeing that, more and more. We really live in a very exciting time.[16]

FROM MIND DYNAMICS TO INWARD BOUND

Alexander Everett was first an exponent of 'self-improvement', but like Shakti Gawain, he moved gradually towards a method based on transcending thought itself. He has been an important influence on such figures as Werner Erhard (founder of est and its later incarnation, Forum), Jim Quinn (Life Stream), Peter and Ruth Honzatko (Alpha Dynamics), and other mind control groups.

07.10 Popular New Age author Shakti Gawain, advocate of creative visualization and positive affirmations.

Born in 1921, Everett fought for six years in the British Army during World War II, became a teacher, then established the private Shiplake School for boys in Henley-on-Thames, near London. In 1968 he moved to the United States, and founded a system of personal development training called Mind Dynamics. Based initially in Texas and later in the San Francisco Bay Area, Everett promoted his ideas to a large audience through seminars and training programmes in which he explained how the mind affected the emotions and how emotions affected the body. But despite financial success, Everett did not find his seminars fulfilling. He discovered that only around ten per cent of people attending benefited substantially from his teaching, and they were already successful in their lives. He wanted to develop new ways of helping a much larger percentage of the population, and he disbanded Mind Dynamics in 1973. He then conducted a spiritual search of his own:

07.11 Alexander Everett, founder of Mind Dynamics and Inward Bound.

I travelled to India and began to realize that there was a power beyond the mind – and that was the *self*. In the West we may be inclined to call it the 'spirit' or the 'soul' – according to the religious tradition we belong to – but I found out that the level of the self is perfect: there is no duality at that point. It seemed to me that if I got into that level, the highest power could control the lower powers. Most people try to find out who they are through the mind and you can't do it. The mind is designed to work at the outer levels. Until you get to the inner levels there is no way you can know about these higher powers. This is the big mistake the Western world makes. The mind is a lower level of consciousness. It cannot perceive that which is above.

Everett incorporated the fruits of his spiritual search into a programme called Inward Bound which he organized from his centre near Eugene, Oregon. Focusing on the idea that the God-principle can be found deep within every human being, he came to believe that there are four levels of human functioning – physical, emotional, mental and spiritual:

I teach that we should stop thinking – that we should still the mind – and when that happens we are awakened to a Higher Source, the Eternal, the I Am, or whatever you care to call it. I train people through a process called 'centering' to make contact, to be open, to wake up to this Higher Source. The idea of Inward Bound is to go to this inner state. When you do that you know. At the lower levels you only think you know. To me, God is not somebody 'out there'. God is a principle. God is within you. As you awaken to that fact, you change. In my seminars I aim for this process of centering on the God part within.[17]

During an interview I conducted with Everett in November 1988, I asked him what he felt were the implications of his approach, both within the human potential movement and in a broader, international context. His response was both encouraging and optimistic:

Human potential in the ultimate sense is developing the highest state of consciousness. When you function at the lower level you want power; you want money, you want possessions, but you are on your own at this level. However, when you open yourself to the highest level, you get a sense of One-ness, you are one with everybody else, and then you realize you can serve other people – you're not in it just for yourself. I believe this is the big quantum leap that is coming to the planet in the next few years. Man is going to have to switch over from the lower self to the level of co-operation and service. At the moment only a minority group is doing this – but it's growing, At the moment man is Homo Sapiens – the 'wise intellectual'. Later man will be known as 'Homo Noeticus' – the knowing man, who is guided by intuition and inspiration, Selfishness is out of date: co-operation is coming. People are going to have to share and work together.[18]

Mystics and Metaphysicians

On one level, as Alexander Everett has suggested, the New Age has been all about developing a capacity for greater intuition, striving for inner spiritual knowledge and for communal co-operation – these are some of its most positive and worthwhile elements. It is also true, however, that many New Age enthusiasts have become excessively eclectic and undiscriminating in their pursuit of mystical enlightenment. The New Age movement offers healing with crystals, metaphysical communication with dolphins, affirmations for prosperity consciousness, and a seemingly never-ending procession of 'spiritual masters' from both East and West – some of whom hold workshops on the perennial wisdom teachings while simultaneously presiding over wealthy, well endowed corporate organizations.

There are those who are attracted to the New Age because they hope that by attaining new levels of mystical self-realization they may come to feel that they are a class apart – exclusive members of a group of more 'evolved' human beings, or 'spiritual illuminati'. There are men who are drawn to the New Age in order to explore their inner feminine natures, and women who seek more dynamic and assertive 'masculine' paradigms for self-renewal. There are business executives who are drawn to the New Age for its promise of material abundance and an end to 'poverty consciousness'. And there are those whose sense of self-confidence is perhaps so fragile that they grasp at all manner of oracles – from predictive astrology and fortune-telling with the *I Ching* or Tarot, through to personal communication with angels.

VOICES OF THE NEW AGE

The New Age has its own superstars. They include motivational speaker and doctor Deepak Chopra; 'angel therapist' Doreen Virtue; 'channeller' Neale Donald Walsch; self-help seminar leaders Anthony Robbins, Louise Hay and Wayne Dyer; holistic therapists Carolyn Myss and Brandon Bays; and Hollywood star and New Age spokesperson Shirley MacLaine. They all, in their respective fields, offer an ultimately positive outlook on life and have inspirational messages to convey. Sometimes, however, these messages lead to misunderstandings.

During a New Age lecture in New York in 1987, emphasizing the divine potential in all human beings, Shirley MacLaine told her audience, 'I am God.' When a woman rose to object, MacLaine is said to have replied, 'If you don't see me as God, that's because you don't see yourself as God.'[1] Maybe she was implying that every human being is animated by the spark of the universal Godhead – a basic principle in the wisdom traditions of both the East and West. As one writer expressed it: 'She believes that each person is the centre of creation and that power, wisdom and the strength to overcome resides in every individual.'[2]

Dr Deepak Chopra has also sent mixed messages during his extraordinary career. He is an articulate and well informed lecturer, and his ability to present a fusion of holistic healing principles with insights into quantum physics, 'cellular intelligence' and transpersonal states of consciousness is impressive. The Dalai Lama himself has endorsed Chopra's book *How to Know God* (2000). Sometimes, however, Chopra seems to be endorsing the cause of spiritual materialism. Born in India, he trained as a doctor, but eventually gave up Western medicine for Indian Ayurvedic medicine because he was less concerned with curing disease than with promoting holistic health. After establishing himself in the USA, Chopra was able to transform himself into what one commentator has called 'the rock star of the new spirituality'. His numerous books – among them *The Seven Spiritual Laws of Success* (1994) – have sold prodigiously, and he earns tens of millions of dollars each year from the sales of his tapes and alternative health products. He also has a close personal following of Hollywood glitterati, among them Elizabeth Taylor, Winona Ryder and Demi Moore, as well as television hostess Oprah Winfrey. Deepak Chopra is possibly the first New Age spiritual guru to claim wealth is God-given. 'I have no qualms about being a millionaire,' he told a journalist from *Newsweek*, 'and I want everyone else to know that they can do it too. People who have achieved an enormous amount of success are inherently very spiritual.'

08.01 Dr Deepak Chopra at a Mardi Gras party at Manray Restaurant and Bar, New York, March 2003.

TRANSFORMATION – FOR A FEE

The blend of 'wealth and wisdom' is a successful mix in the commercial arenas of the New Age. In Western consumerist society, where anything in demand can be marketed, it is unfortunately true that assuaging spiritual thirst has itself become a commodity – and this product usually comes at a cost. There is a vast array of personal and metaphysical 'transformation' seminars, many of them marketed for excessively high fees. Some come with the promotional tag that money is simply 'a unit of power and energy' and that 'prosperity consciousness' is potentially available to all of us if we can 'take the responsibility' to recognize our own self-worth.

08.02 'Angel therapist' Doreen Virtue, a well known figure in contemporary New Age circles.

Techniques like this have certainly worked for 'human potential communicator' Anthony Robbins, author of motivational bestsellers like *Awaken the Giant Within* (1992) and *Notes from a Friend* (1995). Robbins reputedly earns $150,000 a day for his seminars on overcoming fear, and owns an entire island in Fiji. And while he is among the most successful international self-promoters in the consciousness-raising business, there are many others who aspire to follow in his footsteps.

American self-help writer Louise Hay also publishes several motivational authors, who include Dr Doreen Virtue, Wayne Dyer, Stuart Wilde and past-lives therapist Dr Brian Weiss. Hay House has no peer in the holistic marketplace and is one of the most successful independent publishing companies in the United States.

American 'angel therapist' Dr Doreen Virtue is a leading Hay House author. Trained originally as a psychologist and nutritionist, Dr Virtue came from a family interested in psychic and spiritual healing, and this gradually became more important in her work. A highly articulate and personable presenter, with such titles as *Healing with the Angels* (1999), *Divine Guidance* (1999) and *Angel Visions* (2000) to her credit, Doreen Virtue's New Age readership is predominantly female. During her lectures on the healing powers of angels, fairies and Nature spirits, she encourages her audience to call on these supernatural agencies to assist in the treatment of illness or to avoid misfortune.[3]

Clearly the New Age arena is a diverse and wondrous place, and at times its scope seems almost limitless. I possess a 1997 copy of an American New Age magazine called *Interface*, which lists an extraordinary number of personal transformation seminars and workshops – once again, all of them available at a price: 'The Necessity of Meeting God in the Darkness'; 'Embracing the Shadow and Reclaiming our Wholeness'; 'Freedom from Emotional Eating'; 'The Seven Stages of Money Maturity'; 'Evolving Culture through the Chakras'; 'The Tao of Now', and so the list continues.[4] No doubt many of these workshops are meaningful and worthy, but it seems that in popular American culture – a culture that ultimately permeates everywhere around the planet – spirituality and transformation can be purchased in weekend workshops like goods from a supermarket.

Where the New Age seems to have crumbled in its credibility is in its often uncritical mix of self-help, 'channelled' inspiration, confused mythologies and showbiz therapies. There is now a multimillion-dollar international market in experiential workshops, lectures, crystals, relationship counselling and 'rebirthing', presented in a way that often tends to trivialize the more important findings of humanistic and transpersonal psychology. Similarly, there are numerous workshops on loving relationships, discovering the inner child, dialoguing

08.03 Massage is now a mainstream modality in modern healthcare.

with the inner voice, recovering the inner song, or reawakening the inner pulse – all of them variants on Carl Jung's theories or the encounter group therapies of the 1960s.

And still the New Age concentration on self-help and personal transformation remains. It is a truism that one should transform oneself before seeking to transform others. While at times, and often with justification, this may appear to be an extremely self-centred attitude, the broader purpose – at least, in theory – is to move beyond exploring one's own individuality to develop a state of awareness in one's relationship with others, and then with one's immediate environment and the planet as a whole. It is clear, however, that the process of individual integration needs to occur on a number of levels – physical, mental, emotional and spiritual. A whole range of alternative 'mind, body and spirit' modalities, some more authentic than others, has sprung up to cater for this need.

Underlying all these therapies is the common theme of self-transformation and the credo that if we can all make the effort to transform ourselves and raise our culture to the next phase of human evolution, the world will be a better place.[5]

Bodywork therapies like massage, chiropractic, the Alexander Technique and yoga are now mainstream and uncontroversial, and there are many meditation, relaxation and visualization techniques that are both credible and worthwhile. It is in the New Age approaches to the spirit, however, that one finds the most controversial concepts and practices.

CHANNELLING AND CRYSTALS

One of the most popular New Age modalities is 'channelling', or psychic mediumship. Channelling is in fact a more recent name for spiritualism, and as a metaphysical practice it has remained comparatively unchanged since its heyday in the late nineteenth century. In channelling the psychic becomes a vehicle for communications from the spirit-world, entering trance or meditative states and claiming to make contact with spirit-helpers and guides on the inner planes. Clients – or workshop participants – are given advice on how to attain a state of wellbeing, deal with bereavement, or manage day-to-day affairs.

Edgar Cayce, the psychic healer and pioneering explorer of past lives, has influenced contemporary channellers perhaps more than anyone else. Indeed, he can almost be considered a precursor of the New Age, since he spans the period between the spiritualists and Theosophists of the Victorian era and the celebrity channellers of more modern times. Cayce was born on 18 March 1877 in Kentucky, and came from a fundamentalist Protestant Christian background. As a young man he discovered that he could give accurate healing diagnoses for other people by going into a hypnotic trance, where he was assisted by inner guidance, often using medical terms completely unknown to him. On one occasion he gave a diagnosis in fluent Italian even though he was not familiar with this language.

In 1923 he met Arthur Lammers who was interested in occult metaphysics. It seemed to him that if Cayce could correctly diagnose health ailments by going into trance, he might also be able to uncover the metaphysical secrets of life, death and spiritual development. Lammers asked Cayce if he had ever sought to discover our true purpose on earth, the nature of the soul, and what we were doing before we were born. Cayce decided to give Lammers a trance reading. He revealed that Lammers had been a monk in a past life, and also used Sanskrit terms new to him, like *karma* and *akasa* (the Sanskrit term for the Spirit). From this time onwards his trance readings frequently referred to past lives and often used mystical terminology to explain the secrets of the inner world. These life-readings were made in order to reveal both the positive and negative influences

08.04 American healer and psychic Edgar Cayce, who became famous for his 'life-readings'.

08.05 Cayce believed he had been a priest in ancient Egypt during an earlier incarnation. This image of an Egyptian priest is from the *Egyptian Book of the Dead*.

that past lives had brought to bear on present existence, and to demonstrate how certain attitudes and personality characteristics were specifically connected to previous incarnations.

Cayce soon discovered that many of his friends had been relatives or associates in a previous life. He also learned psychically that he had been an Egyptian high priest named Rata in a former incarnation, and his wife Gertrude had also been his wife in ancient Egypt. In other incarnations Cayce had been a Persian physician, an Arab tribal leader named Uhjltd, and the biblical figure Lucius – a relative of Luke and a friend of Paul. He had also incarnated in 1742 as John Bainbridge, a gambler, libertarian and soldier in the British army stationed in America before the War of Independence. His life as Edgar Cayce had been given to him as an opportunity to make up for the sensual excesses and materialism of his life as John Bainbridge.

Edgar Cayce gave some 2,500 life-readings between 1923 and 1945, and these are now housed in the library at the Association for Research and Enlightenment at Virginia Beach in the United States. It is this enormous number of life-readings that has secured his enduring reputation as a psychic and healer. The following narratives are two typical examples from the records.

David Greenwood was fourteen years old when Edgar Cayce gave him his life-reading on 29 August 1927. Cayce told him about five previous incarnations. The first of these could be traced to well before 10,000 BCE when he had been heir to a throne in Atlantis. Then, around 10,000 BCE, Greenwood had been an Egyptian named Isois, and had served as an intermediary between his own people and a conquering army. Later he was Abiel, a court physician in Persia, and in his fourth incarnation Colval, a tradesman who abused his position of power in a city in Thessalonika. Finally he had served Louis XIII and XIV of France as a loyal Master of the Robes. Cayce warned Greenwood about his digestive problems and quick temper, and told him to pursue a trade related to clothing or fabrics. Greenwood became a salesman in a clothing company in 1940, and was very successful. He suffered from food allergies and followed Edgar Cayce's advice by adhering to a strict diet.

Cayce also gave a reading for Patricia Farrier, aged forty-five, a spinster who suffered from claustrophobia and fear of crowds. Attuning himself psychically to the source of her anxieties, he told her that in her previous life, when she was thirteen, an earth tremor had destroyed the floor of a farmhouse, and she had been smothered to death in a cellar as everything crumbled around her.

Cayce was a healer and psychic who was able to utilize trance states in order to tap into previous incarnations and karmic consequences – apparently at will. He came to believe that groups of souls could reincarnate collectively and that people bound by ties of family friendship or common interests would very likely be related, or connected to each other in some way, in successive incarnations. His many publications on psychic healing, past lives and spiritual guidance continue to sell well in New Age bookstores internationally. More than fifty years after his death he remains a superstar among New Age luminaries.

One of the most successful American New Age channellers is Neale Donald Walsch, a former public information officer and radio-show host whose first book, *Conversations with God* (1996),was on the *New York Times* bestseller list for 137 weeks. Walsch claims to communicate not with archangels or spirits but with God himself. From Walsch's own account, his personal life had begun to fall apart during the early 1990s, and both his career and health were in a state of decline. He didn't know why his life had turned out this way, and so he cried out to God the words of Jesus: 'My God, why have you forsaken me?' According to Walsch, God responded to him directly.

Walsch's books – there are now three volumes in the *Conversations with God* series, a sequel titled *Communion with God*, and also an accompanying CD – present a radical and mystical vision of the universe that Walsch claims was channelled directly from God without the intermediary role of the Church. When radio interviewer Rachael Kohn asked him whether any of his readers were indignant that he had written in the voice of God, thereby upturning the authority of the Bible, Walsch responded positively: 'Mostly we receive letters from people who are extraordinarily grateful, who say that "My life has been touched and changed forever," who say "At last, someone who is writing what I have been thinking all of my days." Who say, as one wonderful lady from Portland, Oregon, wrote to us, "Thank you for reintroducing me to a God I can fall in love with." '[6]

08.06 Popular New Age figure Neale Donald Walsch who claims to channel directly to God.

Channelling is an activity associated with many other New Age personalities, among them Shirley MacLaine, Kevin Ryerson, John Edward, Sylvia Browne, J. Z. Knight and Dolores Cannon. The highly regarded New Age classic *A Course in Miracles* (1976), is a channelled work dictated to psychologist Helen Schucman, and this 1500-page manuscript of psycho-spiritual teachings and exercises is thought by some to have emanated from Christ himself.[7]

In November 1987, J. Z. Knight channelled the following insights from a discarnate being called Ramtha: 'God is both male and female and yet neither. That which lives in the woman is as powerful and divine as that which lives in the man.… God is the essence, it permeates your entirety.… Within you lies the ability for profound knowingness. Like the Mother Earth, a wisdom, a courage, a dignity to evolve.' Ramtha also spoke of a huge wave that would soon engulf Sydney. Nearly two decades later, Sydney – the city that hosted the Olympic Games in the year 2000, and the city where I happen to live – has not yet faced this deluge, but several people in J. Z. Knight's audience were so perturbed that they moved to the relative safety of the Blue Mountains, some eighty kilometres (fifty miles) inland. J. Z. Knight also advised participants in her workshop to hoard their gold supplies, and mentioned that governments would soon act to reduce citizens' financial free will – 'psychic' advice that caused unwarranted alarm at the time.

Vulnerability to such messages seems to reflect a sense of individual disempowerment and low self-esteem. Regrettably, there are many in New Age circles who are willing to accept the channelled advice of discarnate entities quite unconditionally without applying any sense of discrimination to the advice that is being given. This is contrary to another dictum that frequently emanates from the New Age: namely, that one can come to valid and worthwhile personal decisions by heeding the 'inner voice'. Those who gravitate towards the pronouncements of venerable discarnate sages are clearly drawn towards the apparent 'authority' of channelled teachings, rather than trusting their own personal judgment and their capacity to make important personal decisions for themselves.

There are other New Age practices that have also attracted widespread media ridicule, and have come to personify the more credulous aspects of the New Age. One is the idea of healing with crystals. In an article of 1985 in an alternative New Age publication called *Southern Crossings* Lynette Mayblom wrote:

> Crystals have wonderful uses in the area of personal healing but they can also be used on a greater scale for world healing. Crystals can be used to focus love and light on important buildings and places, to construct triangles of light in the planet's etheric body, to assist the growth of plants, and to protect and purify your home.... Triangles of light can be set up between three people by meditating daily at the same time with crystals. These people can visualize light flowing from their third eyes to the other two, creating a triangle of light and visualizing the encompassed area filled with light. Distance is of no consequence.[8]

Crystals are by no means cheap, and only the more affluent New Agers could hope to afford crystals of any size. New Age enthusiast Bianca Pace told journalist Mark Chipperfield in 1988 that she marketed quartz crystals for between $600 and $4000 each, and that her crystals had 'the power to cure diseases and transmit human and cosmic thoughts'. Crystals, she maintained, 'are part of the energy grid of the planet.'[9]

In fairness to the less gimmicky aspects of the personal growth movement, however, it must be emphasized that there are also other approaches, philosophies and techniques that have much greater claim to recognition within the New Age

08.07 The Maharishi Mahesh Yogi with The Beatles and other devotees at his ashram in Rishikesh, India, February 1968.

context – especially the proven forms of experiential psychotherapy. One can gauge the respective merits of the various New Age modalities not in terms of the 'quick cosmic fix' they often claim to offer but through their capacity to assist the process of personal transformation.

THE ROLE OF THE GURU

One of the side-effects of the New Age's quest for transformation and the fascination with Eastern mystical traditions has been the proliferation of Indian gurus visiting the West. For many followers these gurus have become the new spiritual authority figures, replacing the more conventional leadership role of Christian priests. The traditional role of the guru is to lead the *chela* – the pupil or follower – towards self-knowledge and mystical transcendence. In theory, the guru represents the sacred divinity within each of us, and is a catalyst for self-enlightenment, the flowering of more complete spiritual awareness.

Some gurus give their *chelas* individual mantras upon which to meditate, and there is usually an unfolding programme of lessons and spiritual exercises appropriate to the pupil's level. At times the interaction between the guru and *chela* may become quite complex and may involve a process whereby the guru challenges the concepts and self-image of the *chela* in order to reduce the ego, in this way allowing a new spiritual awareness to dawn. In some traditions the *chela* is required to submit totally to the spiritual leader. Many believe that without direct guidance from the guru their lives lack meaning, purpose and direction. For these followers, the guru embodies the qualities required for spiritual self-realization and reveals the path to authentic enlightenment.

In the 1960s the top British music group, the Beatles, found their own guru, Maharishi Mahesh Yogi. In 1967 and 1968 the Maharishi attracted enormous publicity during his visit to the West. Adorned in flowing white robes and garlands of flowers, the Maharishi promoted the practice of Transcendental Meditation and his picture was published in most of the leading publications of the day, including *Life*, *Look*, *Time*, *Esquire* and *Newsweek*. Frequently accompanied by public relations personnel and such film stars as Mia Farrow, he appeared as a guest on the Johnny Carson show in the US, and even gave a presentation at Madison Square Gardens in New York. Quite different in appeal from Vivekananda, who had electrified American audiences seventy years earlier, the Maharishi preached a simple message: the purpose of life was to experience happiness. He also claimed that the discipline, concentration and effort associated with traditional forms of yoga and meditation were simply a waste of time. 'Transcendental Meditation,' said the Maharishi, 'is not like Zen or Jnana yoga. It does not employ concentration and contemplation, but is just the opposite of these disciplines. That's what makes it so easy.... TM is a natural process of going to levels of your mind that are the most interesting and the most pleasureable.'[10]

The central technique in Transcendental Meditation was to turn one's attention towards the subtler levels of thought until the mind finally transcended thought altogether. All that was required was to sit comfortably for a few minutes each day and silently repeat a special word or phrase, a mantra. Nothing else was needed, and one could lead whatever sort of life one wanted. In a brochure entitled *Transcendental Meditation; an Introductory Lecture* the Maharishi explained that the quest for higher consciousness was easy:

> Without our having to observe or struggle with ourselves, quite spontaneously our natural inclinations begin to come into greater harmony with the natural laws of the evolution of life. Our desires become increasingly life supporting and simultaneously increasingly fulfilled. This happens gradually. We are not angels from the first meditation, but as the sense of wellbeing grows, naturally the mind becomes well-intentioned, warm, loving and clear, and no longer irritable or fearful.[11]

With his promise of instant Nirvana, the Maharishi quickly attracted a large following of Western devotees. His appeal was especially strong among the young who were no doubt attracted by the idea of an effortless path to enlightenment. At times, it even seemed that he might herald a new spiritual movement – a simplified version of the Eastern wisdom tradition that could replace LSD in the post-psychedelic era.

It was not only the young who were captivated by the Maharishi. Jacob Needleman, Professor of Philosophy at San Francisco State College, recalls that 'tens of thousands from the solid middle-class were also paying for instruction in the magic of transcendental meditation. We saw photographs of huge auditoriums filled with well-tailored adults, their eyes closed, and their minds – the captions told us – plunged into the deeper levels of thought.'[12]

Inevitably there was a catch: all prospective converts to Transcendental Meditation, including the Beatles, had to pay a week's salary to be given their mantra. In hindsight, perhaps this was not such a large fee to pay for enlightenment; it is certainly substantially less than the amounts charged at many transformational seminars today. And there was an ideological gloss to TM as well. Appealing to supporters of the anti-war movement, the Maharishi explained that if only one percent of the world's population were to practise Transcendental Meditation, this would be enough 'to neutralize the power of war for thousands of years'.

Towards the end of 1968 the Maharishi announced he was returning to India and interest in him as a charismatic spiritual figure began to wane. Two years later, however, Transcendental Meditation received support from a surprising source. The 27 March 1970 issue of the prestigious magazine *Science* – the official publication of the American Association for the Advancement of Science – included an article on the 'Physiological Effects of Transcendental Meditation' by Robert K.Wallace from the Department of Psychology at the Center for Health Sciences in Los Angeles. The article reported that Transcendental Meditation had a specific impact on such body functions as oxygen consumption, heart rate, skin resistance and EEG measurements. During meditation oxygen consumption and heart rate decreased, and this could have positive benefits.[13]

The scientific endorsement of meditation as a means for attaining deep states of relaxation is perhaps the most significant legacy of the Maharishi's teachings. There can be little doubt that the Maharishi aimed his message of a simple path to pleasure at a generally uncritical audience. Nevertheless, it is now widely accepted that meditation reduces levels of stress, tension and anxiety in the physical organism. This reduces the level of cortisone which inhibits the immune system, allowing the physical organism to return to a more balanced state of health. The Maharishi deserves acknowledgment for bringing meditation into the awareness of mainstream America and popular consciousness generally. For many, meditation has now become a central part of everyday life.

Another guru who attracted recognition in the West during the post-psychedelic era was Swami Muktananda (1908–82), a leading teacher of Kundalini yoga. (Kundalini, from the Sanskrit for 'spiral' and often symbolized as a coiled serpent, refers to the spiritual and psychic energy aroused by yoga techniques and channelled through the *chakras*, the energy centres.[14]) Muktananda became a disciple of Bhagawan Nityananda in 1947, and claimed that he gained self-realization after nine years of spiritual guidance. When Nityananda died in 1961, he passed on the power of the Siddha yoga lineage to Muktananda. In India Siddha yoga is known as 'the yoga of perfection', and a *siddha* is one who has attained an advanced state of self-knowledge – one who can claim to be a 'perfect master'. Muktananda's message was clear and direct: God dwells within you. 'When the Kundalini has swept away all false impressions and misunderstandings we know our own divinity and we see God everywhere. The whole world is nothing but the play of our own self.'[15]

By definition, a *siddha* is a person whose Kundalini has been already awakened. The *siddha* is then able to awaken the Kundalini in his disciples, initiating the process of their own personal transformation. This, however, requires the all-important 'grace' of the guru, the *shaktipat*, which, according to Swami Muktananda, may be received by the *chela* in one of four ways: through the guru's touch, *sparsha diksha*; through his words, *mantra diksha*; through his gaze, *drik diksha*; or through his power of thought, *manasa diksha*.

Devotees of Siddha yoga believe that simply being in the presence of a master whose Kundalini has been already awakened may act as a stimulus to spiritual growth in itself. As medical practitioner and Siddha yoga devotee Dr Christopher Magarey has noted: 'A holy person, a *siddha*, awakens that awareness spontaneously and initiates the process of inner transformation quite naturally and effortlessly.'[16]

In 1974 Muktananda visited several cities in Australia. In Melbourne he was asked by yoga teacher John Cooper whether it was the will of the guru that actually created the transmission of the Kundalini, or the devotion and openness of the disciple. Muktananda replied:

There are different ways in which Kundalini can be awakened. Kundalini can be awakened just by seeing a guru. It can be awakened by his touch. It can be awakened even by his thought, though you may be at any distance from him. It is also awakened by the grace of the guru, which he transmits deliberately. And the awakening can also take place itself in a natural manner as a result of the disciple's

08.08 17th-century Nepalese painting showing the seven *chakras*, or spiritual energy centres, in the subtle body. The chakras are depicted as lotuses.

devotion to his master. But the important thing is the disciple's love and the guru's grace coming together. Then the Kundalini is awakened.[17]

Muktananda earned widespread respect for his yoga teaching, and by the time he died in 1982 he had established thirty-one ashrams, or meditation centres, around the world. Towards the end of his life, however, there were persistent reports of sexual misconduct with female Siddha yoga devotees, and also claims that the Siddha Yoga Foundation had begun to transfer substantial funds to its bank accounts in Switzerland.[18] These controversial claims (fully detailed in a website dedicated to complaints made by former followers) does not seem to have affected the credibility of the present head of the Siddha yoga lineage, Swami Chidvilasananda (better known as Gurumayi) – Swami Muktananda's youthful and elegant female successor.[19]

Unfortunately, a recurring theme among gurus in the West is the claim that their teaching in some way precludes that of other teachers. In addition, a guru may be elevated to a position of apparent godliness by virtue of his or her claimed achievements. A biography of Indian spiritual leader, artist and musician, Sri Chinmoy – prepared for the news media – related how in one particular calendar year:

Sri Chinmoy painted over 120,000 works of art depicting higher realms of meditation. His poetry and music became just as voluminous. On November 1st… Sri Chinmoy demonstrated the creative dynamism of meditation by writing 843 poems in a 24-hour period. Fifteen days later he painted 16,031 works of art in another 24-hour period. Three days later Sri Chinmoy celebrated a year in which he had completed 120,000 paintings. Since arriving in America he has composed over 5,000 songs and musical compositions, earning the praise of such notable composers as Leonard Bernstein and Zubin Mehta.[20]

Presumably this extraordinary data was intended to establish him as a role model for his prospective followers. As Sri Chinmoy himself explained, 'Our goal is always to go beyond, beyond, beyond. There are no limits to our capacity because we have the infinite divine within us. Each painting, each poem, each thing that I undertake is nothing but an expression of my inner cry for more light, more truth, more delight.'[21] While one can hardly fail to admire the sheer volume of his output, the effect of such statistics upon his followers would surely have been to disempower them, rather than uplift them. There was also a call for devotees to come to his concerts, and a publicity notice for one of his concerts claimed: 'Unlike other musicians, Sri Chinmoy's music is not composed for entertainment but as a guide to higher states of awareness.'

Bhagwan Shree Rajneesh (1931–90) similarly exercised a remarkable charismatic power over his followers before his ashram in Oregon closed. Each day his *sannyasins*, or devotees, would file in procession to watch the Bhagwan drive past in his gleaming Rolls Royce, flanked by security guards armed with Uzi semi-automatic guns. And yet double-think was clearly in evidence at Rajneeshpuram. Bhagwan's principal assistant Ma Anand Sheela described Bhagwan's aims during a cable network interview: 'What he is teaching is to be individual, to become free, free of all limitations, free of all conditioning, and just become an integrated individual, a free being.'[22] The depth of this freedom was clearly limited. Bhagwan gave each of his followers 'spiritual names', insisted on their wearing pendants bearing his photograph, and allowed his devotees to wear clothes only in certain colours. His organization also charged substantial fees for experiential spiritual growth workshops. Such are the paradoxes of spiritual leadership. Meanwhile, Ma Anand Sheela was sentenced in Oregon and then jailed in California in July 1986 for assault, arson and attempted murder at the ashram.[23]

08.09 Bhagwan Shree Rajneesh greeting devotees at his ashram in Oregon.

Admittedly the charismatic Bhagwan Shree Rajneesh and his ashram in Oregon represent an extreme case, but it is shocking and very recent. The ques-

tion must be asked when deciding to follow any guru: 'Are the guru's teachings intended purely for one's spiritual growth and enlightenment? How enlightened is the teacher? Are any other agendas operating? And what is the cost?'

THE GURU WHO WAS NOT A GURU

Jiddu Krishnamurti (1895–1986), meanwhile, allows us to examine the concept of the guru in a different light. Krishnamurti was not only one of the most respected Indian spiritual teachers of the twentieth century, but was also famous for being the guru who renounced the very notion of being a guru. His story raises the important question of whether we need a guru at all, and whether we all have within our own inner resources the capacity for authentic self-realization.

During his lifetime Krishnamurti travelled widely throughout Europe, America and Asia, speaking to millions of people. But rather than seeking followers or disciples, he spoke instead about the issues affecting daily life. His addresses – for which he was renowned – encompassed war, violence, love, fear, death and the nature of time and freedom.[24]

Krishnamurti's father was a Theosophist, and Krishnamurti and his brother grew up on the Theosophical estate at Adyar in India. Krishnamurti came to the notice of leading Theosophist C. W. Leadbeater in 1909 when he was thirteen years old. Leadbeater, who was conducting a clairvoyant investigation into past lives, then claimed to have discovered to his amazement that the boy had once been a disciple of the Buddha.[25] Leadbeater's enthusiasm for Krishnamurti was shared by Mrs Annie Besant, who had succeeded Colonel Henry Olcott in 1907 as the president of the Theosophical Society. Leadbeater now began to refer to Krishnamurti as 'our Krishna', and claimed to take him every night on to the astral plane where he could be instructed by Madame Blavatsky's Tibetan Masters. Before long the message at Adyar was that Krishnamurti had been accepted by Master Koot Hoomi, and he was proclaimed the World Teacher, or Messiah, for whom many Theosophists had been waiting. It was soon said that Krishnamurti was an incarnation of the avatar Lord Maitreya, and a society known as the Order of the Star in the East was established as a vehicle for his teachings.

In 1914 Leadbeater left Adyar for a lecture tour that included Burma, Java, New Zealand and Australia. The following year he decided to settle in Sydney. In 1922 he moved with a group of his students into a large house in Clifton Gardens, a fashionable harbourside suburb. Leadbeater was now deeply involved in the activities of a ritualistic splinter group known as the Liberal Catholic Church whose membership included many Theosophists, but he continued to support the cause of Krishnamurti. In 1923–24 a huge Grecian-style amphitheatre was erected by members of the Order of the Star in the East on the shores of Balmoral

08.10 Krishnamurti and C.W. Leadbeater (left) at Adyar, India 1910. Krishnamurti's brother Nitya is on the right.

beach near Clifton Gardens, and it was announced by Leadbeater and his colleagues that Krishnamurti would enter Sydney by walking across the Harbour, up the beach and into the amphitheatre. Seats for this miraculous event were sold well ahead of time for up to a hundred pounds each.[26]

None of this impressed Krishnamurti himself. He became increasingly disillusioned with Leadbeater's evangelizing tone, and on 3 August 1929 he dissolved the Order of the Star in the East. At the same time he rejected any role as a World Teacher or guru, proclaiming that 'truth is a pathless land' and that all organized systems of religious belief are an 'impediment to inner liberation'.[27]

Having severed his connection with Leadbeater, Krishnamurti now decided to move to California. He had first visited Ojai near Santa Barbara in 1922, and he returned there with Annie Besant in August 1926, staying for eight months. During their visit, she acquired six acres of land in the Ojai Valley which later became the home of the Happy Valley Foundation, a Theosophical residential centre. According to his friend and biographer Pupul Jayakar, Krishnamurti 'cherished his walks in the silences of the mountains surrounding the Ojai Valley. He walked "enormously" for endless miles, spending whole days in the wilderness, alone.'[28] As late as 1927 Annie Besant was still proclaiming that Krishnamurti was the World Teacher and she also told him she would be happy to stand down as president of the Theosophical Society to sit at his feet. Krishnamurti refused these flattering overtures, and resigned from the Theosophical Society in 1930. He then established a new foundation in Ojai, Krishnamurti Writings Inc (KWI). It was here, during the late 1930s, that Krishnamurti met Aldous Huxley and Gerald Heard, who were living in nearby Los Angeles. By the mid-1940s Krishnamurti and Huxley had become close friends and would go for long walks together.[29]

Krishnamurti's essential message was that we can all perceive spiritual truth and no intermediary guru figure or spiritual organization is required. Spiritual liberation is an act of self-discovery. He believed that to achieve spiritual freedom we should practise a form of unconditional self-observation that he called 'attention', because in this way the senses could be fully awakened. He defined 'attention' as a state of 'complete sensory activity', and maintained that by entering a state of authentic self-awareness, one could experience complete harmony and true understanding. Unconditional self-observation involved transcending all aspects of one's prior conditioning, and this meant moving beyond the divisive, analytical aspects of the mind. To achieve true self-awareness, all processes of thought had to become silent and still, for only then could one move beyond thought itself. Krishnamurti had already affirmed, 'Truth is a pathless land'; now he added a further insight. 'Attention', he said,' is a movement to eternity.'[30]

08.11 Krishnamurti in Ojai, 1949. By this time he had become a close friend of Aldous Huxley.

9

Spirit, Myth and Cosmos

'It is not we who invent myth,' wrote Jung, 'rather, it speaks to us as a Word of God.' Jung believed that the origin of mythology lay in the dramatization of images by the archetypes in the unconscious mind. His concept of the collective unconscious has encouraged the examination of myths and fables in order to gain profound insights into the human condition. Jung has had a substantial impact on students of mythology, among them the eloquent and highly regarded Joseph Campbell, and this in turn has contributed much to the New Age movement.

THE POWER OF MYTH

There is little doubt that the American scholar of comparative religion and mythology, Joseph Campbell (1904–87) exerted an enormous influence on the New Age. As a teacher and writer, Campbell produced a number of authoritative but accessible studies on Oriental, indigenous and Western mythology, and essays on metaphor and symbol in comparative religion. This culminated in a series of television interviews in the USA with Bill Moyers, *The Power of Myth* (1985–87), which examined the universality of myth, and brought Campbell's articulate wisdom to millions of viewers across the world.

Campbell's career was one of solid scholarship. With a Master's degree in cultural history from Columbia University in 1927, he studied at the University of Paris from 1927 to 1928, and spent another year at the University of Munich exploring Sanskrit and Oriental religion. He taught at Sarah Lawrence College in Bronxville, New York, for thirty-eight years. It was while he was in Paris that he began to read Freud, Jung and the works of German novelist Thomas Mann, and he also became deeply interested in the universals of the mythic imagination.

> Myths originally came out of the individual's own dream consciousness. Within each person there is what Jung called a collective unconscious. We are not only individuals with our unconscious intentions related to a specific social environment. We are also representatives of the species *homo sapiens*. And that universality is in us whether we know it or not. We penetrate to this level by getting in touch with dreams, fantasies, and traditional myths; by using active imagination.[1]

09.01 Eskimo mask from Alaska, made with painted wood and feathers.

Campbell believed that myths were highly relevant to everyday life. Although on one level they pointed to the mysteries and paradoxes of human existence, myths also validated the social and moral order in specific cultures and marked the pathways through the different stages of life – from childhood, through to adulthood, old age and death. 'Every culture,' said Campbell, 'has rites of passage and related myths that serve this need.'[2]

Myths were also directly relevant to the life-experience of the individual, a source of inspirational guidance for everyday life. Campbell liked to refer to what he called 'the journey of the hero' – the journey that every human makes simply by being purposeful in the world. He thought that each of us, at some point, has to come forth and engage in battle with various obstacles or 'powers of darkness'. During our lives we may encounter demons, angels, dragons or helping spirits, but then, after conquering the obstacles along the way, we finally emerge victorious and return from our adventures with 'the gift of fire', or knowledge.

Campbell believed that as human beings we all have the same sacred heritage: 'We share the same gods, we are informed by the same archetypes. The natural forces that animate us are common and divine.'[3] He also proposed that we should explore those myths that touched us most deeply – the archetypal stories and legends that could help enrich our life's journey. As his biographers, Stephen and Robin Larsen, have observed: 'Campbell urged us to *see through* life metaphorically, and to celebrate the myths *as if* they were alive in us – providing windows for deeper insights into ourselves.'[4] Indeed, it is in his support for the mythic life that he is best remembered. 'Mythology helps you to identify the mysteries of the energies pouring through you,' he once remarked. 'Therein lies your eternity.'[5]

09.02 Joseph Campbell teaching at the Foreign Institute in Washington, D.C., 1957. Campbell emphasized the transformative power of myth.

MYTHIC CONSCIOUSNESS AND SACRED PSYCHOLOGY

Several leading figures in the personal growth movement have played a prominent role in looking at practical and inspirational ways of introducing archetypal mythic realities into everyday consciousness. Dr Jean Houston, an enthusiastic supporter of Joseph Campbell's work, first discovered his ideas at the age of ten when she read his book *The Hero with a Thousand Faces* (1949). Houston is a director of the Foundation for Mind Research now based in Ashland, Oregon. She believes strongly in the transformative power of myth, and this is a central feature of her workshops and training programmes. 'My task is to evoke people into that place of identifying the god or goddess or archetype that is personal to them and allowing that being to speak for them.'[6] She also maintains that not only mythologically, but also quite literally, our origins are in the cosmos:

09.03 Psychologist Dr Jean Houston believes the soul of the world speaks to us through myths.

Earlier peoples saw archetypes in Nature and in the starry Heavens – in the Sun, the Moon, the Earth, the vast oceans – implicitly realizing our descent from these primal entities.... Our ancestors storied this deep knowing into tales of the community of Nature: the marriage of Heaven and Earth; the churning of the ocean to create the nectar of life; the action of the wind upon the waters to bring form out of chaos. In these mythic tellings, our forerunners located higher reality and its values in the larger community – in the things of this world, shining reflections of the community of archetypes. They clearly perceived that the pattern connecting both world and archetype was the essential weave that sustains all life.[7]

Houston believes, like Carl Jung, that, while archetypes are universal, they manifest in unique ways within each individual. Archetypes, she says, 'bridge spirit with nature, mind with body, and self with universe. They are always within us, essential structures within the structure of our psyches.'[8] She claims that one of the key roles of sacred psychology is to assist the individual in transforming his or her life from the 'personal-particular' to the 'personal-universal', thereby bringing a new vision to everyday experience. The deep insights into the nature of personal transformation and renewal supplied by myth and sacred psychology can facilitate this. 'In this time of whole system transition,' she writes, 'the Soul of the World, the *anima mundi*, is emerging. It seems to be with us through all the things and events of the world. Speaking through myths, it enlarges our perception of the deeper story that is unfolding in our time.'[9]

Jean Shinoda Bolen, another leading member of the personal growth movement, shares this passionate interest in sacred psychology. Her concern is to promote the idea that men and women can become increasingly aware of the archetypal processes that influence and inspire their everyday lives. Dr Bolen is a professor of psychiatry at the University of California in San Francisco, a Jungian analyst, and author of *Goddesses in Everywoman* (1985), *Gods in Everyman* (1989) and *The Tao of Psychology* (1979). Like Jung, Bolen believes that the gods and goddesses of mythology represent different qualities in the human psyche:

Myth is a form of metaphor. It's the metaphor that's truly empowering for people. It allows us to see our ordinary lives from a different perspective, to get an intuitive sense of who we are and what is important to us.... Myths are the bridge to the collective unconscious. They tap images, symbols, feelings, possibilities and patterns – inherent, inherited human potential that we all hold in common....[10]

Bolen supports Joseph Campbell's advice that we should all learn to 'follow our bliss' in finding our true calling in life. In her book *Gods in Everyman* she

09.04 Dr Jean Shinoda Bolen feels we must respect the earth as a source of sacred energy.

describes how this personal experience of 'bliss' enables the individual to tap into a universal sense of the sacred:

> Bliss and joy come in moments of living our highest truth – moments when what we do is consistent with our archetypal depths. It's when we are most authentic and trusting, and feel that whatever we are doing, which can be quite ordinary, is nonetheless sacred. This is when we sense that we are part of something divine that is in us and is everywhere.[11]

Like Jean Houston, Bolen believes that this feeling of mythic and archetypal attunement opens out finally into a greater planetary awareness:

> The current need is a return to earth as the source of sacred energy. I have a concept that I share with others that we're evolving into looking out for the earth and our connection with everybody on it. Women seem more attuned to it, but increasingly more men are too. I believe that the human psyche changes collectively, when enough individuals change. Basically, the point of life is to survive and evolve. To do both requires that we recognize our planetary community and be aware that we cannot do anything negative to our enemies without harming ourselves.[12]

DEVELOPING A PERSONAL MYTHOLOGY

Bringing mythic realities into people's daily lives has also been an important part of the work of Dr David Feinstein and Dr Stanley Krippner, authors of *Personal Mythology: The Psychology of Your Evolving Self* (1988). Their book originated in a research project at the Johns Hopkins University School of Medicine, which began by comparing several emerging 'personal growth' therapies with a number of traditional therapies. Feinstein came to believe that each therapy, in its own way, helped people construct an understanding of themselves and where they stood in relation to the world as a whole. He then adopted the term 'personal mythology' to describe what he calls the 'evolving construction of inner reality'. He thinks that all human constructions of reality are, in a sense, mythologies. Krippner, meanwhile, brought to the project an extensive knowledge of dreams, spiritual healing and altered states of consciousness. Together, over several years, Feinstein and Krippner held workshops to help people become aware of the mythologies that had guided them in the past. Soon they were helping participants develop rituals and spiritual practices that would guide them in their lives.

Feinstein and Krippner divided their work with personal mythology into five stages. In Stage One, individuals were asked to recognize and define their own personal myth and to question whether this myth remained an 'ally' or not. Stage

Two involved identifying an 'opposing' personal myth, which had the potential to create conflict within the psyche. The conflicting myths were then examined to see how they were connected to personal experiences from the past. Stage Three provided a sense of synthesis and unified vision. Here the original myth and the conflicting myth were brought into confrontation and then towards a point of resolution, and any obstacles to unity were envisioned as opportunities for personal growth and self-realization. In Stage Four, the therapeutic focus came to an end and participants were asked to make a commitment to the new vision. Finally, in Stage Five, they were encouraged to weave their personal mythologies into their daily lives.

Like Jean Houston and Jean Shinoda Bolen, Feinstein and Krippner have been applying the principles of mythological thought to individual experience, thereby grounding an authentic mythic awareness in the here-and-now.

Each of us is challenged to direct our strength and wisdom toward creating mythological harmonies within ourselves. Within our families. Within our organizations. Within our nation. Within the world. And as we reconcile our logic with our intuition, our egos with our shadows, our old myths with our new ones, and our personal needs with those of our community, we also pave the way for a world steeped in contradictions to move forward in greater peace and creative harmony.[13]

Joseph Campbell, had, perhaps, already anticipated these feelings in his 1972 book *Myths to Live By*:

If you really want to help this world, what you will have to teach is how to live in it. And that no one can do who has not himself learned how to live in it in the joyful sorrow and the sorrowful joy of the knowledge of life as it is. That is the meaning of the monstrous Kirttimukha, 'Face of Glory', over the entrances to the sanctuaries of the god of yoga, whose bride is the goddess of life. No one can know this god and goddess who will not bow to that mask in reverence and pass humbly through.[14]

FEMINISM AND THE GODDESS

It is hardly surprising that the revitalizing themes of sacred psychology have resonated within the New Age movement – the ground had already been prepared by the American counterculture of the early 1970s. With the search for new maps of spiritual awareness that followed the psychedelic revolution, many had already begun to venture down the pathways of magic, witchcraft, shamanism and the mythology of the Goddess. And in a clear and emphatic response to patriarchal forms of religion, the rise of feminism brought with it a resurgence of interest in ancient mythologies that supported an awareness of feminine spirituality.[15]

One of the leading advocates for the new Goddess-based spirituality in the late 1970s was a peace activist named Miriam Simos, otherwise known as Starhawk. She burst on to the American Neopagan scene with the publication in 1979 of her bestselling book *The Spiral Dance*, a handbook of ritual, mythology, spells and inspirational reflections.[16] At the time it was by no means clear whether Starhawk was simply another witch in the same tradition as modern British Neopagan practitioners Doreen Valiente and Janet Farrar, or whether this new expression of feminist spirituality involved something potentially much broader and more comprehensive. When Starhawk was asked several years later what sort of witch she was, this was her reply: 'A witch is somebody who has made a commitment to the spiritual tradition of the Goddess, the old pre-Christian religions of Western Europe. So I am a witch in the sense that that is my religion, my spiritual tradition. I am an initiated priestess of the Goddess.'[17]

Starhawk was a founding member of a community in the San Francisco Bay Area called Reclaiming – a network of women and men working in the Goddess tradition to unify spirituality and politics – and she remains one of the most respected voices in modern Goddess religion and earth-based spirituality. The author or co-author of nine books including *The Fifth Sacred Thing*, and *The Twelve Wild Swans* (with Hilary Valentine), Starhawk is deeply committed to bringing the techniques and creative power of spirituality to political activism. She continues to travel internationally teaching magic, the tools of ritual and the skills of progressive activism. Her award-winning *Webs of Power: Notes from the Global Uprising* (2002), explores these intersections.

Like Jean Houston and Jean Shinoda Bolen, Starhawk maintains that the underlying impetus behind the Goddess movement is a powerful and transformative sense of the sacred. In an interview with Alexander Blair-Ewart in Toronto she explained her perspective:

> What's important about witchcraft and about the pagan movement is, essentially, that it's not so much a way of seeing reality, as it's a different way of valuing the reality around us. We say that what is sacred, in the sense of what we are most committed to, what determines all our other values, is this living Earth, this world, the life systems of the earth, the cycles of birth and growth and death and regeneration; the air, the fire, the water, the land.[18]

In her own writings Starhawk has referred specifically to the nurturing and revitalizing power of the Goddess-energy:

09.05 Goddess devotee and political activist Starhawk, author of *The Spiral Dance*.

09.06 Goddess of Willendorf, *c.* 30,000–20,000 BCE.

The symbolism of the Goddess has taken on an electrifying power for modern women. The rediscovery of the ancient matrifocal civilizations has given us a deep sense of pride in woman's ability to create and sustain culture. It has exposed the falsehoods of patriarchal history, and given us models of female strength and authority. The Goddess – ancient and primeval; the first of deities; patroness of the Stone Age hunt and of the first sowers of seeds; under whose guidance the herds were tamed, the healing herbs first discovered; in whose image the first works of art were created; for whom the standing stones were raised; who was the inspiration of song and poetry – is recognized once again in today's world. She is the bridge, on which we can cross the chasms within ourselves, which were created by our social conditioning, and reconnect with our lost potentials. She is the ship, on which we sail the waters of the deep self, exploring the uncharted seas within. She is the door, through which we pass to the future. She is the cauldron, in which we who have been wrenched apart simmer until we again become whole. She is the vaginal passage, through which we are reborn.[19]

SHAMANISM AND THE NEW SPIRITUALITY

As interest in mythology, magic and sacred psychology became widespread in the counterculture during the 1970s, it was perhaps inevitable that many would become increasingly attracted to indigenous and archaic cultures – cultures for whom the world of myth was still a living reality. It was the rediscovery of the bond that tribal peoples feel with the sacred earth that led many spiritual seekers to the most ancient magical tradition of all – shamanism.

The revival of interest in shamanism owes much to the efforts of one man: writer Carlos Castaneda (1925–98). It can be argued that he was the first to make the shamanic perspective accessible to Westerners – even more so than Mircea Eliade, whose scholarly overview of world shamanism had been published in English in 1964, four years before Castaneda's first book.

Between 1959 and 1973 an elusive South American whose birth name was either Carlos Arana or Carlos Aranha undertook a series of degree courses in anthropology at the University of California, Los Angeles. Although he refused to divulge whether he came from Lima, São Paulo or Buenos Aires, he adopted the name Carlos Castaneda when he acquired United States citizenship in 1959. The following year he travelled to Arizona to study the indigenous use of medicinal plants. Here he met a Yaqui *brujo*, or sorcerer, named don Juan Matus with whom he was able to converse in Spanish. Castaneda entered into a magical apprentice-ship with the shaman which provided him with a completely new outlook on human perception. Under don Juan's guidance Castaneda learned to become a 'man of knowledge', a man who could enter the 'cracks between the worlds'.

Four of Castaneda's early books (published between 1968 and 1974) told of this apprenticeship: *The Teachings of Don Juan*, *A Separate Reality*, *Journey to Ixtlan* and *Tales of Power*.[20] The first told of visionary encounters with the peyote god Mescalito, astral transformations in the form of a crow, and sessions ingesting *datura* and smoking sacred mushrooms. It also described unusual desert skills, including Castaneda's threading of lizards' eyelids with a thorn needle. It seemed a serious work – it had, after all, been published by the University of California Press – but from the beginning there were doubters. No one, not even Castaneda's academic overviewing committee at UCLA, met don Juan or even saw a photograph of him; don Juan didn't seem to fit the Yaqui mould or to have any discernible Native American characteristics; the manuscript was allegedly translated from Spanish fieldnotes since don Juan spoke in this tongue, but no notes were forthcoming; no Yaqui had been known to use *datura*, and sacramental mushroom rites were unknown in the region where Castaneda was said to have done his fieldwork. Peyote specialist Weston La Barre described Castaneda's second book *A Separate Reality* as 'pseudo-profound, deeply vulgar pseudo-ethnography', and when Gordon Wasson – a specialist on sacred mushrooms – wrote to Castaneda requesting detailed background data, he received only half-baked replies.

Later Richard de Mille, a former clinical psychologist who taught at the University of California, Santa Barbara, and who had been working as a writer and editor since 1970, began to take Castaneda's books apart in rigorous detail. His *Castaneda's Journey* (1975) quietly demolished the 'non-ordinary' paradigm of truth that Castaneda was proposing. A main contention was that Castaneda, in writing his account in the form of a diary, mixed up his chronologies. One of don Juan's key magical techniques involved a special way of seeing. 'Seeing,' wrote Castaneda, meant understanding that 'anything can happen in the world and the magician is one who, like a warrior, can take his stand against the totally inexplicable.' In *A Separate Reality*, Carlos asked don Juan: 'What is it like to see?' but don Juan told him that this must remain a secret for the time being. The diary entry was May 1968. Meanwhile, *Journey to Ixtlan* provided a flashback to 1962, in which Castaneda magically located an invisible bush growing in isolation on the side of a hill. 'This spot', said don Juan, 'is yours. This morning you *saw*, and that was the omen. You found this spot by *seeing*.' In de Mille's view such incongruities

09.07 Mexican ceramic from Colima *c.* 200 BCE–AD 100 showing figures dancing around a mushroom. The widespread fascination with sacred mushrooms was renewed during the late 1960s by writers such as Carlos Castaneda and Gordon Wasson.

09.08 Huichol yarn painting by Ramon Medina Silva showing a shaman in search of the soul of a spirit-ancestor.

raised serious doubts about the authenticity of the accounts. He was particularly suspicious about the sewing of the lizards' eyelids. His opinion was that this was a rewrite of an entry in *The Handbook of South American Indians* describing the sewing of a toad's eyes and mouth by a skilled Peruvian sorcerer.[21]

In a later book, *The Don Juan Papers*, published in 1980, de Mille included a conversation with Barbara Myerhoff, who had known Castaneda personally as a student, and was also engaged in the study of shamanism. Castaneda claimed to be studying Yaqui sorcery, but Myerhoff specialized in the Huichol Indians, in particular a shaman named Ramón Medina, whom Castaneda later met. It may be that he borrowed from an actual Huichol occurrence for an incident in *A Separate Reality* – when don Juan's friend, don Genaro, leaps across a precipitous waterfall clinging to it by magical tentacles of power. Barbara Myerhoff and another noted anthropologist, Peter Furst, actually watched Ramón Medina leaping across a waterfall cascading three hundred metres down over slippery rocks. Medina was exhibiting the balance of the shaman in 'crossing the narrow bridge to the other world'. Myerhoff told de Mille how validated she had felt when Castaneda had told her that don Genaro could do similar things. It subsequently seemed to her that Castaneda's own accounts mirrored data from all sorts of sources – including her own.

Nevertheless, while Castaneda was being relentlessly pursued by Richard de Mille, there were others who came to his aid. One was the distinguished anthropologist Dr Michael Harner, who maintained that shamanic techniques of attaining ecstasy or passing through 'the cracks between the worlds' were remarkably similar in all shamanic cultures. In other words, although Castaneda may have been borrowing, he wasn't inventing. According to Harner, the Castaneda books were essentially accurate accounts of how a shaman might be expected to act. Furthermore, Castaneda deserved gratitude for bringing the awesome realities of the shaman's universe to the notice of the general public.

What emerges from the Carlos Castaneda debate is that the writer himself was probably the actual visionary, and many of the shamanic perspectives presented in his books were transferred to the real, partially real, or completely fictitious figure known as don Juan. In one sense it hardly matters whether don Juan was

09.09 Huichol shaman Ramón Medina Silva displaying his remarkable sense of balance on the edge of a waterfall. This may have inspired Carlos Castaneda to describe a similar incident in his bestselling book, *A Separate Reality*.

real or not, since the fiction, if it is that, is authentic enough, but it is interesting that several later Castaneda works were presented in some editions as 'novels'.

ENTER LYNN ANDREWS

It was perhaps inevitable that a feminine counterpart of Carlos Castaneda would appear. Unlike Castaneda, Lynn Andrews' personal history has been more forthcoming. She was raised on a ranch near Spokane, Washington, and moved to Los Angeles with her family when she was fourteen. She studied psychology and philosophy at college, worked for a time as a stockbroker and in film-making, and then became an art-dealer in Beverly Hills. It was while visiting Guatemala to look for a fertility sash for an art-collector that her life changed. On a visit to the Mayan ruins of Tikal-Peten she lost her way in the Grand Jaguar Temple. A tall Indian appeared, and gave her directions back to town. She offered him a twenty-dollar bill in gratitude and, as she recounts in *Medicine Woman* (1981), he then looked at her intently:

> 'This money that you have given me binds you,' he said. 'I will send you two helpers within forty-four days. The first helper will be female. You will not recognise her as your ally. This ally you must conquer. I will also send you a male helper, who will mark your trail.' He ripped the twenty dollar bill in half and gave half back to me, saying, 'Keep this.'[22]

Two months later, back in Los Angeles, she was attracted to a photograph of a beautiful Indian basket in an exhibition: 'it had an intricate pattern resembling a dolphin with a snake, or with lightning.' That night, in the first of several mysterious dreams, she was offered a 'marriage basket' by an Indian woman 'with eyes like polished mirrors'. Next day, intent on purchasing the photograph she had seen, she was told by the gallery that no such photograph existed.

Soon afterwards, at a party in Bel Air, she met the noted shaman-writer Hyemeyohsts Storm, author of *Seven Arrows*. When she asked him about the marriage basket, he replied that he had seen only one in his life and was no longer sure who owned it. He advised Andrews to contact an old *heyoka*, or medicine-woman, called Agnes Whistling Elk on the Cree Reservation in Manitoba, Canada. Ruby Plenty Chiefs, who also lived on the reservation, would know where to find her. Andrews went to the reservation to meet Ruby Plenty Chiefs and went through a 'sort of initiation' with her.

Andrews' acceptance into an exclusive secret society of shaman women – the Sisterhood of Shields – and her descriptions of initiatory practices have caused much of the controversy that now surrounds her writings. In *Medicine Woman* she says she was instructed to gut a deer and eat its still-warm heart, and on another occasion to strip naked before a group of elders in a teepee. These accounts have angered many members of the Cree community, who insist that no such practices exist, and that Agnes Whistling Elk and Ruby Plenty Chiefs are names totally lacking in authenticity.

Andrews followed the bestselling *Medicine Woman* with a number of highly successful sequels, including *Flight of the Seventh Moon*, *Jaguar Woman*, *Star Woman* and *Crystal Woman*. In the last, published in 1987, she writes that Agnes Whistling Elk came with her to Australia and that they travelled with an Aboriginal woman called Ginevee to a ceremonial centre, two hundred and forty kilometres (a hundred and fifty miles) from Ayers Rock (now known as Uluru) in the Northern Territory. 'Our destination was a little known village where many Aboriginal women of high degree or healers were gathered to share their ancient knowledge with apprentices and each other. Their meeting was held in secret, Agnes told me, because there were many warrior societies who were against such a gathering of female power.'[23] Andrews also describes an initiation where a large gathering of Aboriginal women came together and her naked body was smeared with bandicoot grease.

Mr Yami Lester, Chairman of the Pitjantjatjara Council, however, has confirmed that there was no record of Lynn Andrews' visit to the Pitjantjatjara lands in Central Australia, and that no one had any memory of her visit. He also noted that he had never heard of an Aboriginal name like Ginevee, that bandicoots hadn't been seen in these lands for thirty years, and that members of the Women's Council found her ceremony 'laughable'. Furthermore, the Immigration Department records showed that Lynn Andrews had been in Australia for only two weeks. It was apparent that she had little firsthand knowledge of the Aborigines.[24]

But, as with Castaneda, Lynn Andrews' personal philosophy proves to be worth hearing, if somewhat coloured by the audience she is addressing. In an interview published in *Magical Blend* magazine in 1987, Andrews made her personal orientation clear: 'The indigenous cultures of this world know about Mother Earth, and that is why I was drawn to it.… Shamanism, having to do with the balance of the Mother Earth, is something that is probably the answer to the world problem today. And I think that the burden of responsibility lies on women of the west.'[25]

Andrews also seemed intent on claiming that shamanism was a universal language that could be readily understood by any member of the Sisterhood of Shields. In a chapter in Michele Jamal's *Shape Shifters: Shaman Women in Contemporary Society* (1987) – a book that profiles several New Age shamanic

09.10 Author Lynn Andrews in Hawaii, December 2002. Andrew's descriptions of the Sisterhood of Shields have proved popular with New Age readers.

09.11 Chippewa medicine-man Sun Bear, who emphasized that 'we all share the same Earth Mother, regardless of race or country of origin'.

practitioners – Andrews implies that the Sisterhood is a unified spiritual movement with a common goal:

> The Sisterhood of Shields is a secret society of women who work towards self-realisation. The society is based on the ancient traditions of women. Although originally the members were all Native Americans, because of the needs of the time, women of other races are now initiated into the Sisterhood. As we share our wisdom we help bring a balance to the planet.[26]

Such a message obviously has great emotive power, despite the fact that it is anthropologically simplistic. Andrews' books reflect a need to find a secret, feminine society promoting shamanism in every culture she visits (albeit briefly) and are therefore more of a projection of her own desires than an authentic account of what really exists. And yet her personal philosophy appears to stem from a deeply felt intuition that the world is very much in need of a swift dose of enhanced planetary awareness, and that one can address this both individually and collectively: 'We are no longer hunting for buffalo; we are trying to survive a nuclear age and we are trying to bring wisdom into a new way of consciousness.… We may not have the opportunity to have any traditions at all if we don't heal Mother Earth now.'[27] Here, I suspect, we are hearing the real Lynn Andrews. It may well be that she could have come to this position – a powerful summation of the relevance of shamanism in the world today – without the support of her more questionable writings. These words, at least, ring true.

SUN BEAR AND BROOKE MEDICINE EAGLE

Although Carlos Castaneda and Lynn Andrews both succeeded in enchanting New Age readers for over twenty years with their magical exploits, they were not alone in bridging the gulf between traditional shamanism and the American counterculture. There were also Native Americans who could do this. Two in particular – Sun Bear and Brooke Medicine Eagle – went even further in embracing aspects of the personal growth movement.

Sun Bear, or Gheezis Mokwa, was born in 1929 on the White Earth Reservation in northern Minnesota, and died in 1992. A medicine-man of Chippewa descent, he headed a communal organization consisting mainly of people who were not Native Americans, and through his workshops and vision-quests became popular in New Age circles.

As a young child Sun Bear had a vision of a large black bear sheathed in rainbow colours which looked steadfastly at him, stood on its hind legs and gently touched him on the head. It was in this way that Sun Bear received his name. He learnt medicine ways from his uncles and his brothers on the reservation, but didn't practise the medicine path until he was twenty-five years old. In 1961 he started a magazine called *Many Smokes* as a forum for Native American writers and to advocate the ecological cause. It changed its name to *Wildfire* in 1983, and began publishing a broad range of articles on holistic health, vision-quests, wilderness studies, herbalism and New Age philosophy. In this way Sun Bear became a link between Native Americans and urban Americans interested in alternative spiritual paths – an influence that has continued to the present day.

After working for the Intertribal Council of Nevada as an economic development specialist, Sun Bear assisted in a Native Studies programme sponsored by the University of California at Davis, north of San Francisco. It was here, in 1970, that he founded the Bear Tribe, most of whose members were his former students from the Davis campus. Sun Bear maintained that he selected the name for the tribe because the bear is 'one of the few animals that heals its own wounds', and he had in mind an organization whose members 'could join together to help with the healing of the earth'. For a time the Bear Tribe was based outside Placerville, California, before moving to a hundred-acre farm close to Vision Mountain, near Spokane in Washington state. The Spokane community soon became self-sufficient, growing its own food, maintaining a large range of livestock, and running a programme of workshops.

09.12 The original school house on Sun Bear's 100-acre farm near Vision Mountain outside Spokane, Washington. The Bear Tribe soon became self-sufficient.

Sun Bear believed it was no longer appropriate to restrict Native American teachings to his own people, and much of his time was spent spreading this philosophy. To this end he produced several books, among them *The Medicine Wheel*, co-authored with his wife Wabun. He also lectured in Germany, Holland, England, India, Australia and other countries. Whereas Castaneda thrived on secrecy, Sun Bear's ideas were both publicly expressed and essentially global: we should all learn to 'walk in balance on the Earth Mother'. This passage from *The Medicine Wheel* encapsulates his message: 'We all share the same Earth Mother, regardless of race or country of origin, so let us learn the ways of love, peace and harmony and seek the good paths in life'.[28]

Drawing strongly on Native American tradition, Sun Bear taught members of his community and visitors how to undertake a vision-quest, which included fasting, prayers and ritual cleansing in a sweat lodge: 'a symbolic act of entering the womb of the Mother to be reborn'. He also explained that by choosing suitable sites for periods of visionary isolation, it was possible to draw on the vitality of locations where the Earth Mother seemed strong, and where spirits might appear. For Sun Bear it was the presence of spirits, in dreams or in visions, that would provide an authentic sense of personal direction. As he explained to members of his community: 'Each medicine-man has to follow his own medicine and the dreams and visions that give him power.' Sun Bear told his followers that they would always know intuitively when the spirits were near. 'Sometimes,' he said, 'it is just little whisperings, and sometimes a different energy, a change in the air that you feel. It is very recognizable.... You feel and experience things as an energy that comes through the spirit forces at the time.'[29]

Like Sun Bear, Brooke Medicine Eagle has become a bridge between two cultures, showing through her work how shamanism can link the old and the new. Her lineage and ancestry point back to the traditional ways of the Native Americans, but she has also been educated at a Western university and has utilized various holistic health therapies in formulating her worldview.

Brooke Medicine Eagle is of Sioux and Nez Percé extraction although she was raised on the Crow reservation in Montana. The great-great-grandniece of a Nez Percé holy man, Grandfather Joseph, Brooke was brought up in modest circumstances, living sixteen kilometres (ten miles) from the closest reservation village and ninety-five kilometres (sixty miles) over dirt roads from any major town. She says that the initial desire to be a healer-shaman came substantially from within her own experience.

Brooke took her shamanic vision-quest with an eighty-five-year-old Northern Cheyenne shamaness called The Woman Who Knows. With a younger medicine-woman, they journeyed to a place called Bear Butte, near the Black Hills of South Dakota. This region had been used for hundreds of years by the Sioux and Cheyenne as a location for the vision-quest. Here Brooke underwent the traditional preparation of fasting and cleansing. She was expecting to spend up to four days and nights alone on a mountain top, without food and water, praying for her initiatory vision.

After preparing a sage-bed and offering prayers, the other women departed. She recalls that in the evening, as she lay there peacefully, she suddenly became aware of the presence of a woman with long black braided hair, dressed in buckskin. She seemed to be imparting some sort of energy into her navel – the communication between them was not in words. As clouds moved across the sky, allowing the moonlight to filter through, Brooke Medicine Eagle became aware of a 'flurry of rainbows' caused by hundreds of beads on the woman's dress. Now she could also hear drumming, and it seemed then that she was surrounded by two circles of dancing women – 'spirits of the land' – and that these circles were interweaving with each other. One circle included seven old grandmothers, 'women who are significant to me, powerful old women'.[30]

Then the circles disappeared and once again Brooke was alone with the Rainbow Woman. The woman now told her that the land was in trouble – that it needed a new sense of balance, and specifically a more feminine, nurturing

09.13 North American shamaness Brooke Medicine Eagle, a descendant of Nez Percé holy man Grandfather Joseph. Through her writings and workshops she has reached out to a Western audience.

energy and less male aggression. She also said that all dwellers on the North American continent were 'children of the rainbow' of mixed blood, and there could be a balancing between the old cultures and the new. It was clear that the Rainbow Woman was a spirit teacher and not a physical human being because, when she left, 'her feet stayed where they were, but she shot out across the sky in a rainbow arc that covered the heavens, her head at the top of that arc. And then the lights that formed that rainbow began to die out, almost like fireworks in the sky, died out from her feet and died out and died out. And she was gone.'[31]

For Brooke Medicine Eagle the impact of the visitation was both personal and profound, for the communication had touched on the crucial distinction between Native American and Western ways. She had also learnt how she could be of service:

> The Indian people are the people of the heart. When the white man came to this land, what he was to bring was the intellect, that analytic, intellectual way of being. And the Indian people were to develop the heart, the feelings. And those two were to come together to build a new age, in balance, not one or the other.… [The Rainbow Woman] felt that I would be a carrier of the message between the two cultures, across the rainbow bridge, from the old culture to the new, from the Indian culture to the dominant culture, and back again. And in a sense, all of us in this generation can be that. We can help bridge that gap, build that bridge into the new age of balance.[32]

This has become Brooke Medicine Eagle's particular path in shamanism, and one which she brings to her workshops and writings. It is a path she treads with a special conviction, believing as she does that the earth will benefit from more feminine energy and more caring. 'We need to allow, to be receptive, to surrender, to serve.… The whole society, men and women, need that balance to bring ourselves into balance.'

EXPERIENTIAL SHAMANISM IN THE WEST

In addition to Native American teachers, who have drawn primarily on their own tribal shamanic traditions, one of the most influential figures in the international transpersonal movement is former anthropologist Dr Michael Harner, a leading exponent of experiential shamanism. Author of *The Way of the Shaman* (1980), a practical guide to exploring shamanic awareness, Harner has gone to great lengths to make his anthropological research accessible to a Western audience interested in exploring trance states and mystical consciousness. Unlike most of the other shamanic teachers in the West, Harner's material and techniques are drawn from many regions and cultures. He was personally initiated into the use of the 'visionary vine', *ayahuasca*, by the Conibo Indians of the Peruvian Amazon, and has worked with the Jivaro in Ecuador, the Wintun and Pomo Indians in California, the Lakota Sioux of South Dakota and the Coast Salish in Washington State. The techniques of applied shamanism that he now teaches through the auspices of the Foundation for Shamanic Studies in Mill Valley, California, are a synthesis of many cultures, and yet are true to the core essence of the tradition. The Foundation also helps indigenous peoples, including the Sami and the Inuit, to relearn core shamanic techniques that have disappeared from their cultures as a result of missionary activity or Western colonization.

For Michael Harner, shamanism takes the individual 'into the realms of myth and the Dreamtime… and in these experiences we are able to contact sources of power and use them in daily life'. Harner usually holds his shamanic workshops in city tenement buildings or in large open lecture rooms on university campuses, and has also trained many shamanic facilitators to continue this work both in the United States and internationally. Most of his workshop participants are familiar with the concept of the shamanic visionary journey and the idea of 'riding' rhythmic drumming into a state of meditative trance.

Harner's sessions begin as he shakes a gourd rattle to the four quarters in nearly total darkness, summoning the 'spirits' to participate in the shamanic working. He also encourages his group members to sing Native American shamanic chants and to enter into the process of engaging with the mythic world. His techniques include journeying in the mind's eye down the root system of an archetypal 'cosmic tree' or up imaginary smoke tunnels into the sky. As the group participants delve deeper into a state of trance, assisted all the time by the drumming, they enter the 'mythic dreamtime' of their own unconscious minds, frequently having visionary encounters with a variety of animal and humanoid beings and perhaps also exploring unfamiliar locales. They may also make contact with spirit-allies or 'power animals'. Harner's aim is to show his participants that they can discover an authentic mythic universe within themselves.

In the core shamanic model that Harner uses, humanity is said to dwell on Middle Earth, and two other magical domains – the upper and lower universes – may then be accessed through the shamanic trance journey. Often the upper and lower worlds appear to merge into a single 'magical reality' which parallels the familiar world, but which also seems invariably to extend beyond it. The shaman seeks his 'power animals' or spirit allies as a way of obtaining new sources of vitality and sacred knowledge. The main intention is to assist personal growth and healing, with many participants feeling that they have extended the boundaries of their awareness and their being. Sometimes they gain a sense of the extraordinary range of mythological images that become available through the shamanic process. One woman in a Harner workshop ventured to the upper world and had a remarkable 'rebirth' experience:

> I was flying. I went up into black sky – there were so many stars – and then I went into an area that was like a whirlwind. I could still see the stars and I was turning a lot, and my power animals were with me. Then I came up through a layer of clouds and met my teacher – she was a woman I'd seen before. She was dressed in a long,

09.14 Finno-Ugrian shamaness performing a ritual dance.

long gown and I wanted to ask her how I could continue with my shamanic work, how to make it more a part of my daily life. Then she took me into her, into her belly. I could feel her get pregnant with me and felt her belly stretching. I felt myself inside her. I also felt her put her hands on top of her belly and how large it was! She told me that I should stop breathing, that I should take my nourishment from her, and I could actually feel myself stop breathing. I felt a lot of warmth in my belly, as if it were coming into me, and then she stretched further and actually broke apart. Her belly broke apart and I came out of her, and I took it to mean that I needed to use less will in my work, and that I needed to trust her more and let that enter into my daily life. That was the end of my journey – the drum stopped and I came back at that point.[33]

Michael Harner believes that mythic experiences of this sort are common during the shamanic journey, and maintains that they reveal a dimension of consciousness rarely accessed in daily life:

Simply by using the technique of drumming, people from time immemorial have been able to pass into these realms which are normally reserved for those approaching death, or for saints. These are the realms of the upper and lower world where one can get information to puzzling questions. This is the Dreamtime of the Australian Aboriginal, the 'mythic time' of the shaman. In this area, a person can obtain knowledge that rarely comes to other people.[34]

But is this mythic experience real? Harner's reply is persuasive:

Imagination is a modern Western concept that is outside the realm of shamanism. 'Imagination' already pre-judges what is happening. I don't think it is imagination as we ordinarily understand it. I think we are entering something which, surprisingly, is universal – regardless of culture. Certainly people are influenced by their own history, their cultural and individual history. But we are beginning to discover a map of the upper and lower world, regardless of culture. For the shaman, what one sees – that's *real*. What one reads out of a book is secondhand information. But just like the scientist, the shaman depends upon first-hand observation to decide what's real. If you can't trust what you see yourself, then what can you trust?[35]

10
Science and Spirituality

The primal idea of a holistic bond with Nature flows from the idea that the planet itself is a living system. This is a concept reinforced by the Gaia Hypothesis. Gaia was the ancient Greek 'Earth Mother', and from a mythic perspective she is one of the many personifications of Mother Nature – an archetype of renewal and abundance. The Gaia Hypothesis, however, is not only a spiritual metaphor but also a scientific proposition. It was put forward by the British chemist Dr James Lovelock, a former consultant to the California Institute of Technology, who at one time worked on the scientific investigation of life on Mars.

Lovelock's study of the relatively static Martian atmosphere concluded that no life existed on that planet, but he became interested by the dynamics of Earth's atmosphere. He found, for example, that Earth's atmosphere differed greatly from the levels anticipated by physical chemistry. The concentration of atmospheric oxygen is around 21 per cent, and yet in theory – since oxygen is a very reactive gas – it should be almost completely absorbed, resulting in an atmospheric level close to zero. Lovelock was also fascinated by the fact that Earth's atmosphere was

10.01 Gaia, the Goddess of the Earth, in ancient Greek mythology. Panel from the Altar of Augustinian Peace, Rome, 13–9 BCE.

10.02 Native Americans honour the planet as a sacred, living entity. This image depicts ritual activities performed by the Kiowa Sun Dance Lodge, 1876–77.

able to retain a composition suitable for the continuation of life on the planet. His conclusion was that the Earth's atmosphere was affected by a wide range of living processes on the Earth itself, all of which helped maintain the atmosphere and the surface temperature: in short, that the Earth was a type of organically interrelated 'whole'. Gaia came to represent Earth's total biosystem, including the atmosphere, oceans and landforms, and all Earth's plants, animals and fungi. This biosystem contributed to a state of homeostasis, or equilibrium, suitable for the conditions of life.

THE LIVING EARTH

In *Gaia: a New Look at Life on Earth* (1979), Lovelock presented the Gaia model as a 'self-regulating, self-sustaining system, continually adjusting its chemical, physical and biological processes in order to maintain the optimum conditions for life and its continued evolution'.[1] While Lovelock did not take the extra step of identifying the biosphere as a single living organism, the Gaia Hypothesis soon became a powerful metaphor for global environmental awareness. For many in the New Age movement the Earth itself is now seen as a conscious organism – *as fundamentally alive*.

This is also reflected in the animistic beliefs of indigenous peoples across the planet. For Native Americans the planet is the Mother of all living beings – animals, plants, rocks and human beings all have life and are all interrelated – and Mother Earth herself needs to be honoured and nourished. As Sun Bear once said,

10.03 The reckless and destructive power of deforestation.

'The whole earth is sacred…many parts of the sacred earth are hungry right now. They need people to go to them and feed them with prayers and thanksgiving.'[2] And as the Aboriginal writer Miriam-Rose Ungunmerr of the Ngangikurungkurr people has expressed it:

> In our view the Earth is sacred. It is a living entity in which other living entities have [their] origin and destiny. It is where our identity comes from, where our spirituality begins, where our Dreaming comes from; it is where our stewardship begins. We are bound to the Earth in our spirit. By means of our involvement in the natural world we can ensure our well-being.[3]

For the dominant Western cultures, though, Nature is a domain to be exploited and ravaged for her economic resources. Quite apart from feeling any sense of intrinsic respect or reverence for the natural environment, and failing to see – as indigenous people everywhere see – that to ravage Nature is also to destroy ourselves, it often seems that in the West we are actually at war with Mother Earth. We are everywhere engaged in an process of exterminating natural species, reducing regions of native forests and grasslands, poisoning the soil, water and air, and making economic decisions for short-term gain, disregarding acknowledgment of the finite resources of the planet and the needs of human generations yet to come. Dr Ralph Metzner calls this process *ecocide* and sees it as arising through the loss of holistic consciousness:

> The metaphor of man against Nature and the elements is one that many people have formulated. It has a kind of religious worldview rationale in the Christian technological civilization of Europe and North America. It represents the shadow side of our obsession with individual separateness and power. At the same time, there are attitudes of the mystics, or shamanic cultures, and modern holistic worldviews that promise a way out of the self-created dilemmas of humankind.[4]

For Ralph Metzner, the Gaia model points us back in the direction of interconnectedness:

> Once we recognize our inescapable embeddedness in the living, organic ecosystem and our mutual interdependence with all other co-existing species, our sense of separate identity, so strenuously acquired and desperately maintained, recedes more into the background, and the relationships, whether balanced or imbalanced, become the foreground and focus of concern. This is the perceptual basis for the new and ancient points of view of the Gaian scientists and artists: it is holistic and comprehensive, and it is inevitably accompanied by a sense of wonder and reverence.[5]

MORPHIC RESONANCE

The British biologist and biochemist Dr Rupert Sheldrake has suggested that one of the reasons why conventional scientists remain mechanistic and reductionist in their outlook is that they have not yet absorbed the holistic paradigm as a function in Nature. Sheldrake has gained international recognition for introducing his idea of 'morphic resonance' to the study of patterns of natural order. He believes that these patterns in Nature emerge with the passage of time. All biological forms develop from simpler forms through the process of morphogenesis (meaning the coming into being of form, from the Greek 'morphe' and 'genesis'). Mechanistic science uses the hereditary chemical DNA to provide an explanation, but according to Sheldrake this is insufficient. While he acknowledges that DNA is undoubtedly an important factor in heredity, it doesn't explain morphogenesis, the process through which all biological forms develop from simpler forms (like eggs). As he puts it, the process 'brings more from less'.[6] The forms of a human leg or arm, for example, are quite different, even though the individual's DNA is the same. He does not believe that form happens by chance. He supports the vitalist tradition in biology that maintains that there is a formative principle at work in Nature, and that this formative principle directs living processes:

> The mechanistic approach to morphogenesis is challenged by the fact that when we cut a bit off an embryo, very often the embryo manages to grow and to form a complete organism. If a young sea urchin is cut in half, the result is not half a sea urchin, but a complete sea urchin which is about half the normal size. The rest of the cells adjust; although part of the embryo has been removed, the remaining part somehow remains a whole and gives rise to a whole organism.[7]

Sheldrake believes that the concept which best helps explain this situation is that of morphogenetic fields. This was first proposed by the Russian scientist Alexander Gurwitsch in 1922, who suggested that morphogenetic fields gave rise to form, that they directed tissues and cells in such a way that they developed their characteristic shape in the embryo. Sheldrake supports this idea:

10.04 *Diamond Mine*, a fractal image from the Mandelbrot set. According to biologist Dr Rupert Sheldrake the formative principle in Nature directs living processes.

10.05 Computer-generated image of the atomic structure of a DNA double helix.

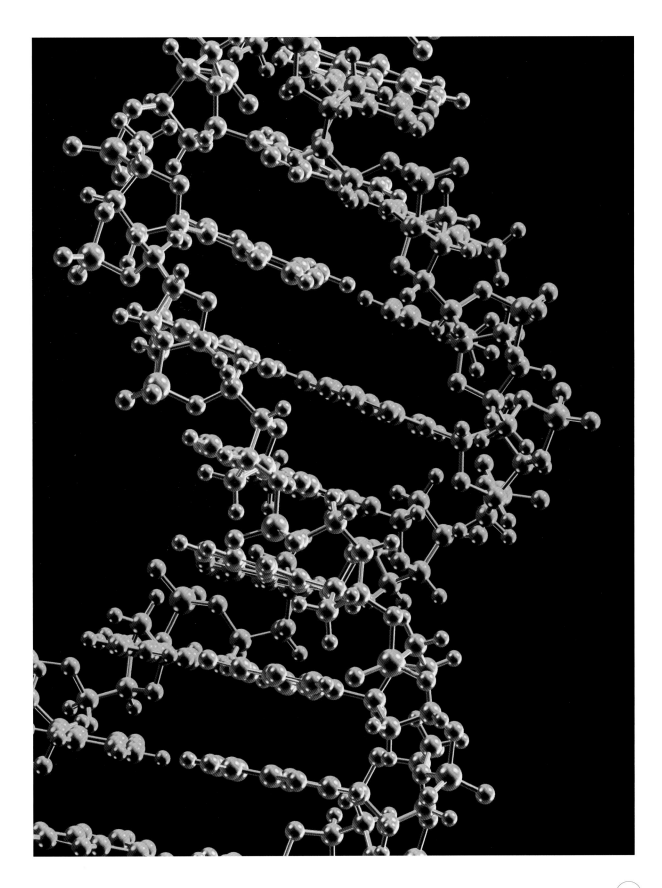

10.06 British biologist and biochemist Dr Rupert Sheldrake, who proposed the concept of 'morphic resonance'.

If part of an embryo is cut away, the remaining part still has the morphogenetic field associated with it. This field has a holistic property, because fields are continuous; they are not atomistic, one cannot cut bits out of fields. The complete form is restored because the field remains a whole… the field is a causal structure that guides the development of form.[8]

Expanding on Gurwitsch's original concept, Sheldrake believes that, with the passage of time, morphogenetic fields may determine what happens to a particular species so that any given species is influenced by, and connected with, all its past members. This is the process that Sheldrake calls *morphic resonance* and it is essentially a holistic concept of natural form and development.[9]

Sheldrake maintains that the problem with mechanistic scientists is that they mistake parts for the whole and also forget that they are dealing at a fundamental level with a profound mystery that finally transcends science itself:

The morphic resonance hypothesis suggests the way patterns and forms are repeated in Nature. It obviously does not explain where the first form, the pattern, or the first creative idea come from.

…

The nature of creativity is really a philosophical question which does not lie within the realm of natural science.[10]

As Sheldrake and Metzner have indicated, there is clearly a marked contrast between what we might call a holistic approach to Nature and its mechanistic, reductionist counterpart. Does this mean, then, that the world of science and the world of spirit can never really meet – that the holistic paradigm and the mechanist approach represent fundamentally different ways of responding to the natural world? This is indeed a crucial question, but before an answer can even be attempted, we must first explore the fundamental issue of objectivity and the types of scientific models we accept as reflections of 'reality'. This in turn leads us to consider some of the paradoxes thrown up by quantum theory and the New Physics.

THE DISAPPEARING UNIVERSE

For most of us operating in the everyday world, our notion of familiar 'reality' draws substantially on the apparent evidence of our senses, and it is entirely reasonable that this should be so. This has given rise in transpersonal psychology to the idea of the 'consensus reality' – the agreed perceptual basis on which language and cultural norms are constructed. In the West our consensus reality is built primarily on the so-called Newtonian-Cartesian model of the universe (based on the ideas of Isaac Newton and René Descartes). In this model the basic elements of the material universe are regarded as solid and ultimately indestructible. The fundamental building blocks of matter – atoms – are subject to gravity and to the laws of cause and effect, and matter itself is mediated through the passage of time. Descartes believed that mind and matter were intrinsically separate, that matter was inert, and that the universe was objectively real – independent of the process of observation.

This model of the universe, however, was challenged by the scientific analysis of light. It became evident that light itself appeared at certain times to consist of particles, while at other times it displayed the characteristics of waves. Einstein then proposed that perhaps space was not three-dimensional but four-dimensional. Time was not separate from the physical world, but was intimately connected with it: together they formed a four-dimensional space/time continuum. Einstein also believed that time was relative, because separate observers would perceive and construct events differently in time if these observers moved at different velocities relative to the events they were observing. This, in turn, suggests that space and time are mental constructs and not absolutes. As transpersonal psychologist Dr Ronald Valle has observed, 'both are merely elements of the language a particular observer uses for his or her description of phenomena'.[11]

The Newtonian three-dimensional model faced a more fundamental challenge when it was discovered that, at the subatomic level, matter does not exist with certainty in any fixed location but only shows a 'tendency to exist'. Werner Heisenberg's Uncertainty Principle affirms that it is not possible to determine with absolute precision both the position and momentum of any given subatomic particle. According to this principle, the wave and particle descriptions of being preclude one another. While *both* are necessary to get a full grasp of what being is, only *one* is available at any given time. We can never measure an electron's exact position (when it expresses itself as a particle) or its momentum (when it expresses itself as a wave) at the same time.[12] As a consequence of this discovery, Heisenberg came to the view that at a fundamental level 'reality' itself was essentially indeterminate: one could no longer rest in the security of a fixed vantage point. The entire universe was characterized by flux and change – by probabilities rather than certainties.

Heisenberg's findings have had an enduring impact on the nature of scientific perception. Indeed, transpersonal psychiatrist Dr Stanislav Grof believes that the very authority of mechanistic science has been eroded because the myth of solid and indestructible matter – its central dogma – soon began to disintegrate once scientists began to understand that atoms, far from being solid, were essentially empty:

> Subatomic particles showed the same paradoxical nature as light, manifesting either particle properties or wave properties depending on the arrangement of the experiment. The world of substance was replaced by that of process, event and relation. In subatomic analysis, solid Newtonian matter disappeared. What remained were activity, form, abstract order and pattern. In the words of the mathematician and physicist Sir James Jeans, the universe began to look less like a machine and more like a thought system.[13]

Quantum theory has also had a profound influence on the study of consciousness. As transpersonal physicist Dr Fritjof Capra has noted in his book, *The Tao of Physics* (1975):

> Quantum theory has… demolished the classical concepts of solid objects and of strictly deterministic laws of Nature. At the subatomic level, the solid material objects of classical physics dissolve into wavelike patterns of probabilities, and these patterns, ultimately, do not represent probabilities of things, but rather probabilities of interconnections. A careful analysis of the process of observation in atomic physics has shown that the subatomic particles have no meaning as isolated entities, but can only be understood as interconnections between the preparation of an

10.07 Dr Fritjof Capra, author of the influential work *The Tao of Physics*. Capra emphasizes the web of relationships within the natural world.

experiment and the subsequent measurement. Quantum theory thus reveals the basic oneness of the universe. It shows that we cannot decompose the world into independently existing smallest units. As we penetrate into matter, Nature does not show us any isolated 'basic building blocks' but rather appears as a complicated web of relations between the various parts of the whole.[14]

THE HOLISTIC APPROACH OF DAVID BOHM

The American quantum physicist Dr David Bohm (1917–92) was Professor at Birkbeck College, University of London, for over twenty years. He had worked with Einstein and went on to develop a theory of quantum physics that treated the whole of existence, including matter and consciousness, as an unbroken whole. In his seminal work *Wholeness and the Implicate Order* (1980) – a classic in transpersonal circles – Bohm proposed that the 'unbroken wholeness of the totality of existence [could be] seen as an undivided flowing movement without borders'.[15] Bohm conceived of an *implicate order* within which the totality of existence was enfolded. This implicate order included space, time and matter, but its presence could only be inferred through observing its manifestations.

In a way reminiscent of the creation process described in various mystical cosmologies – including the Kabbalah and the emanationist systems in Gnosticism – Bohm maintained that the implicate order 'unfolds' into the explicate order – the world of manifestation. According to Bohm, the reductionist methods used in modern science actually prevent scientific observers from grasping that all things owe their existence to an unbroken wholeness – a wholeness nevertheless subject to the unending process of constant flux he termed the 'holomovement'. Bohm believed that the universe is like a total organism in which the constituent parts only make sense in relation to the whole. He also believed that in the final analysis there could be no distinction between mind and matter: 'The mental and the material are two sides of one overall process that are (like form and content) separated only in thought and not in actuality. Rather, there is one energy that is the basis of all reality.... There is never any real division between mental and material sides at any stage of the overall process.'[16]

American Jungian psychologist Dr June Singer, meanwhile, has compared Bohm's perspective with that of Carl Jung:

> We experience the explicate order when we perceive realities with our senses. Our familiar world is one of separate objects subject to various physical forces like gravity etc. We can see that certain things may be in relationship to each other, and in this explicate world of things and thoughts, we can hope to integrate the various disparate parts. Wholeness appears to us as an ideal state of being.... For Jung, the

10.08 Krishnamurti (left) in conversation with the noted quantum physicist Professor David Bohm. Both were fascinated by the nature of human consciousness.

collective unconscious was the fundamental reality, with human consciousness deriving from it. In a similar way, Bohm sees the implicate order as the fundamental reality, with the explicate order and all its manifestations as derivative.[17]

THE OBSERVER AND THE OBSERVED

In quantum theory the very act of observation involves a process of interaction with what is observed – Nature and the observer are not separate and distinct as we have always assumed. Scientific psychology, on the other hand, is based on the principle that if perceptions of the physical world are to be accepted as real, separate observers must be able to agree on, and 'validate', the innate characteristics of what is observed – that there is a clear need for 'objectivity', or an ability to stand apart from what is being observed. Clearly quantum theory and scientific psychology reflect two essentially different perspectives – and in this instance quantum physics appears to favour the mystics. Eastern mysticism and quantum theory are essentially holistic, while scientific psychology is innately reductionist – focusing on discrete and tangible 'facts'. As the transpersonal writers Fritjof Capra and Gary Zukav have observed, quantum theory supports the position of the Eastern mystical tradition in affirming that the observed and the observer are essentially one. As Zukav notes in his influential book *The Dancing Wu Li Masters: An Overview of the New Physics* (1979): 'According to quantum mechanics there is no such thing as objectivity. We cannot eliminate ourselves from the picture. We are a part of Nature, and when we study Nature there is no way around the fact that Nature is studying itself.'[18]

Yet while quantum theory proposes a holistic view of the physical universe, the foundations of Western science still remain entirely grounded in Newtonian-Cartesian thinking. Scientific psychology continues to be strongly influenced by behaviourism, which insists that the observer or experimenter be treated as separate and distinct in relation to the behaviour being observed and measured. This leaves no room whatever for a spiritual component in life because, as Stanislav Grof points out:

> In the reductionist view, human intelligence, creativity, art, religion, ethics and science itself are all byproducts of material processes in the brain. There is no place for mysticism or religion, and spirituality is seen as a sign of primitive superstition, intellectual and emotional immaturity, or even severe psychopathology that science will one day explain in terms of deviant biochemical processes in the brain.[19]

10.09 Physicist Danah Zohar has proposed the notion of the 'quantum self'.

So is there a way out of the impasse? The answer seems to lie in applying the holistic principles of quantum theory to the study of human consciousness itself.

QUANTUM PSYCHOLOGY

An important contribution to the emerging field of 'quantum psychology' has been provided by British-based American physicist Danah Zohar, who relates the principles of quantum mechanics to an understanding of the human condition. Zohar is concerned with issues like the nature of individual identity and its relationship to the universe as a whole. On a physical level the human organism is subject to continual change. It is an intriguing fact, for example, that the neurones in the brain and the cells of the body change entirely every seven years – so where does this leave our sense of self and individuality? Indeed, Zohar asks, if individual people are 'real', what is it that holds them together? Each of us is an organism made up from billions of cells, with each cell in some sense possessing a life of its own. Within our brains alone some ten thousand million neurones contribute to the rich tapestry of our mental life. And yet if our brains consist of all those

10.10 *Mandala* by American artist Robert Venosa – a symbol of cosmic unity and interconnectedness.

myriad neurones, how does the idea of a 'person' actually emerge and how tangible is that person's existence?

Zohar's conclusion is that people, like sub-atomic matter, exhibit the same wave/particle duality identified in Heisenberg's Uncertainty Principle. Our individuality, our sense of apparent separateness, is equivalent to the specificity of a particle, whereas the way we interrelate with others, and with the world as a whole, has more the characteristic of a wave. According to Zohar, if we consider the human being from the perspective of quantum theory – as a *quantum self* – both aspects emerge. Seen this way, 'the quantum self is simply a more fluid self, changing and evolving at every moment, now separating into sub-selves, now reuniting into a larger self. It ebbs and flows, but always in some sense being itself.'[20]

Zohar rejects computer-based models of consciousness because they are essentially impersonal and offer no insights into the continuity of individual identity and the nature of human relationships. All computer models of the brain assume that the brain itself functions like a giant computer, but, assuming that to be the case, where do we find the 'central committee of neurones' overseeing the whole process that provides us with our sense of individuality and the will to make spontaneous decisions? Clearly, without a sense of wholeness, as distinct from a myriad variety of brain functions, there is no sense of self. And yet we all know from our own experience that human consciousness is characterized by a sense of unbroken wholeness and continuity that provides cohesion in daily life:

> The whole corpus of classical physics, and the technology that rests on it (including computer technology), is about the separateness of things, about constituent parts and how they influence each other across their separateness, as the separate neurones in the brain act on one another across the synapses. If there were no other good reasons to reject the computer model of the brain, the argument pointing towards the unity of consciousness would be the most damning.[21]

Zohar believes that quantum theory leads us towards the realization that all sentient beings are ultimately connected and share a common destiny on the planet:

> On a quantum view of the person, it is impossible *not* to love my neighbour as myself, because my neighbour *is* myself.... In a quantum psychology, there are no isolated persons. Individuals do exist, do have an identity, a meaning and a purpose, but, like particles, each of them is a brief manifestation of a particularity.... Each of us, because of our integral relationship with others, with Nature, and with the world of values, has the capacity to beautify or to taint the waters of eternity.[22]

The implications of the New Physics and the theories of such thinkers as Bohm, Capra, Sheldrake, Grof, Metzner and Zohar are far-reaching. We begin to understand that at a core level everything in the known universe seems to be interconnected, that totally separate and individual identity is ultimately an illusion, and that what we know as 'individual' consciousness contains in essence all the potentials of universal consciousness.

All of this, of course, comes close to the shamanic perspective of indigenous peoples: they, too, conceive of a holistic, interconnected universe that is alive with meaning, and grounded in a reality far more profound and sacred than reductionist concepts of causality. From an animist view, everything is alive, and consciousness, or spirit, is the very basis of life. For Fritjof Capra, this awareness reinforces an ecological awareness that honours both the planet and our place upon the Earth:

> The new vision of reality is ecological, but it goes far beyond immediate concerns with environmental protection. It is supported by modern science, but rooted in a perception of reality than reaches beyond the scientific framework to an intuitive awareness of the oneness of all life, the interdependence of its multiple manifestations, and its cycles of change and transformation. When the concept of the human spirit is understood in the transpersonal sense, as the mode of consciousness in which the individual feels connected to the cosmos as a whole, it becomes clear that ecological awareness is truly spiritual.[23]

SEEKING A NEW PARADIGM

Few have tackled the relationship between science and spirituality in more depth than American transpersonal theorist Ken Wilber. Psychologist Daniel Goleman was moved to write in *The New York Times* that Wilber has joined 'the ranks of the grand theorists of human consciousness like Ernst Cassirer, Mircea Eliade and Gregory Bateson', and Dr Roger Walsh of the University of California Medical School at Irvine has called him 'the foremost writer on consciousness and transpersonal psychology in the world today'. Wilber started young, writing his first book, *The Spectrum of Consciousness*, in 1973 when he was still finishing graduate studies. He has now produced over a dozen substantial books on the history and development of consciousness, including *No Boundary* (1979), *Up from Eden* (1981) and *Sex, Ecology and Spirituality* (1995).

Ken Wilber studied chemistry and biology at Duke University and later at graduate school in Nebraska. But he was also extremely interested in psychotherapy, philosophy and religion, and eventually began to perceive a major gulf between Freudian psychology, which emphasized the strength of the ego, and the Buddhist concept of surrendering the ego in an act of transcendence. He came gradually to the view that there is a hierarchy, or spectrum, of levels of consciousness, with each part of the spectrum comparatively valid and apparently 'real' on its own level. For Wilber the different levels are rather like boxes within larger boxes, each potentially more all-encompassing than the others. 'Just as Newtonian physics is a subset of Einsteinian physics,' he maintains, 'so existentialism is a smaller box – correct as far as it goes – which is encompassed by the larger box of the transcendentalists.'[24]

Wilber himself has been substantially influenced by Theosophy, by the teachings of Krishnamurti, and by Zen practitioner Philip Kapleau, Eido Roshi, and American spiritual teacher Da Free John. Wilber's own meditative practices derive from the Vajrayana Buddhist tradition of Tibet, which consists of oral instructions and secret teachings intended to develop wisdom and compassion; his principal teachers have been Kalu Rinpoche and Trungpa Rinpoche. Yet Wilber's spectrum model derives not so much from his meditative experience as from his remarkably far-ranging scholarly review of the 'Perennial Philosophy' – the wisdom tradition of both East and West. According to Wilber:

> Human personality is a multi-levelled manifestation or expression of a single Consciousness, just as in physics the electro-magnetic spectrum is viewed as a multi-banded expression of a single, characteristic electro-magnetic wave…each level of the Spectrum is marked by a different and easily recognized sense of individual identity, which ranges from the Supreme Identity of cosmic-consciousness through several gradations or bands to the drastically narrowed sense of identity associated with egoic consciousness.[25]

Wilber believes that man's 'innermost' consciousness is identical to the absolute and ultimate reality of the Universe known variously as Brahman, Tao, Dharmakaya, Allah, the Godhead. He refers to these collectively as 'Mind', for, according to the Perennial Philosophy, this is all that exists in the ultimate sense. A problem arises, however, because humans usually operate in a dualistic state of consciousness – characterized, for example, by the distinction between 'subject' and 'object' – and each of us tends to lose sight of this overriding One-ness. As Wilber notes in *The Spectrum of Consciousness* (1973), dualism gives rise to psychological boundaries that are perceived as real. 'We divide reality,' he writes, 'forget that we have divided it, and then forget that we have forgotten it.'[26] So each level of mind below the level of Unity Consciousness represents a progressive distortion of Mind's truly unified reality. These levels of consciousness (or illusion) represent the different states of perception which all human beings must pass through in their quest for self-knowledge.

According to Wilber's model, the levels below the state of Unity Consciousness are like bands in a spectrum. The 'lowest' level is a stage of consciousness he calls the 'Shadow', where individuals identify with an impoverished self-image and have repressed part of their psyche as 'alien', 'evil' or 'undesirable'. On the next level of 'Ego', the individual identifies with a mental image of himself but perceives himself to exist '*in* his body and not as his body'. This, for Wilber, is a substantially intellectual level of reality. At the next level – the existential level –

individuals identify with the 'total psycho-physical organism'. Wilber would say that here there has been a profound development towards individual integration because the person now accepts all facets of his or her total organism. He quotes Gestalt therapist Fritz Perls as embodying this process: 'Lose your mind and come to your senses!'

Wilber recognizes, though, that beyond the individual level of psychophysical awareness, and at a higher existential level, may be found what he calls 'Biosocial Bands' of consciousness. Here we are considering the individual in the context of society. But social patterns filter our capacity for feeling and perceiving into culturally accepted modes, so, to this extent, cultural patterns distort or restrict consciousness. All societies consist of people in a web of relationships and a certain amount of social cohesion and stability is required, but, as a consequence, human consciousness is prevented from attaining complete self-realization.

At the transpersonal levels of the spectrum we arrive at a perceptual domain where consciousness is able to transcend the individual level. But even here, as Wilber puts it, transpersonal awareness may not yet be 'completely identified with the All'. The transpersonal levels of consciousness have been associated by some theorists with Jungian archetypes and the Collective Unconscious – the realm of mythic, primordial consciousness – and Jung himself defined mystical experience as the 'experience of archetypes'.[27] However, Wilber has made it clear, in his somewhat extravagantly titled *A Brief History of Everything* (1996), that he disagrees with Jung on this point. For Wilber, 'the *collective* is not necessarily *transpersonal*. Most of the Jungian archetypes… are simply archaic images lying in the *magic* and *mythic* structures. … There is nothing transrational or transpersonal about them… they are not themselves the source of a transpersonal or genuinely spiritual awareness.'[28]

Many commentators, though, myself included, would disagree with Wilber on this point, and such a view demarcates Wilber strongly from those within the personal growth movement – Jean Houston and Jean Shinoda Bolen, among many others – who, in continuing the work of scholars like Joseph Campbell, have sought to enrich the exploration of mystical consciousness with mythic diversity. In the final analysis, it may come down to how one defines magic and myth. For Wilber, magical and mythic dimensions of consciousness are 'pre-rational' and therefore regressive, whereas for others mythic archetypes enliven what would otherwise be a comparatively sterile collective psyche. It is also of interest that in his experiential work Stanislav Grof has confirmed the existence of archetypal levels of mythic awareness at profoundly transpersonal levels of consciousness and he believes they have a defining, rather than regressive, role.[29]

For Wilber, nevertheless – and few transpersonal theorists would disagree on this point – the supreme level is reached only when Mind alone exists, when there is no distinction whatsoever between subject and object. Wilber reminds us, for example, that there is still a hint of dualism when the mystic feels he is *witnessing* something beyond himself. The truth of Unity Consciousness is only realized, says Wilber, when 'the witness and the witnessed are one and the same'.[30]

Wilber's spectrum model embraces the non-dualist position of Vedanta and Vajrayana Buddhism, and the breadth of his study has been widely acclaimed. It has to be said, however, that Wilber's tendency to categorize and label different religious, psychological and philosophical traditions – necessary if one is considering 'boxes within boxes' – has been found, by its very nature, to be a limiting process. At times his approach in defining levels of human consciousness seems too cerebral in its construction to be completely convincing, and the dynamism – the sheer awesomeness of metaphysical consciousness and the rich poetic tapestry of archetypal imagery – sometimes seems diminished by highly structured models like this. I myself share some of these concerns, for structures tend to imply their own sense of certainty, and when we embrace them, we are inclined to forget that models and maps of mystical and visionary consciousness are only that: they draw finally on metaphors, symbols and allusions.

Ken Wilber's spectrum model of spiritual consciousness nevertheless remains one of the most all-encompassing structures yet proposed. With Stanislav Grof's framework of perinatal and transpersonal levels of consciousness, and John Lilly's model of positive and negative mystical states, the Wilber model has helped define transpersonal concepts of human evolution, bringing science and spirituality closer together within a coherent holistic paradigm.

Meanwhile, if the developing transpersonal view affirms the idea of a holistic universe grounded in a matrix of universal order, mind or consciousness, what does this say to us about the nature of death? We all face the inevitable trauma of our own impending death and there are many fundamental issues to consider. Does the death of the brain bring with it the extinction of our personal identity, as the reductionist model in science would imply? Is our sense of personal worth and individuality nothing other than a by-product of our human biochemistry? How significant are spiritual and religious beliefs in the dying process? And what actually happens when we die?

11

The Challenge of Death

From a transpersonal viewpoint, studying the experience of death is perhaps the greatest remaining challenge in the study of human consciousness. Knowing more about death would not only teach us about what to expect when we die, but also how we should live our lives. Fortunately, the scientific investigation of the near-death experience is beginning to provide useful insights into the possible nature of death itself. Thanatology – the study of death and the dying process – is now a major realm of enquiry within the international personal growth movement, and may yet challenge current ideas of the mind/body relationship.

DEATH – THE FINAL STAGE OF GROWTH

The Swiss psychiatrist Dr Elisabeth Kübler-Ross used the phrase, 'Death – the Final Stage of Growth', as the title of one of her many books on dying (1975), and it conveys a clear sense of optimism. Dr Kübler-Ross thinks that, although many people associate death with trauma and crisis, it is also possible to regard death as a challenge. Death then becomes just another transitionary state of consciousness. The final stage of growth, yes. The end of identity and awareness? On the basis of the evidence, probably not.

We usually define death as the absence of all visible signs of life – there is no heartbeat or respiration, and brainwave activity has apparently ceased (any EEG monitoring of electrical brain impulses would register as zero). To all intents and purposes, a body in this state is clinically dead. The issues we are considering here relate to the experiences of people who have been pronounced clinically dead, and yet revived to recount their often mystical and visionary experiences, known as near-death experiences, or NDEs. They provide us with the best scientifically based data on what may happen to us when we die, and to that extent they represent a possible meeting ground between the worlds of science and spirituality.

The term 'near-death experience' was coined in 1975 by the American philosopher and teacher Dr Raymond Moody, author of the bestseller *Life After Life*. Moody began collecting anecdotal accounts of near-death incidents in 1972, and his book was based on 150 accounts from people who contacted him as a result of articles he had written or lectures he had given on this topic.

The NDE by definition involves the return from apparent clinical death to waking consciousness. It can be considered a substantially modern phenomenon because the techniques of medical resuscitation and life-support are now so sophisticated.[1] We have a burgeoning literature that describes the accounts of people who have seemingly 'died' and yet lived to tell the tale. These accounts, and the scientific and medical commentaries accompanying them, provide a new focus for the philosophical issues of mind and body in the debate over the nature of human consciousness and the 'soul'.

Among the first modern accounts anticipating the NDE studies was the work of Swiss geologist Professor Albert Heim whose writings were translated in the 1970s by Russell Noyes and Ray Kletti.[2] Heim collected data on the experiences of people who had nearly died in mountain-climbing accidents or warfare and included instances where people faced with the prospect of imminent death experienced a panoramic life-review or heard transcendental music.

There were also the findings of Dr Karlis Osis, a Latvian-born parapsychologist based in the United States, who conducted a survey of deathbed visionary experiences. Osis sent questionnaires to 10,000 physicians and nurses in late 1959, and received 540 responses. On the basis of these, he published a book titled *Death-bed Observations by Physicians and Nurses* in 1961, and followed it with a more substantial volume, *At the Hour of Death*, in 1977. In these works Osis noted that terminal subjects often experienced periods of bliss and spiritual peace prior to death. Some also saw apparitions of deceased relatives or friends coming to greet them, and seemed to realize intuitively that these figures were about to help them through the transition of death itself.

It was Raymond Moody's book, *Life After Life* (1978), however, that became the principal catalyst and inspiration for others interested in NDEs, and there have been several systematic research studies of the phenomenon since then – in the United States, Britain and Australia. Among those who have played a prominent role in this work are Dr Kenneth Ring, former Professor of Psychology at the University of Connecticut; his British colleague Dr Margot Grey, founder of the International Association for Near-Death Studies (IANDS) in the United Kingdom; psychiatrist Dr Elisabeth Kübler-Ross; Australian psychologist Dr Cherie Sutherland; and Dr Michael Sabom of Emory University in Atlanta.

Kenneth Ring's *Life at Death*, published in 1980, was the first scientific study of NDEs and was based on over a hundred interviews with medical subjects who had survived near-death. Ring followed it in 1984 with *Heading Toward Omega*, a lucid overview of the spiritual implications of the NDE. Ring and his international colleagues have described the 'core' NDE in broadly the same way: an 'altered state' of feeling (peace, joy, serenity); a sense of movement or separation from the body (an aerial perspective on the body, generally heightened awareness); a journey through a tunnel towards either a transcendent dimension or some other, more tangible realm (a celestial valley, garden or city), the experience of light and beauty; encounters in the spirit world with deceased relatives, spirits or 'guides' and sometimes religious figures like Jesus or 'God'. They have also sought to evaluate the impact such visionary experiences have had on the lives of the NDE subjects themselves.

Ring, Grey and Sutherland have all come to the conclusion that the 'core' NDE is largely *invariant*, that it occurs in much the same form – though not with all the characteristics present in every case – irrespective of nationality, social class, age, sex, educational level or occupation. What is highly significant about this finding is that the core aspects are comparatively constant whether or not that person is a religious believer, atheist or agnostic: in other words, the NDE seems to be pointing towards characteristics of human consciousness rather than towards the disjointed or divergent sensory experiences one might expect if the experience were purely hallucinatory. To this extent the NDE seems to be telling us about the process of dying itself and the various stages or transitions of human perception that might occur beyond bodily death.

Once again, we have the difficult issue of body, mind and spirit to resolve. During an NDE, is the subject projecting consciousness beyond the confines of the physical body and, if so, how is such a thing possible? In Kenneth Ring's *Life at Death* survey of core experiencers:

  97.4 per cent felt that their bodies were light or absent

  94.6 per cent found their sense of time either expanded or absent

  81.8 per cent experienced space 'as either extended, infinite or absent'.

As Ring noted: 'For most respondents, body, time and space simply disappear – or, to put it another way, they are no longer meaningful constructs.'[3]

Such aspects of the NDE are problematic for reductionist researchers keen on explaining away the phenomenon as illusory or hallucinatory. Among the most commonly reported 'explanations' from this camp are that NDEs are delusory experiences which result from temporal lobe seizure or loss of oxygen as one approaches death; that they are simply re-enactments of the birth process; that they are caused by anaesthetic drugs; and that they are the symptoms of psychological factors related to the likely onset of death.

The following summary of these explanations provides comments on their relevance in each case:

11.01 The near-death experience (NDE) is often described as an otherworld journey towards the light. Aspects of the NDE are depicted in this well known painting by Hieronymus Bosch, *The Ascent of the Blessed*, c. 1450–1516.

Hallucinations and delusions

Dr Michael Sabom was particularly impressed in his medical survey by the ability of autoscopic (out-of-the-body/self-observing) NDE subjects to report details of actual events (medical equipment, surgical procedures, real conversations) from a detached and elevated position. 'The details of these perceptions were found to be accurate in all instances where corroborating evidence was available.' Dr Sabom also reported that some NDE subjects experienced hallucinations during their coma states and were able to distinguish clearly between the two categories of perception.[4]

Temporal lobe seizure

Seizures deriving from the temporal lobes (or non-motor portions) of the brain involve sensory distortions of the size or location of objects close by, and sometimes a feeling of detachment from the environment. They are also characterized by feelings of fear and loneliness and visual or auditory hallucinations. On the other hand, many NDE subjects report accurate, undistorted perceptual fields and may feel elated or relaxed about their dissociated condition.

Loss of oxygen in the brain

Under normal circumstances, if the oxygen supply to the brain is reduced, this produces a state of mental confusion and cognitive dysfunction. This is certainly not characteristic of the core NDE, which is often described by subjects as profoundly real and perceptually coherent. Some subjects suffering from brain hypoxia (oxygen loss) – for example, mountain climbers who have trekked in rarefied atmospheres – find they experience an onset of laziness and irritability, and they may also find it difficult to remember what they were thinking or doing at the time. Many NDE subjects, on the other hand, are so awed by the clarity and detail of their experiences that they remember them for many years afterwards.

Reliving the birth process

If NDEs, which are characterized by feelings of passing through a tunnel towards light, are somehow related to the normal birth process, then people born by Caesarian section should not experience them. Dr Susan Blackmore – a well known sceptic in relation to the NDE data – gave a questionnaire to 254 people, of whom 36 had been born by Caesarian section. 'Both groups reported the same proportion of out-of-the-body and tunnel experiences,' she has written. 'It could be that the experiences are based on the idea of birth in general, but this drastically weakens the theory.'[5]

Anaesthetic drugs

There are several cases of NDE subjects who received no anaesthetic during their hospitalization, so this explanation, if indeed it is one at all, would not apply in many instances. While it is true that some dissociative anaesthetics like ketamine hydrochloride (Ketalar) may produce an experience in which one's consciousness appears distinct from the body and there may also be an awareness of journeying through tunnels in space, Ketalar is not widely used in human medical treatment, and is now for the most part restricted to veterinary practice. In general, drug-induced hallucinations seem to be markedly different from NDEs. Dr Sabom notes that drug experiences are 'highly variable and idiosyncratic' and 'markedly different from NDEs, which always show a remarkable degree of invariance'.

Psychological factors

One psychological view of NDEs is that the experience derives from 'depersonalization'. This theory, advanced by Noyes and Kletti (who translated the Heim material) argues that the ego has to protect itself from impending death, and thus creates a perceptual scenario which supports the feeling of continuing mental integration. As Dr Noyes has said: 'As an adaptive pattern of the nervous system it alerts the organism to its threatening environment while holding potentially disorganizing emotion in check.' Dr Sabom rejects this view as a blanket explanation of the NDE because there were subjects in his survey who had out-of-the-body NDEs without being aware of any likelihood of imminent death. Some of these were subjects who experienced loss of waking consciousness without warning, due to a stoppage of the heart. Also, as Dr Margot Grey has indicated, 'depersonalization' is unable to account for NDE subjects who have claimed to meet relatives who had recently died but whom the NDE subject did not know at the time had died. Here the NDE subject would learn of the relative's actual death only after recovering from the NDE.

WHAT HAPPENS DURING THE NDE?

It may be worthwhile at this point to quote a few brief but characteristic examples of what NDE subjects actually report, because their testimonies are our starting point, and they provide insights into the processes involved:

I felt as though I was looking down at myself, as though I was way out here in space…. I felt sort of separated. It was a wonderful feeling. It was marvellous. I felt very light and didn't know where I was…. And then I thought that something was happening to me…. This wasn't night. I wasn't dreaming…. And then I felt a wonderful feeling as if I was out in space.

I felt myself being separated: my soul drawing apart from the physical being, was drawn upward seemingly to leave the earth and to go upward where it reached a greater Spirit with whom there was a communion, producing a remarkable new relaxation and deep security.

I went into this kind of feeling of ecstasy and just started moving outward energetically… and then I experienced a replay of all of my life… from my birth to the actual operation… it was like it was on a fast-forward video… people, places, everything.

It is not uncommon for NDE subjects to report contact with deceased relatives or friends. In Dr Sabom's survey of 116 NDE subjects, 28 described encounters with other personages. One of Dr Sabom's case studies involved a seriously injured soldier, and his account of his deceased colleagues is interestingly matter-of-fact:

I came out of my body, and perceived me laying on the ground with three limbs gone.… What makes this so real was that the thirteen guys that had been killed the day before, that I had put in plastic bags, were right there with me. And more than that, during the course of that month of May, my regular company lost forty-two dead. All forty-two of those guys were there. They were not in the form we perceive the human body, and I can't tell you what form they were in because I don't know. But I know they were there. I felt their presence. We communicated without talking with our voices. There was no sympathy, no sorrow. They were already where they were. They didn't want to go back. That was the basic tone of our communication… that we were all happy right where we were.[6]

In a potentially highly significant research study, Kenneth Ring and his colleague Sharon Cooper have explored near-death experiences among the blind. If it could be demonstrated that blind people have their sight restored to them during a near-death experience, the entire relationship between body, mind and spirit would have to be re-assessed. In 1997 Ring and Cooper approached eleven national and regional American associations for the blind in order to locate people who had experienced near-death experiences (NDEs) or out-of-the-body experiences (OOBEs). Screened for the research study were 46 individuals, of whom 31 qualified for inclusion. They included 20 females and 11 males, most of them Christian and all of them Caucasian. Nearly half of the participants had been blind from birth. The research study took two years.[7]

One of the subjects – a forty-five-year-old woman named Vicki – had been born blind: her optic nerve had been completely destroyed at birth because of

11.02 Encountering the 'Being of Light': *Unio Mystica*, 2002, by American painter A. Andrew Gonzalez.

excess oxygen received in an incubator. Nevertheless, Vicki appeared to be able to 'see' during her NDE. Vicki found herself floating above her body in the emergency room of a hospital following an automobile accident. She was aware of being up near the ceiling of the room and she could see a male doctor and female nurse working on her body. At first she thought she must be dead: 'I just briefly saw this body,' she said later, 'and I knew that it was mine because I wasn't in mine.' She then went on to identify features of her clothing and personal possessions:

> I think I was wearing the plain gold band on my right finger and my father's wedding ring next to it. But my wedding ring I definitely saw…. That was the one I noticed the most because it's most unusual. It has orange blossoms on the corners of it. This was the only time I could ever relate to seeing and to what light was, because I experienced it.[8]

During her NDE, Vicki also reported visiting a very bright realm 'where everybody…was made of light'. She saw herself surrounded by trees and flowers and a vast number of people. It was here she became aware of specific people whom she had known in real life but who had since died. Two of them were blind schoolmates who had died some years before. She also encountered her grandmother who had died two years before her accident.[9]

Ring and Cooper's research provides evidence that the blind are indeed able to experience some sort of vision during their NDEs, even though their normal sight organs are not functioning. Ring and Cooper have speculated that this may involve a unique type of telepathic perception they call 'mindsight'. Their research is continuing, and may prove to be of considerable importance because mindsight clearly involves an ability to perceive in a manner beyond the currently known limits of the material brain.

There are several categories within the NDE. A number of the experiences involve a substantially physical frame of reference. Many subjects perceive themselves to be just slightly dissociated from the physical plane of events – perhaps observing their comatose bodies, before rising into the sky above their house, or observing themselves being resuscitated by a doctor in a hospital. In such instances it is not uncommon for subjects to also hear and accurately report conversations that have taken place at that time. At a more removed level, though – perhaps at a level that brings the subject closer to physical death – a different experiential domain reveals itself, one that the American parapsychologist D. Scott Rogo has referred to as 'eschatological' (opening out into an otherworld journey and perceptions of the final resting-place of the soul).[10] It is here that the

NDE subject may have visionary, religious or spiritual experiences – usually shaped by cultural expectations or by the person's individual belief system. The visionary material itself can be of varying degrees of profundity, ranging from a dreamlike or surreal flow of imagery through to powerful archetypal experiences. In instances like these, subjects report encounters with celestial beings, superhuman beings from classical mythology or encounters with 'God'. And sometimes they even transcend these levels of imagery, experiencing a dissolving of personal boundaries as the ego melts into other beings or forms, or seems to unite with the entire manifested universe.

IMPLICATIONS FOR AN AFTERLIFE

Psychiatrist Elisabeth Kübler-Ross's medical work with dying patients predates scientific research into NDEs – it extends back some thirty years – although her contribution to thanatology is continuing. Much of her original medical work and her earlier publications on the process of death and dying were concerned primarily with the various stages of engaging with death, including denial and self-questioning, the role of grief, and the idea of death as an integral part of human development. It is only comparatively recently that Kübler-Ross has expressed her ideas on the afterlife in any detail. A small book entitled *On Life After Death*, published in 1991, brought together Kübler-Ross's principal writings on the afterlife for the first time.

Perhaps more than any other living person, Kübler-Ross has been associated with the process of death and dying. She acknowledges cultural variations in the visionary episodes different individuals might have after death, but maintains that there is substantial evidence for post-mortem survival. 'For me,' says Kübler-Ross, 'it is no longer a matter of belief, but rather a matter of knowing.'[11] She maintains that her views are based on a study of more than 20,000 people who have had near-death experiences, although, unlike the Ring and Sabom studies, many of her references are anecdotal.

She believes that none of us dies alone, that those of our loved ones who have preceded us in death will be there to assist our transition through death, and that death, like life, is 'a birth into a different existence'.[12] Kübler-Ross says that she became convinced about the reality of meeting loved ones after death when researching family car accidents. She was particularly interested in the evidence from accidents where most, but not all, of the people had been killed. Fatally injured children were generally taken to trauma units in hospitals, and Kübler-Ross was able to visit them two or three days before they died. She found that children about to experience death in these circumstances were invariably calm and serene, and were always somehow assured that others would be waiting for them after death. These children had not been told by the medical staff that their parents or siblings had died, as it was thought that children in crisis would not fight to stay alive if they knew that the other members of their family had died. Nevertheless, says Kübler-Ross, 'In fifteen years I have not had a single child who did not somehow know when a family member had preceded them in death.'[13]

Kübler Ross says quite categorically that none of her patients who has had an out-of-body experience was ever again afraid of dying:

> Death is simply a shedding of the physical body like the butterfly shedding its cocoon. It is a transition to a higher state of consciousness where you continue to perceive, to understand, to laugh, and to be able to grow. The only thing you lose is something that you don't need any more, your physical body. It's like putting away your winter coat when spring comes. You know that the coat is shabby and you don't want to wear it any more. That's virtually what death is about….[14]

> After we pass through this visually very beautiful and individually appropriate form of transition, say the tunnel, we are approaching a source of light that many of our patients describe and that I myself experienced in the form of an incredibly beautiful and unforgettable life-changing experience. This is called cosmic consciousness. In the presence of this light, which most people in our western hemisphere call Christ or God, or love or light, we are surrounded by total and absolute unconditional love, understanding and compassion.[15]

Kübler-Ross's emphasis on the positive and loving aspects of the afterlife transition is also supported by Kenneth Ring's NDE data, although he does not draw the same final conclusion. Ring believes that the almost universal occurrence of *positive* visionary states of consciousness experienced during a NDE (as distinct from negative, hell-like states) may simply be a mapping of one's initial contact with the Inner Light and may by no means represent the total spectrum of visionary after-death encounters. It may well be that works like the *Tibetan Book of the Dead* present a more complete picture, and that what Kübler-Ross is describing is simply the first stage of a much more extensive process. Considered in this context, if the *Tibetan Book of the Dead* is in any sense correct, at the point of physical death we will all encounter the Great Light and the positive deities – or archetypes of the psyche – first, and the negative images will emerge later. According to the Tibetan model of post-mortem consciousness, if we are unable to transcend these powerful visionary encounters we may then find ourselves being gradually drawn back into the more tangible dimensions of physical awareness prior to entering a new human incarnation.

Two maverick figures on the fringe of the transpersonal movement have played a unique role in the exploration of consciousness states related to death and near-death. The first is Ian Stevenson (born 1918), Alumni Professor of Psychiatry at the University of Virginia School of Medicine, whose systematic international research into claimed cases of reincarnation among young children has attracted widespread respect. The second is the late Robert Monroe (1915–95) whose research into out-of-the-body experiences and the transitional states following death may yet redefine our understanding of what it is like to die. Both Stevenson and Monroe are highly regarded in the New Age movement. Stevenson's best known work is *Twenty Cases Suggestive of Reincarnation* (1966, revised in 1995); Monroe's exploration of out-of-the-body states was documented in his three books: *Journeys out of the Body* (1971), *Far Journeys* (1985) and *Ultimate Journey* (1994).

Ian Stevenson believes that children under the age of five or six years are less worldly than teenagers or adults, have scant access to information from other regions, and therefore have little inclination or capacity to fabricate evidence. He has therefore considered reincarnation evidence in young children to be of special interest, particularly in those instances when it is possible to verify independently the claims these children make.

Over several decades Professor Stevenson and his staff have travelled to many different countries – including India, Sri Lanka, Brazil, Lebanon, Turkey and Thailand – in their search for evidence of reincarnation. They have also visited Tlingit communities in south-eastern Alaska where several reincarnation cases have been reported. As a consequence, Stevenson has now documented over 2,000 cases of claimed reincarnational memories in young children and has published his findings in a number of scholarly books and journals. An analysis of these cases suggests that reincarnational memories in the children of different cultures are remarkably similar – even in those from isolated communities that have had little contact with other cultural groups.

Professor Stevenson has said that in some instances other factors, such as telepathy, 'racial memory', and sometimes even fraud, could also be involved in the reincarnational memories of young children. But it is not only the reincarnation accounts themselves that attract him. In recent times he has also begun to explore what he calls the relationship between biology and reincarnation. He is particularly interested in the existence of birthmarks that appear to correspond to bullet or stab wounds inflicted in previous lives, and he has explored the issue of whether a violent death is more likely to lead to a rapid reincarnation. The Tlingit, for example, believe it is better to be killed than to die a natural death because they maintain this will result in a quick rebirth. Members of the Druse sect in Lebanon believe that a dead person's spirit will be reincarnated immediately after death, but they maintain that this happens swiftly, regardless of how a person dies.

Birthmark evidence is especially prevalent among the Inuit and the Tlingit of Alaska, occurring in approximately half of all reported reincarnation cases. Both cultures are familiar with violent death and wounds caused by wild animals. They also report frequent injuries inflicted by spears, guns, knives or axes as the result of fights. Stevenson has examined several hundred cases where the birthmarks that appear on a person's body are claimed to be linked to surgical procedures or stab and bullet wounds that occurred in previous lives.

One of Stevenson's numerous case studies involved a man known as Victor Vincent, a full-blooded Tlingit who lived on an island in southern Alaska.[16] In 1946, towards the end of his life, he became very close to his niece, Mrs Corliss Chotkin, his sister's daughter, and told her that he would be reborn as her next son. Vincent had a distinctive scar on his back and another on the right side of his nose near its base. He told Mrs Chotkin that he would imprint these scars on to the body of his next incarnation to prove that he had indeed been reborn.

In December 1947, fifteen months after her uncle Victor died, Mrs Chotkin gave birth to a son, whom she named Corliss Junior, and the baby was born with birthmarks in exactly the same places as Victor Vincent's scars. The scar near the boy's nose became less noticeable as he grew older but the mark on his back became even more distinctive, and had all the characteristics of a surgical incision that had healed over. It was raised and pigmented and also itched like a wound that was on the mend.

Around the age of thirteen months he said to his mother, 'Don't you know me? I'm Kahkody.' This was Victor Vincent's tribal name, and Mrs Chotkin was amazed that her son seemed to speak with the same accent as her deceased uncle. Later, when he was two and being wheeled along the street in Sitka, where the family lived, Corliss Junior recognized one of Victor Vincent's stepdaughters and called her correctly by her name, Susie. Later that year he recognized Victor Vincent's son William, who was visiting Sitka unannounced, and said to his mother, 'There is William, my son.'[17] At the age of three Corliss Junior identified Victor Vincent's widow, Rose, in a large crowd – spotting her even before Mrs Chotkin had noticed her – and on another occasion he recognized a close family friend of Victor's who happened to be in Sitka. Later he identified other friends of Victor's, referring to them correctly by their tribal names. By the age of nine, however, Corliss was able to recall fewer and fewer memories of his former life, and by the age of fifteen he could recall nothing whatever from his previous incar-

11.03 The Tlingit of Alaska accept reincarnation as a fact of everyday life. This photograph shows Tlingit people in ceremonial finery at a potlach in 1904.

nation. In most cases like this, the memories of past lives seem to disappear with the passage of the time.

Over the years Stevenson has been circumspect when asked whether he believes his research has established the existence of reincarnation. In Tom Shroder's biography (1999) Stevenson is quoted as saying that reincarnation is difficult to prove scientifically but that the evidence tends to support it. 'Of the cases we know now, at least for some, reincarnation is the best explanation we have been able to come up with. There is an impressive body of evidence, and I think it is getting stronger all the time.'[18]

Robert A. Monroe went further than Ian Stevenson in supporting the reality of reincarnation – as we will see, he claimed it as a 'known' rather than a belief. And it has to be emphasized that Monroe was by no means a natural mystic. Of all the pioneers of altered states of consciousness, Monroe stands out as a surprising and atypical example because he stumbled upon the paranormal almost by accident. His research into out-of-the-body experiences was an unexpected consequence of his use of sleep-learning techniques.

Having studied engineering and journalism at Ohio State University, he went to New York in 1939, where over a period of twenty-one years he created and produced some four hundred radio and television programmes. Later he formed his own production company, generating twenty-eight radio network shows weekly. He subsequently became a director and Vice-President of Mutual Broadcasting Inc., a position he held until 1956.

In the spring of 1958 Monroe had the first of a series of out-of-the body experiences. He had been experimenting with techniques of absorbing data while asleep, using a tape recorder. One afternoon he was lying quietly on his couch at home when he felt a 'warm light' on his body and began to 'vibrate' quite strongly. At the same time he found himself unable to move, as if he had been trapped in a metal vice. During the following months the same condition recurred several times. Monroe gradually discovered, however, that he could move his fingertips during the onset of the vibrations, and he was surprised to find that he could 'extend' them to feel things beyond his normal reach. It also became apparent that his fingers were not feeling in the physical sense because they were able to penetrate through normally solid surfaces.

Shortly afterwards he had a similar experience, except that he now found himself extended and floating in his entirety, just below the surface of the ceiling in his room. Beneath him lay his immobile body, clearly visible on the bed. He panicked, thinking he had died, and in desperation sought hurriedly to return to his body. These initial fears proved groundless, however, and gradually he acquired more confidence. He subsequently began to explore the new dimensions

11.04 Robert A. Monroe (1915–95), a pioneering researcher of out-of-body experiences.

of awareness made available to him in an out-of-the-body state. On several occasions he would 'travel' to see his friends – sometimes at unscheduled times. He was able to set up a number of double-blind experiments with friends and colleagues where he could later confirm what he had seen, checking such details as the time of his encounters, and their clothes, movements and activities.

He gradually identified different 'locales' that he was able to visit while journeying out-of-the-body. Locale I was the familiar realm of everyday experience, viewed simply from a new perspective. This was where he encountered his everyday colleagues while out-of-the-body, and as a perceptual realm it contained no strange beings, environments or imagery. He soon became aware of a dimension that he called Locale II. This was a realm described in esoteric literature as the 'astral plane'. It encompassed regions one might associate with Heaven and Hell, and included imagery associated with fantasies and raw emotions. It also seemed to be home to various discarnate beings, some of whom were unaware that they had died. Monroe noted that beings in Locale I could not normally detect beings resident in Locale II. A further domain that he visited, which he called Locale III, seemed to be some kind of 'anti-matter duplicate of our physical world.'[19]

Robert Monroe's study of altered states continued after the publication of his first book, *Journeys out of the Body*, in 1971. Encouraged by the enthusiastic reception he had received for his work internationally, he established a laboratory to research the out-of-the-body experience more systematically. Located in the foothills of Virginia's Blue Ridge Mountains, the centre eventually became known as the Monroe Institute of Applied Sciences. Drawing on his experience as a sound engineer, he was soon able to establish that when sounds of different wavelengths are played into each ear through stereo headphones, the brain assimilates the two pulses and 'hears' the difference between them. For example, if 100 cycles per second (Hz) were fed into one ear and 110 Hz into the other, the difference would be a 10 Hz wave. This corresponds to a low alpha-wave frequency in the brain – a pattern associated with meditative states. He was able to establish that OOBEs were primarily associated with the theta wave frequency which ranges from 4–7 Hz, although other frequencies were also involved.

Monroe subsequently developed a sound system known as the Hemi-Sync process to feed identical wave forms into both brain hemispheres, making it possible for research participants to utilize fully the potential in the right side of their brains as well as the left.[20] In *Ultimate Journey* (1994), Monroe describes the right brain as 'that portion of our mind-consciousness that emanates from our Core Self which was present when we began the human experience'.[21]

At the Institute, Monroe then established the Gateway Programme where individuals could experience altered states for themselves – including the possibility of the OOBE. Specially designed isolation booths were built with individual headphones – these were then wired to allow participants to receive audio and electro-magnetic signals from a central location. Each person could be monitored for EEG (brain waves), EMG (muscle-tone), pulse rate and body voltage. Wearing their headphones and relaxing in a state of total darkness, participants would then progress from meditation and visualization exercises through to out-of-the-body journeys, in a series of carefully graded steps. By the mid-1990s over 8,000 people had attended the Institute's programmes, among them Dr Elisabeth Kübler-Ross, Dr Rupert Sheldrake, and psychologist Joseph Chilton Pearce.

It was perhaps inevitable that a theoretical cosmology would result from the Institute's research programmes. In this cosmology post-mortem states are associated with different vibratory levels of awareness, strongly suggesting that after death human consciousness functions on an entirely different vibratory frequency. According to Robert Monroe, the world is surrounded by 'rings' of discarnate entities, reflecting different levels of spiritual evolution. Many of these beings remain in an intermediate state, unaware that they are dead, while others appear to envelop themselves in 'emotionally based fears and drives which they attempt to act out but never conclude'. These discarnate beings are very much in need of psychic assistance to help them avoid remaining in a 'locked-in state' – a situation that experienced researchers at the Institute have sought to remedy through what is known as the Lifeline Programme. Lifeline helpers have been trained to journey out-of-the-body into experiential realms where their assistance is most needed. By the mid-1990s Monroe claimed to have trained hundreds of people at his Institute to help guide the souls of the dead.[22]

Robert Monroe maintained that one should approach the different vibrationary levels associated with the after-death state with care, gradually becoming acclimatized to a range of altered states. He identified the basic levels of modified awareness, which he labelled Focus 1 through to Focus 10, as levels where the mind remained awake while the body gradually fell asleep – a basic pre-condition for inducing an out-of-the-body state. He associated Focus 12 with a state of 'expanded awareness' and Focus 15 with a level of awareness where there was no sense of time. Focus 21, meanwhile, was identified as a place to explore one's true inner nature, and Focus 22 as a place where 'humans still in physical existence [had] only partial consciousness…remembered as dreams or hallucinations'.

In *Ultimate Journey,* Monroe went on to describe Focus 23, as a 'level inhabited by those who have recently left physical existence but who either have not been able to recognize and accept this or are unable to free themselves from the Earth Life System.'[23] It was here that some research participants made direct contact with deceased family members and loved ones, in some cases concluding

11.05 The Monroe Institute, Virginia.

11.06 An isolation unit at the Institute where individuals are monitored for brain waves, muscle tone, pulse rate and body voltage.

11.07 F. Holmes Atwater, who has published his own account of out-of-body consciousness.

unfinished business that had been interrupted by the process of death. But there were further levels still. Monroe identified Focus 24, 25 and 26 as levels associated with various religious belief systems, and it was clear to him that many discarnate beings would choose to immerse themselves after death in imagery associated with their personal religious beliefs. But he maintained that one could pass through these 'belief system territories' and then enter what he called Focus 27. Here was a place he called the Park – a place where discarnate spirits were taken for rest and renewal.

Monroe's associate F. Holmes Atwater, who published his own account of out-of-the-body research in 2001, describes Focus 27 as a type of spiritual 'way station' intended to 'ease the trauma and shock of the transition out of physical reality and assist in evaluating options for the next steps in growth and development.[24] The Park is a visionary construct that Monroe says has been intentionally created by discarnate human intelligence to provide a comforting psychic environment for those in a state of spiritual transition. Interestingly, many near-death subjects completely unconnected with the research at the Monroe Institute have

reported entering paradisiacal gardens that provided a profound sense of solace and peace. Sometimes, too, these NDE subjects report that they have encountered deceased relatives in such settings.[25] Meanwhile, some Monroe Institute researchers now say they have begun to explore the realms beyond Focus 27, entering uncharted territory where 'it is nearly impossible to relate experiences in human terms'.[26]

Six years before his death in 1995 I interviewed Robert Monroe at his Institute in Virginia and asked him about his own conception of the afterlife.[27] He told me that one of the most important challenges we all face as human beings is to convert our religious beliefs into 'knowns' – so that our ideas and concepts can then be based on personal experience. He told me he had been able to establish reincarnation as one of his personal 'knowns' – for him a knowledge of past lives was no longer a matter of faith or belief but the result of direct experience. He also said that those who did not embrace a belief in rebirth would not reincarnate in the future – electing to be reborn was very much a matter of choice. He also spoke of spiritual freedom, describing it as the ability to step outside the hologram of the known physical universe.

All previous knowledge and information relating to the lifetimes is within the hologram. All of our belief systems are within the hologram. When you step out of the hologram, as an intelligent energy that is nevertheless separate and apart from it, you are no longer human, and you are no longer part of time and space. Then you can have an experience of all your lifetimes – it is like a dream of all the things that happened within the hologram.[28]

A CELEBRATORY VIEW OF DEATH

On 21 April 1997 a satellite-bearing Pegasus rocket was launched above the Atlantic Ocean with a number of small containers strapped to one of its booster engines. Inside the containers were the cremated remains of Dr Timothy Leary, Gene Roddenberry – creator of *Star Trek* – and twenty-two other posthumous space travellers. In what was to become the world's first space funeral, the Pegasus soared into space and then jettisoned both its engines and the ashes, allowing them to fall into orbit in a blaze of light.

Carol Rosin, a close personal friend of Leary's, had helped co-ordinate the mission to put his ashes into orbit. She says that Leary's message to her during the last phase of his life was that all of us are 'free to ride the light' on earth and into space. It is an optimistic message, and Leary both believed it and put it into practice. His approach to death was essentially celebratory. After being told by his doctors in January 1995 that he was terminally ill with an advanced prostate

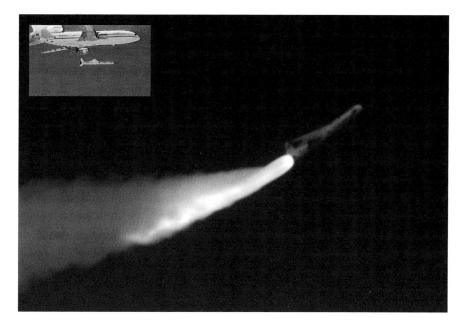

11.08 Launch of the Pegasus rocket carrying the cremated remains of Timothy Leary, *Star Trek* creator Gene Roddenberry and 22 others into Earth's orbit in April 1997 – the world's first space funeral.

cancer, Leary decided to gather his friends around him, 'to reflect on the past, help plan and design my future death, and just plain hang out and have a good time'. For Leary there could be no morbidity – he simply wanted his friends around him in a spirit of joy and friendship. 'Instead of treating the last act in your life in terms of fear, weakness and helplessness,' wrote Leary in his posthumously published book *Design for Dying*, 'think of it as a triumphant graduation.'[29]

Forever a showman and always hostile to the dicta of the status quo, Leary believed in the idea that you should live fully and joyously until you die. 'The house party is a wonderful way to deal with your divinity as you approach death,' said Leary, 'I can't recommend it enough.… Invite people to your house party who share your celestial ambitions.' No stranger to controversy, Leary was happy to flaunt contemporary taboos around death by maintaining a running commentary about his dying process on a home web-site.

Leary always maintained that death is a trip to higher realms of consciousness, and reminded us that it was 'the single transcendent experience that every person will undergo.'[30] This makes death special. If we are to follow Timothy Leary's advice, it is something we should all plan for, and hope to do well when our time comes.

12

The Future of the New Age

A crucial question – one that has been raised by enthusiasts and critics alike – is whether the New Age movement is likely to endure. My own view is that its immediate future seems assured because at the deepest level of this movement – the transpersonal level – the New Age perspective draws our attention to issues that are of global spiritual concern.

Central among these issues is the view, widely held among members of the transpersonal movement, that the scientific thinking that currently governs our definitions of 'reality' should be supplemented by a spiritual or holistic dimension. It is also generally agreed that this should be an authentic and well-informed spirituality, one based not on narrow definitions of doctrinal religion but using frameworks for studying universal aspects of the spiritual experience, thereby transcending cultural differences. Transpersonal psychologist Frances Vaughan, addressing an international conference on integrating ancient wisdom and modern science, expressed it well when she said: 'Science without wisdom can destroy the world; wisdom without science remains ineffectual. The transpersonal perspective sees the Eastern and Western approaches as complementary, and recognizes the transcendental mystical unity of all religions.'[1]

A RECEPTIVE SPIRITUALITY

One especially positive aspect of the New Age movement is its sense of spiritual open-endedness and receptivity. The fact that it has no dominant or entrenched doctrinal position, and is willing to absorb perennial wisdom teachings from both East and West while also accommodating insights based on new scientific discoveries, seems to me to be very much in its favour. In orthodox Judaism, Christianity and Islam, by way of contrast, it is much more difficult to maintain the same degree of intellectual and spiritual flexibility. These religions are based on unique spiritual revelations from founder-prophets, and in turn became grounded in doctrinal frameworks. This explains the contradiction, for example, that even now, in the twenty-first century, Christian Creationists choose to ignore the presence of the fossil record, reverting instead to a fundamentalist interpretation of *The Book of Genesis* that is clearly at odds with scientific discoveries. The

12.01 From the transpersonal perspective, the scientific thinking that currently governs our definitions of 'reality' should be complemented by a spiritual or holistic dimension. Photograph shows subatomic particles whirling in space.

lack of a consolidated doctrinal position within the transpersonal movement, on the other hand, means that the New Age remains much more open to new ideas and scientific advances. To this extent, what some Christian critics of the New Age, like Dr David Tacey, have seen as a weakness of the New Age – namely, the absence of a formal religious tradition – may yet emerge as a major strength.[2]

Another positive aspect of the New Age viewpoint is its willingness to subject personal spiritual beliefs to the test of experience – or as consciousness researcher Robert Monroe has expressed it, to convert 'beliefs' into 'knowns'. New Agers are undoubtedly eclectic in their spiritual tastes, but their choices are generally based on what feels true – on what measures up as 'real'. And, clearly, evaluations based on broad-based human experience give us a useful yardstick for measuring spiritual 'reality'. Gautama Buddha made the same point over two thousand years ago:

Do not believe in what you have heard. Do not believe in traditions because they have been handed down for many generations. Do not believe anything because it is rumoured and spoken of by many. Do not believe merely because the written statement of some old sage is produced. Do not believe in conjectures. Do not believe merely in the authority of your teachers and elders. After observation and analysis, when it agrees with reason and it is conducive to the good and benefit of one and all, then accept it, and live up to it.[3]

As in the Buddhist teachings, the New Age credo stresses that all individuals need to take responsibility for their own lives and their own personal spiritual beliefs. At the same time it is necessary to remember that all belief systems are themselves metaphors or constructs that seek, in their own limited and incomplete way, to describe what we believe to be true. Spiritual beliefs – especially those trying to explain 'God' or concepts of ultimate spiritual causality – should remain as open-ended as possible. As transpersonal neurophysiologist Dr John C. Lilly observed in his influential book *Simulations of God* (1975):

[the concept of God] must be huge – in order to include one's ignorance, the unknown, the ineffable. Instead of God as the Belief, the Simulation, the Model, one adheres to God as Mystery, God as the Unknown. The explorer of inner spaces cannot afford the baggage of fixed beliefs. This baggage is too heavy, too limited and too limiting to allow further exploration.[4]

12.02 Tibetan brass Shakyamuni Buddha sculpture. Gautama Buddha urged his followers to base their beliefs on personal experience and not to rely solely on traditions handed down from one generation to the next.

As Lilly points out, religious dogmas arise when followers assert the exclusiveness and 'truth' of a belief system – when they narrow the options and assert that their interpretation alone is valid.

Transpersonal viewpoints avoid references to exclusive sources of spiritual authority. Similarly, New Agers tend towards body, mind and spirit practices that are experientially effective in the 'here-and-now' – which accounts for the widespread popularity of meditation and yoga. From the New Age standpoint there is little value in retaining religious teachings conceived for another time and place if their orientation and function are no longer relevant. To this extent, no one can afford the complacency of allowing his or her spiritual horizons to become frozen in time.

THE NEW AGE AND FUNDAMENTALISM

In the future we may well find an increasing polarization across the spectrum of spiritual beliefs – with a clear division between those who embrace an eclectic form of non-institutionalized New Age spirituality and those who turn in the opposite direction towards religious fundamentalism with its promise of doctrinal certainty. Fundamentalism has an undoubted appeal in uncertain and troubled times, with its clear distinction between good and evil and its emphatic demarcation between supporters and disbelievers. Fundamentalist religions of all kinds, however, signal a return to the authority of the past. The fundamentalist position resists doctrinal change. The very authority of any religious institution is grounded in orthodoxy – and any move for fundamental change is likely to be branded as deviance or heresy and fiercely resisted. Indeed, religious institutions are obliged, by their very nature and innate conservatism, to become substantially inflexible.

Paradoxically, something similar to religious fundamentalism is also found in some scientific circles. When supporters of particular scientific models become so closely aligned with certain interpretations of scientific data that their minds are closed to any new information that might challenge their position, this changes science into what transpersonal psychologist Dr Charles Tart has referred to as 'scientism', when science itself is converted into a belief system. Dr Tart notes that when science acts like a belief system it ossifies instead of providing a continual challenge to further thought.[5]

The transpersonal movement has been subject to attack from those who practise a form of scientism. The transpersonal perspective promotes a holistic concept of Nature and the universe, and a corresponding movement away from more limited mechanistic models. But there are many who cling to the old mechanistic paradigm, despite the findings of quantum theory and the New Physics. As is becoming increasingly obvious, prevailing paradigms often take some time to change, even when the scientific evidence points in a new direction.

12.03 The groundswell supporting the new paradigm in consciousness is already underway. Fractal geometry image, *Chaotic Attractors*.

PARADIGM SHIFTS

Transpersonal ideas have so far made little impact on reductionist scientific models of reality and perception. A work by American philosopher Daniel C. Dennett entitled *Consciousness Explained* (1993) makes no mention of any of these thinkers, and neglects the transpersonal perspective altogether. But Dennett – who is himself an exponent of computer-based models of consciousness – has at least been bold and honest enough to assert: 'The prevailing wisdom is *materialism*: there is only one sort of stuff, namely matter – the physical stuff of physics, chemistry and physiology – and the mind is somehow nothing but a physical phenomenon. In short, the mind is the brain.'[6]

For many in the transpersonal movement, nevertheless, it is just a matter of time before a sense of the wider view makes its presence felt. The groundswell supporting the new paradigm in physics is already underway, and a change is inevitable. As Dr Stanislav Grof has noted:

One of the most important achievements of the Western philosophy of science is the recognition that scientific theories are but conceptual models organizing the data about reality available at the time. As useful approximations to reality, they should not be mistaken for correct descriptions of reality itself. The relationship between theory and the reality which it describes is like that between a map and territory… to confuse the two represents a violation of scientific thinking.[7]

Since scientific enquiry is often highly subjective and value-laden, and at times akin to a belief system itself, paradigm shifts affect science in the same way that they affect the social and philosophical impact of religious beliefs. In his influential book *The Structure of Scientific Revolutions* (1970), philosopher Thomas Kuhn explains the dynamics as one paradigm replaces another. Initially the dominant paradigm consolidates a body of scientific data, helps define areas of research, provides methodology for experiments and also proposes acceptable criteria for evaluating the data. For a time the dominant paradigm will go unchallenged – and vocal critics may even be denounced as scientific heretics – but eventually new data emerges that is incompatible with the prevailing view. An accumulation of such data challenges the prevailing paradigm and forces a revision of the dominant interpretation. And so the process continues.

According to Kuhn, all scientific revolutions are paradigm shifts. In relation to the scientific study of human consciousness the quantum/transpersonal model, with its holistic implications, presents a clear challenge to the model of reductionist materialism. Yet who can predict when a point of critical mass will be reached enabling the emergent paradigm to gain widespread currency? It is also true, as Ian Barbour points out in his book *Myths, Models and Paradigms* (1974), that while paradigms may help determine the way a scientist sees the world, it is also the case that scientists with rival paradigms may gather quite different data in order to support their own personal cause.[8]

GLOBAL SPIRITUALITY

Transpersonal and New Age approaches to the spiritual life extend beyond the familiar social context to the idea of the mythic self – towards the idea that everyday life can encompass mythic and sacred realities. Today many sense a profound existential crisis, a fragmentation of both self and society as the world's political situation becomes increasingly unstable. Many also feel that the deep inner self of our being is becoming ever harder to sustain. In shamanic terms it is as if we have become collectively 'dis-spirited'. We are suffering from a collective withdrawal of the human spirit, and our increasingly fractured world has begun to reflect this reality. As shamanic counsellor and author Sandra Ingerman has observed, 'the planet is mirroring back to us our own soul loss'.[9]

The transpersonal solution to this is to look for progress in incremental stages, from personal self-transformation through to the transformation of communities and whole societies, thereby moving gradually towards a broader international context. Aimed squarely against this holistic vision of human development are the enormous forces of wealthy transnational corporations and the manoeuvrings of long-established, self-interested organizations and economic blocs whose power has an effect on human and global resources everywhere. Nevertheless the transpersonal movement encourages the personal drive towards physical, mental and spiritual self-empowerment, despite the widespread feeling that the odds are increasingly stacked up in opposition.

A deep sense of the sacred and the mythic takes us, in human terms, beyond the realms of secular power towards the very ground of our being. As Jean Houston has written: 'When myths are actively pursued… they can lead us from the personal-particular concerns and frustrations of our everyday lives to the personal-universal, with its capacity to broaden the context of our lives and our vision.'[10]

In effect, the transpersonal movement and the New Age are calling for a collective drive towards re-sacralizing the world; towards reaffirming the perennial wisdom principle that there is a spiritual basis to our existence, a unifying mystical purpose that transcends the ebb and flow of secular power and influence. This is a global interpretation of spirituality, a necessary perspective if we are to accept a holistic vision of our place and purpose on the planet. Jean Houston affirms this as eloquently as anyone else in the international transpersonal movement:

> This shift from the personal-particular to the personal-universal may well be a deep and essential requirement for an emerging planetary society. Otherwise, locked into our own experience and culture, we will have neither the passion for the possible nor the moral energy to co-create with others of different cultures and beliefs a world that works. We are now in the process of learning to see with our souls – combining our life's experience with our deepest archetypal knowings.[11]

It seems to me that the rise of the transpersonal movement and its New Age counterpart has lasting and challenging implications for religious belief and doctrinal orthodoxy in the West. The message that emerges from these movements is that we should all seek in our own individual way to become visionaries, to explore every way possible of expanding our spiritual horizons. New Agers believe that each of us will find that sacred source in different ways. Some through the guidance of a guru, spiritual teacher, or religious organization; others through meditation, shamanic practice or devotional prayer. Still others will tap that source by wandering in wilderness regions – mountains or rainforests – thereby opening their hearts and souls to the rhythms and spirit of Nature.

In its belief that there are many different, but nonetheless valid and authentic, paths to spiritual self-realization, the New Age movement recognizes that teachings and practices that may open one person to the sacred and infinite may seem inappropriate to another. Nevertheless, the aim of attaining a state of Oneness with the sacred and unifying ground of being remains the ultimate goal of all mystical paths. In a sense, the New Age questions all spiritual paths and traditions by urging us to ask ourselves:

Is the path I am following broad enough for all the aspects of body, mind and spirit that are part of my spiritual search?

Are my frameworks of 'reality' sufficiently open-ended to allow the transcendent dimension to enter my life?

Are the practices and teachings I follow essentially liberating or restrictive?

Do they encourage inner personal growth and connectedness with others, leading to powerful possibilities for social transformation, or do they perpetuate an outdated and restrictive belief system?

We stand at a very interesting crossroads in spiritual history. The New Age movement affirms that we should all have the opportunity to explore the many and diverse ways that lead towards spiritual self-realization, and that this will lead inevitably towards new paradigms for human development. The main alternative is to retreat into the security of formal doctrinal belief systems that have persisted for centuries as explanations of the perceived relationship between humanity and God. A continuing problem with this is that many of these doctrines exclude the rights of outsiders and non-conformists, including those who have chosen to search for the sacred in other ways or through other belief systems. Many doctrinal definitions of God are essentially tribal in nature. We would do well to heed the Buddhist rejection of any concept of a god who protects only one people and whose power stops at certain frontiers. As the Dalai Lama, Tenzin Gyatso, has observed, 'Whoever excludes others will find himself excluded in turn. Those who affirm that their god is the only God are doing something dangerous and pernicious because they are on the way to imposing their beliefs on others, by any means possible.'[12]

New Age and transpersonal perspectives take the view that our belief systems should be reinforced by personal experience of the deeper, inner realities. At the same time, it is important to remember that any particular spiritual path is but

12.04 According to the Dalai Lama, Tenzin Gyatso, there are many authentic spiritual paths. We should avoid imposing our beliefs on those who follow other teachings and traditions.

one of many possibilities – an essential attitude if we are to have any hope of nurturing religious tolerance in an increasingly polarized world. It is also crucial to translate beliefs and spiritual insights into practice. As Frances Vaughan has explained:

> We cannot just talk about spirituality; it needs to be an experiential realization. Enlightenment does not come simply from following the wisdom teachings. It comes from direct experience.… This work is also important in our emphasis on community, which translates intellectual work and personal transformation into community service.[13]

In this present phase of our cultural history, perhaps for the first time on a wide scale in modern Western society, it has become possible to formulate our spiritual and developmental paradigms on the basis of what we have collectively experienced, rather than what we have simply hoped for or have been brought up to believe. From the viewpoint of the New Age movement, shared knowledge and cumulative experiential wisdom are likely to be the crucial determinants of our future spiritual journey.

Notes

Most sources cited are listed with full details in the Bibliography

Introduction
pp. 8–11

1 There are two great schools of Buddhism: Mahayana (the Great Vehicle) and Hinayana (the Small Vehicle, a term used only by Mahayana followers). The latter is also known as Theravada (Teaching of the Elders) or Southern Buddhism. Historically, Mahayana grew out of Hinayana Buddhism. While Hinayana Buddhism seeks the liberation of the individual, the practitioner of Mahayana Buddhism seeks to attain enlightenment on behalf of all beings. Buddhas and *bodhisattvas* play a key role in Mahayana tradition. *Bodhisattvas* seek buddhahood through systematic practice of perfect virtues, but renounce complete entry into *nirvana* until all beings are saved.

2 The term 'transpersonal' was used earlier by the Jungian philosopher Erich Neumann, as well as by Ira Progoff and Dane Rudhyar. It was later adopted by Abraham Maslow and Stanislav Grof in 1967 for the new 'fourth force' psychology emerging from humanistic psychology.

Chapter 1 Wisdom from the East, Wisdom from the West
pp. 12–35

1 Tafel, *Documents 1*, 1890, pp. 35–36.
2 Swedenborg, *Arcana Coelestia*, para. 68.
3 Van Dusen, *The Presence of Other Worlds*, 1974, p. 16.
4 See *Arcana Coelestia*, paras 904, 5470, 5848, 6189.
5 This observation anticipates the findings of many researchers of modern near-death experience (NDE). See Chapter 11.
6 Swedenborg, *Heaven and Hell*, para. 495.
7 Swedenborg, *True Christian Religion*, para. 763.
8 Swedenborg, *Arcana Coelestia*, para. 1285.
9 Swedenborg, *Apocalypse Explained*, para. 20.
10 Van Dusen, *The Presence of Other Worlds*, p. 222.
11 In a paper published in 1779 Mesmer stated that all the heavenly bodies, the earth and life on it, were interconnected. He believed that the common medium uniting these natural forms was a magnetic fluid that was 'so continuous as not to admit of a vacuum and incomparably subtle'.
12 For further details see Drury, *The Healing Power*, 1981, p. 92.
13 Fodor, *An Encyclopaedia of Psychic Science*, 1974 edn, p. 240.
14 *The Memoirs of Count Witte*, translated from original MS and edited by A. Yarmolisky, London, 1921.
15 Symonds, 'Madame Blavatsky', *Man, Myth and Magic*, vol. 10, 1970, p. 286.
16 Colonel Olcott produced 15 articles on the Eddy brothers and the psychic phenomena at Chittenden. These were first published in book form as *People from the Other World* in 1875.
17 According to Peter Washington, Madame Blavatsky and Colonel Olcott were never lovers but regarded each other as 'chums' – see Washington's fascinating and informative book *Madame Blavatsky's Baboon*, 1993, p. 43.

18 Quoted in Roe, *Beyond Belief: Theosophy in Australia 1879–1939*, 1986, p. 1.
19 *Isis Unveiled*, 1972 edition, vol. 1. p. xi.
20 See Roe, *Beyond Belief*, 1986, p. 4.
21 Ellwood points out in his book *Alternative Altars* (1979, p. 131) that Olcott is honoured in Sri Lanka for his contribution to Buddhism and has even been featured on a local postage stamp.
22 Roe, *Beyond Belief*, 1986, pp. 4–5.
23 Ibid, p. 18.
24 This statement was published in the A*ustralian Herald*, October 1890, p. 21, a newspaper published by an eclectic, broad-based organization sympathetic to Theosophy called the Australian Church.
25 Christmas Humphreys, 'Helena Petrovna Blavatsky' in Wilson (ed.), *Men of Mystery*, 1977, p. 58.
26 Vivekananda said of Ramakrishna, 'I learnt from my Master…that the religions of the world…are but various phases of one eternal religion': *Collected Works*, vol. 4, p. 180 – quoted in Rawlinson, *The Book of Enlightened Masters*, 1997, p. 596.
27 Webb, *The Flight from Reason*, 1971, p.40
28 See Steven F. Walker, 'Vivekananda and American Occultism' in Kerr and Crow (eds), *The Occult in America*, 1983, p. 165.
29 Bridges, *American Mysticism*, 1971, p. 73.
30 See Isherwood (ed.) *Vedanta for Modern Man*, 1962 edn, p. 442.
31 Bridges, *American Mysticism*, p. 86.
32 Gerald Heard actively encouraged Esalen co-founders Michael Murphy and Richard Price to establish their new personal growth centre.
33 Vajrayana developed from Mahayana Buddhism in northern India around the middle of the first millennium, and extended to Tibet, China and Japan. In this school, the 'master' of the group initiates his followers by empowering their connection to a specific deity who then becomes a focus of the practitioner's meditation practice. Practitioners recite mantras, contemplate mandalas and ritual gestures and seek to sublimate individual dualistic awareness so that they can experience the fundamental 'oneness' of spiritual enlightenment.
34 Pauwels, *Gurdjieff*, 1972.
35 Quoted in Travers, 'Gurdjieff', *Man, Myth and Magic*, 1970, vol. 42, p. 1168.
36 Having separated from Gurdjieff in 1923, Ouspensky rejected Gurdjieff's theories outright in 1931. Orage also formally rejected Gurdjieff in 1931.
37 Quoted in Ouspensky, *In Search of the Miraculous*, 1949, p. 297.
38 See Travers, 'Gurdjieff', *Man, Myth and Magic*, 1970, vol. 42, p. 1189.
39 Ibid.
40 For further information on the enneagram, see Kathleen Riordan's chapter, 'Gurdjieff', in Tart (ed.) *Transpersonal Psychologies*, 1975.
41 Guiley, *Harper's Encyclopedia of Mystical and Paranormal Experience*, 1991, p. 248.

Chapter 2 Pioneers of the Psyche
pp. 36–53

1 James, *Psychology: Briefer Course*, 1892, p. 1.
2 James, *The Variety of Religious Experience*, 1958 edn., p. 298.
3 James always denied that he was himself a mystic and claimed he had never had a mystical experience. Nevertheless, on 9 July 1898 he wrote a letter to his wife after hiking in the Adirondack Mountains. It was a clear, still night, and while his companions lay sleeping, James entered a state of 'spiritual alertness' and then spent much of the night 'in the woods, where the streaming moonlight lit up things in a magical checkered play, and it seemed as if the Gods

of all the nature-mythologies were holding an indescribable meeting in my breast with the moral Gods of the inner life…. It was one of the happiest lonesome nights of my existence, and I understand now what a poet is.' See Hal Bridges, *American Mysticism*, 1970, p. 13.
4 Quoted in Murphy and Ballou (eds), *William James on Psychical Research*, 1960, p. 324.
5 See Robert Galbreath, 'Explaining Modern Occultism' in Kerr and Crow (eds), *The Occult in America*, 1983, p. 31.
6 See Murphy and Ballou, *William James on Psychical Research*, 1960, pp. 44–45 and 46–47.
7 James, *The Will to Believe and Other Essays*, 1902, p. 232.
8 James, *The Principles of Psychology*, vol. 2, 1950, p. 560 (first published 1890).
9 James, *Talks to Teachers on Psychology and to Students on Some of Life's Ideals*, 1899, p. 100 (republished 1962).
10 See Fadiman and Frager, *Personality and Personal Growth*, 1976, p. 201.
11 James, *Talks to Teachers on Psychology*, 1899, p. 100.
12 Jung, *Memories, Dreams, Reflections*, 1989 edn, pp. 168–69
13 Dilman, *Freud and the Mind*, 1986 edn, p. 7.
14 See Fadiman and Frager, *Personality and Personal Growth*, 1976, p. 14.
15 Alexander Lowen was associated with Reich from 1940, and in 1956 established the Institute of Bioenergetic Analysis. Bioenergetics aims to integrate mind and body processes so that a heightening of energy flow and the pleasure of self-awareness are experienced. Physical tensions are alleviated by paying attention to the psychological problems causing them.
16 Freud, *New Introductory Lectures on Psychoanalysis*, vol. 22, 1949 edn, p. 80.
17 See Fadiman and Frager, *Personality and Personal Growth*, 1976, p. 20.
18 Dilman, *Freud and the Mind*, 1986 edn, p. 125.
19 Sulloway, *Freud: Biologist of the Mind*, 1979, p. 338.
20 Freud, *The Interpretation of Dreams*, quoted in Fadiman and Frager, *Personality and Personal Growth*, 1976, p. 21.
21 Jung, *Memories, Dreams, Reflections*, 1989 edn, pp. 155–56
22 Ibid, pp. 150–51
23 Jung, *Man and his Symbols*, 1968, p. 13.
24 Ibid, pp. 41–42.
25 Jung, *Two Essays on Analytical Psychology*, 1928, p. 68.
26 Quoted in McGuire and Hull (eds), *C. G. Jung Speaking*, 1978 edn, p. 348.
27 Jung, *Memories, Dreams, Reflections*, 1989, p. 340.
28 Jung, *Two Essays in Analytical Psychology*, 1928, p. 70.
29 Ibid, pp. 65–66
30 Jung, 'The Relations Between the Ego and the Unconscious' in *Two Essays on Analytical Psychology: Collected Works*, vol. 7, 1928, p. 175.
31 Tacey, *Jung and the New Age*, 2001.
32 Readers are referred to Johnson, *Owning Your Own Shadow*, 1991, Gawain, *Living in the Light*, 1986 and Jeffers, *Feel the Fear and Do it Anyway*, 1987.
33 G. Adler (ed.), *C. G. Jung: Letters*, vol. 1, Routledge & Kegan Paul, London, 1973, p. 203.
34 Jung, 'Spirit and Life', in *Contributions to Analytical Psychology*, 1928, p. 78.
35 Quoted in Dunne: *Carl Jung: Wounded Healer of the Soul*, 2000, p. 200.
36 Segal, *The Gnostic Jung*, 1992, p. 48.
37 Segaller and Berger, *Jung and the Wisdom of the Dream*, 1989, p. 179.
38 Ansbacher and Ansbacher (eds), *The Individual*

Psychology of Alfred Adler, 1956, p. 104.
39 See Fadiman and Frager, *Personality and Personal Growth*, 1976, p. 99.
40 Ansbacher and Ansbacher (eds), *The Individual Psychology of Alfred Adler*, 1956, p. 177.
41 Fadiman and Frager, *Personality and Personal Growth*, 1976, p. 99.
42 Ansbacher and Ansbacher (eds), *Alfred Adler: Superiority and Social Interest*, 1964, p. 69.
43 See Reich, *The Function of the Orgasm*, 1973, for Reich's views on character analysis and bioenergy. This is widely regarded as his best book.

Chapter 3 Towards the Transpersonal
pp. 54–63
1 Watson, 'Psychology as the Behaviorist views it', *Psychological Review*, vol. 20, 1913, p. 158 ff.
2 Skinner, *About Behaviorism*, 1974, p. 225.
3 Phenomenology was a modern school of philosophy founded by German thinker Edmund Husserl (1859–1938) based on the descriptive study of consciousness for the purpose of discovering the structure of experience. According to Husserl it was just as legitimate to draw data from the imagination as from the objective world. Anything that could be seen – either subjectively or objectively – could affect consciousness and the meaning of a perceived object could be understood intuitively. Husserl's model introduced an element of subjectivity to the social sciences, extending legitimacy beyond the collection of 'objective data'. It is far removed from the objectivity of behaviourism. See Chapter 9 for Carlos Castaneda's 'magical reality' which meshed well with the phenomenological approach.
4 Maslow, *Motivation and Personality*, 2nd edn 1970, p. 150.
5 Maslow, *The Further Reaches of Human Nature*, 1971, p. 47.
6 Quoted in Sutich, 'The Emergence of the Transpersonal Orientation: A Personal Account', *Journal of Transpersonal Psychology*, vol. 8, no. 1, 1976, p. 6.
7 Sutich, 'The Founding of Humanistic and Transpersonal Psychology', dissertation presented to the Humanistic Psychology Institute, April 1976, p. 22.
8 Ibid, p. 23.
9 Ibid, p. 29.
10 Ibid, p. 35.
11 Zen was brought to the United States by two monks: Sokei-an Sasaki founded the First Zen Institute of America in 1930 and directed it until his death in 1945; Nyogen Senzaki established a Zen centre in Los Angeles in 1931 and served as its spiritual leader until his death in 1958 (see Bridges, *American Mysticism*, 1970, p. 98). Interest in Zen developed in the counterculture during the 1950s and 1960s following the publication of works by Daisetz T. Suzuki who was resident in the United States 1897–1909 and 1949–57, and became a professor of religion at Columbia University, New York, in 1951. His best known American publications include *Zen Buddhism* (1956), *Zen and Japanese Culture* (1959) and *Manual of Zen Buddhism* (1960). Alan Watts also helped introduce Zen Buddhism to a broad readership in the US. Watts's first book *The Spirit of Zen* (1936) was a popularization of Suzuki's works, and was first published in the UK in 1936 and then in New York in 1960. Watts also published the influential *The Way of Zen* in 1957, and three years later released a collection of essays entitled *This is It* (1960), which included his article 'Beat Zen, Square Zen, and Zen'. Another influential American Zen teacher was Philip Kapleau, a former businessman, who trained for thirteen years in Japan and became a Zen priest in 1965. In 1966 he returned to the USA and founded the Zen Meditation Center of Rochester, New York. Kapleau is best known for his compilation *The Three Pillars of Zen* (1966), *Zen: Dawn in the West* (1980) and *The Wheel of Life and Death* (1989).
12 Sutich, 'The Founding of Humanistic and Transpersonal Psychology', April 1976, p. 45.
13 Ibid, pp. 59–60.
14 Ibid, p. 114.
15 Ibid, p. 115.
16 Ibid, p. 148.
17 Ibid, p. 150.
18 Ibid, p. 155.
19 Ibid, p. 167.
20 Ibid, p.172.
21 Hoffman, *The Right to be Human: A Biography of Abraham Maslow*, 1988, p. 266.

Chapter 4 Esalen, Gestalt and Encounter
pp. 64–75
1 Hoffman, *The Right to be Human: A Biography of Abraham Maslow*, 1988, pp. 289–90
2 Perls, *In and Out the Garbage Pail*, 1969, p. 115.
3 Quoted in Shepard, Fritz, 1975, pp. 8–9.
4 Perls, *In and Out the Garbage Pail*, p. 272.
5 Quoted in Shepard, *Fritz*, p. 214.
6 Perls, *Gestalt Therapy Verbatim*, 1969, p. 4.
7 Ibid, p. 68.
8 Schutz, *Joy*, 1967, p. 15.
9 LSD-25 was synthesized in 1938 by Swiss chemist Albert Hofmann (born 1906) while he was working as a researcher for the Basle-based pharmaceutical company Sandoz. On 19 April 1943, Hofmann took the first consciously induced LSD 'trip', and he has continued to support the sacramental value of psychedelics.
10 The popular drug 'ecstasy', a drug of choice at modern 'rave parties' and clubs, is related to MDA.

Chapter 5 The Psychedelic Years
pp. 76–97
1 Huxley, 'Wings that Shape Men's Minds,' *Saturday Evening Post*, New York, 18 Oct. 1958, pp. 111–13.
2 Watts, *The Joyous Cosmology*, 1962, p. 1.
3 See Furlong, *Genuine Fake: A Biography of Alan Watts*, 1987 edn, pp.115–16
4 Leary, *Flashbacks*, 1983, p. 29.
5 Leary, *High Priest*, 1968, p. 25.
6 Leary, *Politics of Ecstasy*, 1970, p. 112.
7 Ibid, p. 131.
8 Quoted in Leary, *High Priest*, 1968, p. 215.
9 See Pahnke, 'Drugs and Mysticism', in Aaronson and Osmond, *Psychedelics*, 1970, pp. 148–51.
10 See Stace, *Mysticism and Philosophy*, 1960.
11 Leary, *The Politics of Ecstasy*, 1970, p. 15.
12 Quoted in Anthony, *The Summer of Love*, 1980, p. 29.
13 Hunter S.Thompson, 'The "Hashbury" is the Capital of the Hippies', in *The Great Shark Hunt: Strange Tales from a Strange Time*, 1979, p. 385.
14 Brown (ed.), *The Hippies*, 1967, pp. 39–40.
15 See Whitmer and Van Wyngarden, *Aquarius Revisited*, 1987, p. 201.
16 The best known and most vivid account of the Merry Pranksters is Tom Wolfe's bestselling book *The Electric Kool-Aid Acid Test*, 1968.
17 Quoted in *The High Times Encyclopedia of Recreational Drugs*, 1978, p. 145.
18 Quoted in Anthony, *The Summer of Love*, 1980, p. 129.
19 Ibid, p. 155.
20 Ibid, p. 156.
21 Quoted in Webb, *The Occult Establishment*, 1981, p. 462. The 'Yippies' (a name adopted by Jerry Rubin and Abbie Hoffman in 1967) advocated a form of 'clowning protest' in the American counterculture, and this included their attempt to levitate the Pentagon. The Yippie leaders were among the Chicago Seven who were prosecuted by the Nixon administration in late 1969. See Ellwood, *The Sixties' Spiritual Awakening*, 1994, pp. 269–70.

Chapter 6 Maps for Inner Space
pp. 98–113
1 The *Bardo Thodol* is a Tibetan Buddhist text from the Nyingma (or Nyingmapa, 'Old School'), one of the four principal schools of Tibetan Buddhism; the other three are Kagyüpa, Sakyapa and Gelugpa schools, and all are within the Mahayana tradition. Each has its own doctrinal traditions and philosophical theories. The *Bardo Thodol* was first committed to writing in the time of Padma Sambhava (8th century). Sambhava was the founder of Lamaism, or Tantric Buddhism – a form of Mahayana Buddhism.
2 Leary (et al.), *The Psychedelic Experience*, 1964, pp. 47–49.
3 W. Y. Evans-Wentz (ed.), *The Tibetan Book of the Dead*, 1960 edn, p. 32.
4 For additional background information see Lilly, *The Center of the Cyclone*, 1972, and *The Human Biocomputer*, 1968.
5 Ichazo's *Psychology Today* interview is included in Sam Keen's anthology *Voices and Visions*, 1976.
6 The Lilly/Ichazo model allows for comparisons with the chakras in Kundalini yoga (see Chapter 8) and the *sephiroth* in the Jewish mystical Kabbalah, in which there is the concept of various symbolic 'energy' levels between normal waking consciousness and transcendental states of being.
7 See Jeffrey and Lilly, *John Lilly, So Far…*, 1990, p. 172.
8 Ibid, p. 272.
9 Stanislav Grof interviewed by the author at the Esalen Institute, Dec. 1984.
10 See Grof, *Realms of the Human Unconscious*, 1975, p. 49ff.
11 Tarnas, *LSD, Psychoanalysis and Spiritual Rebirth*, unpublished MS, Esalen Institute, 1976, p. 37.
12 See Grof, *Realms of the Human Unconscious*, 1975, p. 10.
13 See Grof, *LSD Psychotherapy*, 1980, p. 76, and also Grof, *The Holotropic Mind*, 1992, pp. 45–56.
14 See Grof, *Realms of the Human Unconscious*, 1975, p. 132.
15 Ibid, p. 142.
16 See Grof, 'Modern Consciousness Research and the Quest for a New Paradigm', *Re-Vision*, vol. 2, no. 1, Winter/Spring 1979. pp. 42–43.
17 See Grof, *The Holotropic Mind*, 1992, p. 83.
18 Ibid, p. 84.
19 Stanislav Grof interviewed by the author at the Esalen Institute, Dec. 1984.

Chapter 7 The Holistic Perspective
pp. 114–126
1 For interesting insights into the counterculture transition from psychedelics to Zen meditation see Rick Fields, 'A High History of Buddhism in America', in Badiner and Grey (eds), *Zig Zag Zen: Buddhism and Psychedelics*, 2002.
2 Miller et al., *Dimensions of Humanistic Medicine*, 1975.
3 See Pelletier, *Holistic Health*, 1979, p. 10.
4 See President Carter, 'Preventive Health Care' in *The Holistic Health Handbook*, 1978, p. 29.
5 For further information readers are referred to multi-authored *The Holistic Health Lifebook*, compiled by the Berkeley Holistic Health Center, 1984, and Bliss (ed.), *The New Holistic Health*

Handbook, Stephen Greene Press, Lexington, Mass., 1985. These sourcebooks provide an excellent overview of the holistic health paradigm that began to emerge during the 1970s.
6 See Hans Selye, 'Stress: The Basis of Illness' in Goldwag (ed.) *Inner Balance: The Power of Holistic Healing*, 1979, and Selye, *The Stress of Life* (revised edn), 1976.
7 Friedman and Rosenman, *Type A Behavior and Your Heart*, 1974.
8 See Le Shan, *You Can Fight for Your Life*, 1977.
9 See Simonton and Matthews-Simonton, 'Belief Systems and Management of the Emotional Aspects of Malignancy' in Bliss (ed.), *The New Holistic Health Handbook*, 1985, p. 210.
10 See Carl and Stephanie Simonton, 'The Role of the Mind in Cancer Therapy', in Carlson (ed.), *The Frontiers of Medicine*, 1975. See also Simonton, Simonton and Creighton, *Getting Well Again*, 1978.
11 For further information on psychoneuroimmunology see Lloyd (ed.), *Explorations in Psychoneuroimmunology*, 1987.
12 See Pert, *Molecules of Emotion*, 1997.
13 Wechsler, 'A New Paradigm: Mind Over Malady', *Discover* magazine, Feb. 1987, p. 59.
14 Quoted in Bartley, *Werner Erhard*, 1978, p. 74.
15 Reprinted in *New Age News*, vol. 2, no. 1, April 1988.
16 Ibid.
17 Alexander Everett interviewed by the author, Sydney, Nov. 1988.
18 Ibid.

Chapter 8 Mystics and Metaphysicians
pp. 127–143
1 Reported in an article by Deborah Cameron, 'Satan and the Showgirl: The New Age under Fire', *Good Weekend* magazine, Sydney, 11 March 1989, p. 20.
2 Ibid.
3 As manager of a leading New Age bookshop in Sydney, I helped to arrange in-store author promotions for New Age writers. Dr Doreen Virtue, both in our shop, and later at a large public seminar, recounted her tale of an angel interceding to prevent the theft of her car. During Dec. 2000 to Sept. 2002 when I worked in this bookshop, Doreen Virtue shared equal billing with the Dalai Lama as the shop's top-selling authors.
4 *Interface*, Boston, Fall 1997.
5 Those interested in spiritual responses to the global crisis post-Iraq may wish to read *A Way Forward: Spiritual Guidance for our Troubled Times*, 2003, which my wife Anna Voigt and I co-wrote.
6 Interview by Rachael Kohn, *The Spirit of Things*, ABC Radio National, Sydney, 19 January 2003.
7 See Arthur C. Hastings, 'Channeling and Spiritual Teachings', in Tart (ed.) *Body Mind Spirit*, 1997, and also Hastings' definitive study of channelling, *With the Tongues of Men and Angels*, 1991.
8 *Southern Crossings*, Sydney, August 1985, p. 7.
9 Mark Chipperfield, 'New Age Inc.', *The Australian Magazine*, Sydney, 10 Dec. 1988.
10 Quoted in Henderson, *Awakening*, 1975, p. 113.
11 Needleman, *The New Religions*, 1972, p. 130.
12 Ibid, p. 129.
13 See Cohen, *The New Believers*, 1976, p. 78.
14 Christopher Magarey, 'Meditation: The Essence of Health', in Drury (ed.) *Inner Health*, 1985, p. 141.
15 The chakras ('wheels'), the spiritual nerve centres that align with the central nervous column, *sushumna*, from the base of the spine to the crown of the forehead, are mystical rather than biological in nature, and do not correspond to the body organs.
16 Magarey, 'Meditation: The Essence of Health', in Drury (ed.) *Inner Health*, 1985, p. 143.

17 John Cooper, 'Swami Muktananda and the Yoga of Power,' in Drury (ed.) *Frontiers of Consciousness*, 1975, p. 138.
18 Interested readers are referred to the articles 'O Guru, Guru, Guru' by Lis Harris and 'The Secret Life of Swami Muktananda' by William Rodarmor, published on the website cyberpass.net/truth/secret.htm.
   Rodarmor says wryly in his article that 'when crowds saw Muktananda step from a black limousine to a waiting Lear jet, it was clear that the diminutive, orange-robed Indian was an American-style success.'
19 Originally both Swami Chidvilasananda (Gurumayi) and her brother Swami Nityananda were nominated to succeed Swami Muktananda after his death. Swami Nityananda, however, later admitted to sexual transgressions and to breaking his vow of celibacy. He withdrew from the Siddha Yoga Foundation, which is now headed by Gurumayi alone.
20 Included in the media press-kit for Sri Chinmoy's tour of Australia and New Zealand, Nov.–Dec. 1987.
21 Ibid.
22 'Ma Anand Sheela interview on Cable News Network', *The Rajneesh Times*, vol. 3, no. 5, 9 Aug. 1985, p. 4.
23 See Kate Strelley, *The Ultimate Game: The rise and fall of Bhagwan Shree Rajneesh*, 1987, p. 380
24 Krishnamurti was not averse to the material benefits of the Western lifestyle. He liked well-cut Savile Row suits and expensive shoes, and was also a very accomplished golfer – almost professional standard.
25 Pupul Jayakar, *Krishnamurti*, 1986, p. 26.
26 See Drury and Tillett, *Other Temples, Other Gods*, 1980, p. 24. The amphitheatre was demolished in 1951.
27 Ibid.
28 Pupul Jayakar, *Krishnamurti*, p. 85.
29 Ibid, p. 88.
30 Ibid, pp. 403–404.

Chapter 9 Spirit, Myth and Cosmos
pp. 144–163
1 Interview with Joseph Campbell (1971) in Keen (ed.), *Voices and Visions*, 1976, p. 73.
2 Ibid, p. 72.
3 Ibid, p.76.
4 Larsen and Larsen, *A Fire in the Mind*, 1991, pp. xix–xx.
5 Osbon (ed.), *A Joseph Campbell Companion*, 1991, p. 40.
6 Daab and Smith, 'Midwife of the Possible: an Interview with Jean Houston', part 3, *Magical Blend*, Fall 1988, p. 22.
7 Houston, *The Hero and the Goddess*, 1992, p.10.
8 Ibid, p. 13.
9 Houston, *The Passion of Isis and Osiris*, 1995, p. 6.
10 See Mirka Knaster, 'The Goddesses in Jean Shinoda Bolen', *East West*, March 1989, p. 45. An interesting interview with Bolen is also included in Alexander Blair-Ewart, *Mindfire*, 1995.
11 Bolen, *Gods in Everyman*, 1989, p. 287.
12 Bolen inteviewed by Mirka Knaster, *East West*, March 1989, p. 73.
13 Feinstein and Krippner, *Personal Mythology*, 1988, p. 231.
14 Campbell, *Myths to Live By*, 1972, p. 104.
15 I have described the rise of modern magic, Wicca and neo-shamanism in *Magic and Witchcraft: From Shamanism to the Technopagans*, 2003.
16 Starhawk, *The Spiral Dance*, 1979.
17 Blair-Ewart, *Mindfire*, 1995, p.127.
18 Ibid, p. 128.
19 Starhawk, 'The Goddess', in Gottlieb (ed.), *A New*

Creation, 1990, p. 213.
20 Castaneda's first four books have been his most influential: *The Teachings of Don Juan* (1968), *A Separate Reality* (1971), *Journey to Ixtlan* (1972) and *Tales of Power* (1974).
21 De Mille, *Castaneda's Journey*, 1975, p. 42.
22 Andrews, *Medicine Woman*, 1981, p. 9.
23 Peter Benesh, 'White Woman write with Forked Typewriter', *The Sydney Morning Herald*, 2 July 1988, p. 25.
24 Ibid.
25 Richard Daab, 'An interview with Lynn Andrews', *Magical Blend*, No. 16, 1987, p. 36.
26 Jamal, *Shape Shifters*, 1987, pp. 25–26.
27 Daab, 'An interview with Lynn Andrews', *Magical Blend*, No. 16, 1987, p. 38.
28 Sun Bear and Wabun, *The Medicine Wheel*, 1980, p. xiii.
29 Ron Boyer, 'The Vision Quest', in *The Laughing Man*, vol. 2, no. 4, p. 63.
30 Quoted in Halifax (ed.), *Shamanic Voices*, 1991, p. 68.
31 Quoted in Jamal, *Shape Shifters*, 1987, pp. 89–90.
32 Ibid.
33 Personal communication during filming for the Cinetel Productions documentary *The Occult Experience*, New York, November 1984, for which I was interviewer. This documentary, screened in Australia by Channel 10 and released in the United States through Sony home video, included a section on this particular shamanic drumming workshop.
34 Quoted in Drury, *The Occult Experience*, 1987, p. 145.
35 Ibid.

Chapter 10 Science and Spirituality
pp. 164–181
1 Russell, *The Awakening Earth*, 1982, p. 12.
2 Sun Bear, 'Honouring Sacred Places', in Lehrman (ed.), *The Sacred Landscape*, 1988, pp. 139–40.
3 Voigt and Drury, *Wisdom from the Earth*, 1998, p. 66.
4 Ralph Metzner, 'Gaia's Alchemy', in Lehrman (ed.), *The Sacred Landscape*, 1988, pp. 118–19.
5 Ibid.
6 Sheldrake, 'Morphic Resonance' in Grof (ed.), *Ancient Wisdom and Modern Science*, 1984, p. 150.
7 Ibid, p. 49. See also Sheldrake, *A New Science of Life*, 1981, p. 151.
8 Ibid.
9 Ibid, p. 156.
10 Ibid, p. 166.
11 Ronald Valle, 'Relativistic Quantum Psychology' in Valle and von Eckartsberg (eds), *The Metaphors of Consciousness*, 1981, p. 424.
12 See Zohar, *The Quantum Self*, 1991, p. 5.
13 Grof (ed.), *Ancient Wisdom and Modern Science*, 1984, p. 10.
14 Capra, *The Tao of Physics*, 1975, pp. 56–57.
15 Bohm, *Wholeness and the Implicate Order*, 1980, p. 172.
16 David Bohm, 'A New Theory of the Relationship of Mind and Matter', in *The Journal of the American Society of Psychical Research*, 1986, vol. 80, no. 2, p. 126.
17 Singer, *Seeing Through the Visible World*, 1980, p. 66.
18 Zukav, *The Dancing Wu Li Masters*, 1980, p. 55.
19 Grof (ed.) *Ancient Wisdom and Modern Science*, 1984, p. 9.
20 See Zohar, *The Quantum Self*, 1991, p. 106.
21 Ibid, p. 51.
22 Ibid, p. 151.
23 Fritjof Capra, 'The New Vision of Reality', in Grof, *Ancient Wisdom and Modern Science*, 1984, p. 136.

24 See Catherine Ingram, 'Ken Wilber', *Yoga Journal*, Sept./Oct. 1987, p. 44.
25 Ken Wilber, 'Psychologia Perennis: The Spectrum of Consciousness' in Walsh and Vaughan (ed.), *Beyond Ego*, 1980, pp. 74–75.
26 Wilber, *The Spectrum of Consciousness*, 1977, p. 241.
27 Jung, *Analytical Psychology*, 1968, p. 110.
28 Wilber, *A Brief History of Everything*, 1996, p. 214. See also Wilber's chapter 'The Pre/Trans Fallacy' in his collection *Eye to Eye*, 1988.
29 For further insights into this debate, readers are referred to the multi-authored volume *Ken Wilber in Dialogue*, Rothberg and Kelly (eds) 1998 – where both Wilber and Grof present their differing positions.
30 Ken Wilber, 'Psychologia Perennis', in Walsh and Vaughan (eds) *Beyond Ego*, 1980, p. 83.

Chapter 11 The Challenge of Death
pp. 182–201
1 Nevertheless, there are a significant number of historical cases that could also be considered as NDEs. Readers are referred to Carol Zaleski's *Otherworld Journeys: Accounts of Near-Death Experience in Medieval and Modern Times*, 1987.
2 See Russell Noyes and Roy Kletti, 'The Experience of Dying from Falls', *Omega*, vol. 2, 1972, pp. 45–52. This article includes a translation of Albert Heim's 'Remarks on Fatal Falls'.
3 See Ring, *Life at Death*, 1980, pp. 96–97.
4 See Michael Sabom, *Recollections of Death*, Corgi Books, London, 1982, pp. 70–71.
5 Susan Blackmore, 'Visions of the World Beyond,' *The Australian*, 14 May 1988 (reprinted from *The New Scientist*).
6 See Michael Sabom, *Recollections of Death*, 1982, pp. 70–71.
7 See Ring and Cooper, *Mindsight: Near-Death and Out-of-Body Experiences in the Blind*, 1999.
8 Ring and Cooper, 'Mindsight: How the Blind can "see" during Near-Death Experiences', *The Anomalist*, no. 5, Summer 1997, p. 1.
9 Ibid, p. 2.
10 See D. Scott Rogo, *The Return from Silence*, 1989, p. 19.
11 See Kübler-Ross, *On Life After Death*, 1991, p. 10.
12 Ibid, p. 10.
13 See interview with Elisabeth Kübler-Ross, in Blair-Ewart (ed.), *Mindfire*, 1995, p. 223.
14 Kübler-Ross, *On Life After Death*, 1991, pp. 30–31.
15 Ibid, pp. 60–61.
16 See Ian Stevenson, *Twenty Cases Suggestive of Reincarnation*, 1966, pp. 231–40.
17 Ibid, p. 233.
18 See Shroder, *Old Souls*, 1999, p. 33.
19 Jean-Noel Bassior, 'Astral Travel: an Interview with Robert Monroe', *New Age Journal*, Nov./Dec. 1988, p. 47.
20 Monroe felt at the time that too much emphasis had been placed in modern society on 'left hemisphere' brain functions, such as rational, verbal and analystic skills, and not enough on 'right hemisphere' skills, such as non-verbal holistic learning.
21 Monroe, *Ultimate Journey*, 1994, p. 275.
22 For further information on ways of assisting the 'earth-bound spirits of the dead', readers are also referred to Terry and Natalia O'Sullivan, *Soul Rescuers*, 1999.
23 Monroe, *Ultimate Journey*, 1994, p. 249.
24 Atwater, *Captain of My Ship, Master of My Soul*, 2001, p. 167.
25 See Ring, *Heading Toward Omega*, 1984; Sutherland, *Within the Light*, 1993; and Lundahl and Widdison, *The Eternal Journey*, 1997 – among many other books on near-death experiences.
26 Atwater, *Captain of My Ship, Master of My Soul*, 2001, p. 169.
27 See 'Journeys Beyond the Body: An Interview with Robert Monroe' in Drury, *The Visionary Human*, 2002, p. 127ff.
28 Ibid, p. 129.
29 See Leary and Sirius, *Design for Dying*, 1997, p. 99.
30 Ibid, p. 132

Chapter 12 The Future of the New Age
pp. 202–211
1 Frances Vaughan, 'The Transpersonal Perspective', in Grof (ed.), *Ancient Wisdom and Modern Science*, 1984, p. 25.
2 For a 21st-century example of a largely dismissive Christian response to the New Age, readers are referred to David Tacey, *Jung and the New Age*, 2001.
3 From the *Kalamas Sutra*, cited in Boorstein (ed.), *Transpersonal Psychotherapy*, 1980, p. 5.
4 Lilly, *Simulations of God*, 1975, p. 157.
5 Tart, *Open Mind, Discriminating Mind*, 1989, p. 219.
6 Dennett, *Consciousness Explained*, 1993, p. 33.
7 See Grof (ed.), *Ancient Wisdom and Modern Science*, 1984, p. 5.
8 Barbour, *Myths, Models and Paradigms*, 1976, p. 105.
9 Interview between Lynn Siprelle and Sandra Ingerman, *Grandmother Spider's Spirit Web*, published on the Internet at: www.grandmother-spider.com/bookstore/ingerman.html
10 Houston, *The Hero and the Goddess*, 1992, p. 15.
11 Ibid, p. 23.
12 Voigt and Drury, *A Way Forward*, 2003, p. 120.
13 Frances Vaughan, 'The Transpersonal Perspective', in Grof (ed.), *Ancient Wisdom and Modern Science*, 1984, p. 30. i

Bibliography

Abdullah, S., 'Meditation: Achieving Internal Balance', in E. Goldwag (ed.), *Inner Balance*, Prentice-Hall, Englewood Cliffs, New Jersey, 1979

Abraham, R., McKenna, T., and Sheldrake, R., *Trialogues at the Edge of the West: Chaos, Creativity and the Resacralization of the World*, Bear & Co., Santa Fe, New Mexico, 1992

Achterberg, J., *Imagery in Healing*, Shambhala, Boston, 1985

Swami Akhilananda, *Hindu Psychology: Its Meaning for the West*, Harper & Brothers, New York, 1946

Anderson, W. T., *The Upstart Spring: Esalen and the American Awakening*, Addison Wesley, Reading, Mass., 1983

Andrews, L., *Crystal Woman*, Warner Books, New York, 1987

—, *Flight of the Seventh Moon*, Harper & Row, San Francisco, 1984

—, *Jaguar Woman*, Harper & Row, San Francisco, 1985

—, *Medicine Woman*, Harper & Row, San Francisco, 1981

—, *Star Woman*, Warner Books, New York, 1986

Ansbacher, H. L., and R. (eds) *Alfred Adler: Superiority and Social Interest, a Collection of Later Writings*, Northwestern Univ. Press, Illinois, 1964

— (eds) *The Individual Psychology of Alfred Adler*, Basic Books, New York, 1956; George Allen & Unwin, London, 1958

Anthony, D., Ecker, B., and Wilber, K. (eds) *Spiritual Choices*, Paragon House, New York, 1987

Anthony, G., *The Summer of Love: Haight-Ashbury at its Highest*, Celestial Arts, Millbrae, California, 1980

Atwater, F. H., *Captain of my Ship, Master of my Soul*, Hampton Roads, Charlottesville, Virginia, 2001

Badiner, A. H., and Grey, A. (eds) *Zig Zag Zen: Buddhism and Psychedelics*, Chronicle Books, San Francisco, 2002

Barbour, I. G., *Myths, Models and Paradigms: A Comparative Study in Science and Religion*, Harper & Row, New York, 1974

Bartley, W. W., *Werner Erhard*, Clarkson Potter, New York, 1978

Bassior, J.-N., 'Astral Travel: An Interview with Robert Monroe', *New Age Journal*, Nov.–Dec. 1988

Bays, B., *The Journey*, Simon & Schuster, New York, 2002

Bednarowski, M. F., and Starret, B., 'Women in Occult America', in H. Kerr and C. L. Crow (eds), *The Occult in America: New Historical Perspectives*, Univ. of Illinois Press, Urbana and Chicago, 1983

Benz, E., *Emanuel Swedenborg: Visionary Savant in the Age of Reason*, Swedenborg Foundation, New York, 2002

Berkeley Holistic Health Center (ed.), *The Holistic Health Handbook*, And/Or Press, Berkeley, California, 1978

—, *The Holistic Health Lifebook*, Stephen Greene Press, Lexington, Mass., 1984

Bharati, A., *The Light at the Center*, Ross-Erikson, Santa Barbara, California, 1976

Blackmore, S., *Dying to Live: Science and the Near-Death Experience*, Grafton, London, and Prometheus Books, Buffalo, New York, 1993

—, 'Visions of the World Beyond', *The Australian*, Sydney, 14 May 1988 (reprinted from *The New Scientist*)

Blair-Ewart, A. (ed.), *Mindfire: Dialogues in the Other Future*, Somerville House, Toronto, 1995

Blavatsky, H. P., *Isis Unveiled*, Theosophical Publishing House, Wheaton, Illinois, 1972; Theosophical Publishing Society, London, 1910 (first published New York, 1877)

—, *The Key to Theosophy*, Theosophy Company, Bombay, 1930 (first published London, 1889, and later by Theosophical Univ. Press, Pasadena, California, 1972)

—, *The Secret Doctrine*, (vols. 1 and 2), Theosophical Univ. Press, Point Loma, California, 1999 (first published London, 1888)

Bliss, S. (ed.), *The New Holistic Health Handbook*, Stephen Greene Press, Lexington, Mass., 1985

Boadella, D., *Wilhelm Reich: The Evolution of his Work*, Vision Press, London, 1973

Bohm, D., 'A New Theory of the Relationship of Mind and Matter', *The Journal of the American Society of Psychical Research*, vol. 80, no. 2, 1986

—, *Wholeness and the Implicate Order*, Routledge & Kegan Paul, London and Boston, 1980

Bolen, J. S., *Goddesses in Everywoman*, Harper & Row, New York, 1985

—, *Gods in Everyman*, Harper & Row, New York, 1989

—, *The Tao of Psychology*, Harper & Row, New York, 1979

Boorstein, S. (ed.), *Transpersonal Psychotherapy*, Science and Behavior Books, Palo Alto, California, 1980

Boyer, R., 'The Vision Quest', *The Laughing Man*, vol. 2, no. 4, 1981

Bridges, H., *American Mysticism: From William James to Zen*, Harper & Row, New York, 1970

Brown, J. D. (ed.), *The Hippies*, Time-Life Books, New York, 1967

Brown, M., *The Spiritual Tourist: A Personal Odyssey through the Outer Reaches of Belief*, Bloomsbury, London, 1998

Cameron, D., 'Satan and the Showgirl: The New Age Under Fire', *Good Weekend*, Sydney, 11 March 1989

Campbell, J., *The Hero with a Thousand Faces*, 2nd edn, Princeton Univ. Press, New Jersey, 1972 (first published Pantheon Books, New York, 1949)

—, *The Inner Reaches of Outer Space: Metaphor as Myth and as Religion*, A. van der Marck Editions, New York, 1985

—, *Myths to Live By*, Viking Press, New York, 1972

Capra, F., 'The New Vision of Reality', in S. Grof (ed.), *Ancient Wisdom and Modern Science*, State Univ. of New York Press, Albany, 1984

—, *The Tao of Physics*, Shambhala, Boulder, Colorado, 1975

—, *The Turning Point*, Simon & Schuster, New York, 1982

—, *Uncommon Wisdom*, Simon & Schuster, New York, 1988

Carlson. R. J. (ed.), *The Frontiers of Science and Medicine*, Regnery, New York, 1975

Castaneda, C., *The Active Side of Infinity*, HarperCollins, New York, and Thorsons, London, 1998

—, *Journey to Ixtlan*, Simon & Schuster, New York, 1972; Bodley Head, London, 1973

—, *A Separate Reality*, Simon & Schuster, New York, and Bodley Head, London, 1971

—, *Tales of Power*, Simon & Schuster, New York, 1974; Hodder & Stoughton, London, 1975

—, *The Teachings of Don Juan*, Univ. of California Press, Berkeley and London, 1968

—, *The Wheel of Time*, LA Eidolona Press, Los Angeles, 1998; Allen Lane, London, 1999

Chipperfield, M., 'New Age Inc.', *The Australian Magazine*, Sydney, 10 December 1988

Chopra, D., *How to Know God*, Crown Publishers, New York, 2000

—, *The Seven Spiritual Laws of Success*, Amber-Allen Publishing, San Rafael, California, 1994

Cohen, D., *The New Believers: Young Religion in America*, M. Evans, New York, 1975

Combs, A., *The Radiance of Being: Complexity, Chaos and the Evolution of Consciousness*, Floris Books, Edinburgh, 1995; Paragon House, Minnesota, 1996

Cooper, J., 'Swami Muktananda and the Yoga of Power', in N. Drury (ed.), *Frontiers of Consciousness*, Greenhouse Publications, Melbourne, 1975

Daab, R., and Smith, S., 'Midwife of the Possible: An Interview with Jean Houston', *Magical Blend*, issues 18–20, Berkeley, California, 1988

Dalai Lama, *Ancient Wisdom, Modern World*, Abacus/Little, Brown, London 2001

—, *The Meaning of Life*, Wisdom Publications, Boston, 2000

Daly, M., *Gyn/Ecology: The Metaethics of Radical Feminism*, Beacon Press, Boston, 1978

Davis, J., and Weaver, J., 'Dimensions of Spirituality', *Quest*, 1:1975

De Mille, R., *Castaneda's Journey*, Capra Press, Santa Barbara, California, 1976

—, *The Don Juan Papers*, Ross-Erikson, Santa Barbara, California, 1980

Dennett, D. C., *Consciousness Explained*, Little, Brown, Boston, 1991; Penguin Books, London, 1993

Dilman, I., *Freud and the Mind*, Blackwell, Oxford, 1984

Drury, N. (ed.), *The Bodywork Book*, Harper & Row, Sydney, 1984

—, *The Elements of Shamanism*, Element, Dorset, 1989

— (ed.), *Frontiers of Consciousness*, Greenhouse Publications, Melbourne, 1975

—, *Healers, Quacks or Mystics?* Hale & Iremonger, Sydney, 1983

—, *The Healing Power*, Muller, London, 1981

— (ed.), *Inner Health*, Harper & Row, Sydney, 1985

—, *Magic and Witchcraft: From Shamanism to the Technopagans*, Thames & Hudson, London and New York, 2003

—, *The Occult Experience*, Hale, London, 1987

—, *The Visionary Human: Mystical Consciousness and Paranormal Perspectives*, Chrysalis/Vega, London, 2002

—, and Tillett, G., *Other Temples, Other Gods; the Occult in Australia*, Methuen, Sydney, 1980

Dunne, C., *Carl Jung: Wounded Healer of the Soul*, Parabola Books, New York, 2000

Dyer, W., *Manifest Your Destiny*, HarperCollins, New York, 1997

—, *There's a Spiritual Solution to Every Problem*, HarperCollins, New York, 2001

—, *Your Sacred Self*, HarperCollins, New York, 1995

Edinger, E., *Ego and Archetype*, Putnam, New York, 1972

Eliade, M., *Shamanism*, Princeton Univ. Press, New Jersey, 1964 (first published in French by Librairie Payot, 1951)

Ellwood, R. S., *Alternative Altars: Unconventional and Eastern Spirituality in America*, Univ. of Chicago Press, Chicago, 1979

—, *The Sixties Spiritual Awakening*, Rutgers Univ. Press, New Brunswick, New Jersey, 1994

Evans-Wentz, W. Y. (ed.), *The Tibetan Book of the Dead*, 3rd edn, Oxford Univ. Press, New York, 1960 (first published London, 1927)

Everett, A., 'Interview with Alexander Everett', *Nature & Health*, Sydney, September 1989

Fadiman, J., and Frager, R., *Personality and Personal*

Growth, Harper & Row, New York, 1976

Farrar, J., and S., *The Witches' Way*, Hale, London, 1984

Feinstein, D., and Krippner, S., *Personal Mythology: The Psychology of Your Evolving Self*, Tarcher, Los Angeles, 1988

Ferguson, D. S. (ed.), *New Age Spirituality*, Westminster/John Knox Press, Louisville, Kentucky, 1993

Ferguson, M., *The Aquarian Conspiracy*, Tarcher, Los Angeles, 1980

Fields, R., 'A High History of Buddhism in America', in A. H. Badiner and A. Grey (eds) *Zig Zag Zen: Buddhism and Psychedelics*, Chronicle Books, San Francisco, 2002

Fodor, N., *An Enyclopaedia of Psychic Science*, Citadel Press, Secaucus, New Jersey, 1974 (first published London, 1934)

Freud, S., *The Interpretation of Dreams*, Avon, New York, 1954 (first published London, 1933)

—, *New Introductory Lectures on Psychoanalysis*, Norton, New York, 1949 (first published London, 1933)

Friedman, M., and Rosenman, R. H., *Type A Behavior and Your Heart*, Knopf, New York, 1974

Furlong, M., *Genuine Fake: A Biography of Alan Watts*, Unwin Hyman, London, 1987 (first published by Heinemann, London, and by Houghton Mifflin, Boston, in 1986)

Gawain, S., *Creative Visualization*, Whatever Publishing, Mill Valley, California, 1978

Gawain, S., with King, L., *Living in the Light*, Whatever Publishing, Mill Valley, California, 1986

Getty, A., *A Sense of the Sacred*, Taylor Publishing, Dallas 1997

Glock, C. Y., and Bellah, R. N., (eds), *The New Religious Consciousness*, Univ. of California Press, Berkeley, 1976

Goldenberg, N., *Changing of the Gods*, Beacon Press, Boston, 1979

Goldwag, E. (ed.), *Inner Balance*, Prentice-Hall, Englewood Cliffs, New Jersey, 1979

Goleman, D. (ed.), *Consciousness: Brain, States of Awareness and Mysticism*, Harper & Row, New York, 1979

—, *The Meditative Mind*, Tarcher, Los Angeles, 1988

Gottlieb, R. S., *A New Creation: America's Contemporary Spiritual Voices*, Crossroad, New York, 1990

Grey, M., *Return from Death: An Exploration of the Near-Death Experience*, Arkana, Boston, Mass., and London, 1985

Grof, S., *The Adventure of Self-Discovery*, State Univ. of New York Press, Albany, 1988

— (ed.), *Ancient Wisdom and Modern Science*, State Univ. of New York Press, Albany, 1984

—, *Beyond the Brain*, State Univ. of New York Press, Albany, 1985

—, *The Cosmic Game*, State Univ. of New York Press, Albany, 1998

—, *The Holotropic Mind*, HarperCollins, San Francisco, 1992

—, *LSD Psychotherapy*, Hunter House, Pomona, California, 1980

—, 'Modern Consciousness Research and the Quest for a New Paradigm', *Re-Vision*, vol. 2, no. 1, Winter/Spring 1979

—, *Realms of the Human Unconscious*, Viking, New York, 1975

—, and Halifax, J., *The Human Encounter with Death*, Dutton, New York, 1977

—, and Valier, M. L. (eds), *Human Survival and Consciousness Evolution*, State Univ. of New York Press, Albany, 1988

Guiley, R. E., *Harper's Encyclopedia of Mystical & Paranormal Experience*, HarperSanFrancisco, San Francisco, 1991

Gurdjieff, G. I., *Beelzebub's Tales to his Grandson*, Dutton, New York, 1973 (first published Toronto, 1971)

—, *Life is Real Only Then, When 'I Am'*, 2nd edn, Dutton, New York, 1981 (first published New York, 1975)

—, *Meetings with Remarkable Men*, Routledge & Kegan Paul, London, and Dutton, New York, 1963

Hagon, Z., *Channelling*, Prism Press, Dorset, 1989

Halifax, J., (ed.) *Shamanic Voices*, Arkana, London and New York, 1991

Hanegraaff, W. J., *New Age Religion and Western Culture*, State Univ. of New York Press, Albany, 1998

Harner, M., *The Way of the Shaman*, Harper & Row, San Francisco, 1980

Hastings, A., *With the Tongues of Men and Angels: A Study of Channeling*, Holt, Rinehart and Winston, Fort Worth, Texas, 1991

—, Fadiman, J., and Gordon, J. (eds) *Health for the Whole Person*, Westview Press, Colorado, 1980

Haule, J. R., *Perils of the Soul: Ancient Wisdom and the New Age*, Weiser, York Beach, Maine, 1999

Hay, L., *Heal Your Body*, Hay House, Carlsbad, California, 1988

—, *You Can Heal Your Life*, Hay House, Santa Monica, California, 1987

Heelas, P., *The New Age Movement*, Blackwell, Oxford and Cambridge, Mass., 1996

Henderson, C. W., *Awakening: Ways to Psycho-spiritual Growth*, Prentice-Hall, Englewood Cliffs, New Jersey, 1975

The High Times Encyclopedia of Recreational Drugs, Stonehill, New York, 1978

Hoffman, E., T*he Right to be Human: A Biography of Abraham Maslow*, Tarcher, Los Angeles, 1988

Hofmann, A., *LSD: My Problem Child*, Tarcher, Los Angeles, 1983

Houston, J., *The Hero and the Goddess*, Ballantine, New York, 1992

—, 'Myth and Pathos in Sacred Psychology', *Dromenon*, vol. 3, no. 2, Spring 1981

—, *A Mythic Life*, HarperSanFrancisco, San Francisco, 1996

—, *A Passion for the Possible*, HarperSanFrancisco, San Francisco, 1997

—, *The Passion of Isis and Osiris: A Union of Two Souls*, Ballantine, New York, 1995

—, *The Possible Human*, Tarcher, Los Angeles, 1982

—, *The Search for the Beloved: Journeys in Sacred Psychology*, Tarcher, Los Angeles, 1987; Crucible, Wellingborough, 1990

Humphreys, C., 'Helena Petrovna Blavatsky', in C. Wilson (ed.), *Men of Mystery*, W. H. Allen, London, 1977

Huxley, A., *The Doors of Perception: Heaven and Hell*, Chatto & Windus, London, and Harper, New York, 1954

—, *Moksha: Writings on Psychedelics and the Visionary Experience*, Stonehill, New York, 1977

—, *The Perennial Philosophy*, Harper & Brothers Publishers, New York, 1945; Chatto & Windus, London, 1946

—, 'Wings that Shape Men's Minds', *Saturday Evening Post*, New York, 18 October 1958

Ingerman, S., *Soul Retrieval*, HarperSanFrancisco, San Francisco, 1991

Inglis, B., *Natural and Supernatural*, Prism Press, Dorset, 1992 (first published London, 1977)

—, *Trance: A Natural History of Altered States of Mind*, Grafton, London, 1989

Ingram, C., 'Ken Wilber: The Pundit of Transpersonal Psychology', *Yoga Journal*, Sept.–Oct. 1987

Isherwood, C. (ed.), *Vedanta for Modern Man*, Collier Books, New York, 1962 (first published New York, 1951)

Jamal, M., *Shape Shifters*, Arkana, New York and London, 1987

James, W., *The Principles of Psychology*, vol. 2, Dover, New York, 1950 (first published 1890)

—, *Psychology: The Briefer Course*, Holt, New York, 1892

—, *Talks to Teachers on Psychology and to Students on Some of Life's Ideals*, Dover, New York, 1962 (first published New York, 1899)

—, *The Variety of Religious Experience*, New American Library, New York, 1958 (first published 1902)

—, *The Will to Believe and Other Essays in Popular Philosophy*, Longmans, Green & Co., New York, 1902

Jayakar, P., *Krishnamurti: A Biography*, Harper & Row, San Francisco, 1986

Jeffers, S., *Feel the Fear and Do it Anyway*, Harcourt Brace Jovanovich, San Diego, 1987

Jeffrey, F., and Lilly, J. C., *John Lilly So Far…*, Tarcher, Los Angeles, 1990

Johnson, R. A., *Owning Your Own Shadow: Understanding the Dark Side of the Psyche*, HarperSanFrancisco, San Francisco, 1991

Jung, C. G., *Analytical Psychology: Its Theory and Practice*, Vintage Books, New York, 1968

—, *Man and his Symbols*, Aldus, London, 1964; Dell, New York, 1968

—, *Memories, Dreams, Reflections*, Random House, New York, 1989 (first published 1961)

—, 'The Relations Between the Ego and the Unconscious', in *Two Essays on Analytical Psychology*, Routledge & Kegan Paul, London, 1928

—, 'Spirit and Life', in *Contributions to Analytical Psychology*, Kegan Paul, Trench, Trubner & Co, London, and Harcourt, Brace & Co., New York, 1928

—, *Symbols of Transformation*, Bollingen Foundation, New Jersey, 1956

—, *Two Essays on Analytical Psychology*, Routledge & Kegan Paul, London, and Dodd, Mead & Co., New York, 1928

Jung, C. G. and Wilhelm, R., *The Secret of the Golden Flower*, Kegan Paul, London, 1931

Kalweit, H., *Dreamtime and Inner Space*, Shambhala, Boston, 1988

Keen, S. (ed.), *Voices and Visions*, Harper & Row, New York, 1976

Kerr, H., and Crow, C. L. (eds) *The Occult in America: New Historical Perspectives*, Univ. of Illinois Press, Urbana and Chicago, 1983

Knaster, M., 'The Goddesses in Jean Shinoda Bolen', *East West*, March 1989

Knight, J. Z., *A State of Mind*, Warner Books, New York, 1987

—, *Ramtha: The Mystery of Birth and Death*, JZK Publishing, Yelm, Washington, 2001

Koestler, A., and Smythies, J. R. (eds), *Beyond Reductionism*, Beacon Press, Boston, 1969

Krishnamurti, J., and Bohm, D., *The Ending of Time: Thirteen Dialogues*, Gollancz, London, and Harper & Row, San Francisco, 1985

Kübler-Ross, E. (ed.), *Death: The Final Stage of Growth*, Prentice-Hall, Englewood Cliffs, New Jersey, 1975

—, Interview in A. Blair-Ewart (ed.), *Mindfire: Dialogues in the Other Future*, Somerville House, Toronto, 1995

—, *On Life After Death*, Celestial Arts, Berkeley, California, 1991

Kuhn, T., *The Structure of Scientific Revolutions*, 2nd edn, Univ. of Chicago Press, Chicago, 1970

Langley, N., *Edgar Cayce on Reincarnation*, Hawthorn Books, New York, 1967

Larsen, R. (ed.), *Emanuel Swedenborg: A Continuing Vision*, Swedenborg Foundation, New York, 1988

Larsen, S., *The Shaman's Doorway*, Harper & Row, New York, 1976

—, and R., *A Fire in the Mind: The Life of Joseph Campbell*, Doubleday, New York, 1991

Leary, T., *Flashbacks*, Tarcher, Los Angeles, 1983

—, *High Priest*, World Publishing, New York, 1968

—, *The Politics of Ecstasy*, Putnam, New York, 1968; Paladin, London, 1970

—, et al., *The Psychedelic Experience*, University Books, New York, 1964

—, and Sirius, R. U., *Design for Dying*, HarperCollins, San Francisco, 1997

Lehrman, F. (ed.), *The Sacred Landscape*, Celestial Arts, Berkeley, California, 1988

Le Shan, L., *The Medium, the Mystic and the Physicist*, Viking, New York, 1974

—, *You Can Fight for Your Life*, Evans, New York, 1977

Lewis, J. R., and Melton, J. G. (eds), *Perspectives on the New Age*, State Univ. of New York Press, Albany, 1992

Lilly, J. C., *The Center of the Cyclone*, Julian Press, New York, 1972

—, *The Human Biocomputer*, Communication Research Unit, Miami, 1968; Abacus, London, 1974

—, *Simulations of God*, Simon & Schuster, New York, 1975

Lloyd, R. (ed.), *Explorations in Psychoneuroimmunology*, Grune & Stratton, Orlando, Florida, 1987

Lovelock, J., *Gaia: A New Look at Life on Earth*, Oxford Univ. Press, London and New York, 1979

Lowry, R., *Dominance, Self-esteem, Self-actualization*, Brooks/Cole, Monterey, California, 1973

Lundahl, C. R., and Widdison, H. A., *The Eternal Journey*, Warner Books, New York, 1997

Luton, L., 'Reichian and Neo-Reichian Therapy', in N. Drury (ed.), *The Bodywork Book*, Harper & Row, Sydney, 1984

McGuire, W., and Hull, R. F. C. (eds) *C. G. Jung Speaking: Interviews and Encounters*, Princeton Univ. Press, New Jersey, 1977; Thames & Hudson, London, 1978

MacLaine, S., *Don't Fall off the Mountain*, Norton, New York, 1971

—, *Going Within*, Bantam, New York, 1989

—, *You Can Get There From Here*, Norton, New York, 1975

Magarey, C., 'Meditation: The Essence of Health', in N. Drury (ed.), *Inner Health*, Harper & Row, Sydney, 1985

Maltz, M., *Psycho-Cybernetics*, Prentice-Hall, Englewood Cliffs, New Jersey, 1960

Maslow, A., *The Farther Reaches of Human Nature*, Viking, New York, 1971

—, *Motivation and Personality*, 2nd edn, Harper & Row, New York, 1970

—, *Toward a Psychology of Being*, 2nd edn, Van Nostrand, Princeton, New Jersey, 1968

Masters, R., and Houston, J., *The Varieties of Psychedelic Experience*, Holt, Rinehart and Winston, New York, 1966

Meade, M., *Madame Blavatsky: The Woman Behind the Myth*, Putnam, New York, 1980

Medicine Eagle, B., *Buffalo Woman Comes Singing*, Ballantine, New York, 1991

—, *The Last Ghost Dance: A Guide for Earth Mages*, Ballantine Wellspring, New York, 2000

Mehta, G., *Karma Cola*, Simon & Schuster, New York, 1979; Jonathan Cape, London, 1980

Metzner, R. (ed.), *The Ecstatic Adventure*, Macmillan, New York, 1968

—, 'Gaia's Alchemy: Ruin and Renewal of the Elements,' in F. Lehrman (ed.), *The Sacred Landscape*, Celestial Arts, Berkeley, California, 1988

—, *Maps of Consciousness*, Macmillan, New York, 1971

—, *Opening to Inner Light*, Tarcher, Los Angeles, 1986

—, *The Unfolding Self: Varieties of Transformative Experience*, Origin Press, Novato, California, 1998

Miller, S., et al., *Dimensions of Humanistic Medicine*, Institute for the Study of Humanistic Medicine, San Francisco, 1975

Millikan, D., and Drury, N., *Worlds Apart? Christianity and the New Age*, Australian Broadcasting Corporation, Sydney, 1991

Monroe, R. A., *Far Journeys*, Doubleday, New York, 1985

—, *Journeys out of the Body*, Doubleday, New York, 1971

—, *Ultimate Journey*, Doubleday, New York, 1994

Moody, R. *Life After Life*, Bantam Books, New York, 1978

Murphy, G., *An Historical Introduction to Modern Psychology*, Routledge & Kegan Paul, London, 1967 (first published in London and New York, 1929)

—, and Ballou, R. (eds) *William James on Psychical Research*, Viking, New York, 1960

Myss, C., *Anatomy of the Spirit*, Harmony Books, New York, 1996

Naranjo, C., *The One Quest*, Viking Press, New York, 1972

Needleman, J., *The New Religions*, Doubleday, New York, 1970

Neher, A., *The Psychology of Transcendence*, Prentice-Hall, Englewood Cliffs, New Jersey, 1980

Neville, R., *Play Power*, Jonathan Cape, London, 1970

Noyes, R., and Kletti, R., 'The Experience of Dying from Falls', *Omega*, vol. 2, 1972

Olcott, H. S., *People from the Other World*, Tuttle, Rutland, Vermont, 1972 (first published Connecticut, 1875)

Ornstein, R., *The Psychology of Consciousness*, Jonathan Cape, London, and Penguin, New York, 1975

Osbon, D. K. (ed.), *A Joseph Campbell Companion*, HarperCollins, New York, 1991

Osis, K., *Deathbed Observations by Physicians and Nurses*, Parapsychology Foundation, New York, 1961

—, and Haraldsson, E., *At the Hour of Death*, Avon, New York, 1977

O'Sullivan, T., and N., *Soul Rescuers*, Thorsons, London, 1999

Ouspensky, P. D., *In Search of the Miraculous*, Harcourt, Brace, New York, 1949

Pahnke, W. N., 'Drugs and Mysticism', in B. Aaronson and H. Osmond, *Psychedelics*, Anchor/Doubleday, New York, 1970

Pauwels, L., *Gurdjieff*, Weiser, New York, 1972

Pelletier, K., *Holistic Medicine*, Delacorte Press, New York, 1979

Perls, F. S., *Gestalt Therapy Verbatim*, Real People Press, Moab, Utah, 1969

—, *In and Out the Garbage Pail*, Real People Press, Moab, Utah, 1969

Pert, C., *Molecules of Emotion*, Scribner, New York, 1997

Peters, T., *The Cosmic Self*, HarperSanFrancisco, San Francisco, 1991

Ram Dass, *Be Here Now*, Lama Foundation/Crown, New York, 1971

—, *Doing Your Own Being*, Spearman, London, 1973

—, *Grist for the Mill*, Unity Press, Santa Cruz, California, 1977

—, *The Only Dance There Is*, Doubleday, New York, 1974

—, *Still Here*, Riverhead, New York, 2000

Rawlinson, A., *The Book of Enlightened Masters: Western Teachers in Eastern Traditions*, Open Court, La Salle and Chicago, 1997

Reich, W., *The Function of the Orgasm*, Farrar, Straus & Giroux, New York, 1973

Ring, K., *Life at Death: A Scientific Investigation of the Near-Death Experience*, Coward, McCann & Geoghegan, New York, 1980

—, *Heading Toward Omega*, Morrow, New York, 1984

—, and Cooper, S., 'Mindsight: How the Blind can "see" during Near-Death Experiences', *The Anomalist*, no.5, Summer 1997

—, and —, *Mindsight: Near-Death and Out-of-Body Experiences in the Blind*, William James Center for Consciousness Studies, Palo Alto, California, 1999

—, and Valarino, E. E., *Lessons From the Light: What we can learn from the Near-Death Experience*, Plenum, New York, 1998

Riordan, K., 'Gurdjieff', in C. Tart (ed.), *Transpersonal Psychologies*, Harper & Row, New York, 1975

Robbins, A., *Awaken the Giant Within*, Fireside/Simon & Schuster, New York 1992

—, *Notes from a Friend*, Fireside, New York, 1995

Roberts, J., *Seth Speaks*, Prentice-Hall, Englewood Cliffs, New Jersey, 1972

Roe, J., *Beyond Belief: Theosophy in Australia 1879–1939*, New South Wales Univ. Press, Sydney, 1986

Rogers, C., *Carl Rogers on Encounter Groups*, Harper & Row, New York, 1970

Rogo, D. S., *The Return from Silence: A Study of the Near-Death Experience*, Aquarian, Wellingborough, and Sterling Publishing Company, New York, 1989

Rosen, E. J. (ed.), *Experiencing the Soul*, Hay House, Carlsbad, California, 1998

Rossman, M., *New Age Blues: On the Politics of Consciousness*, Dutton, New York, 1979

Roszak, T., *The Making of a Counter Culture*, Anchor, Garden City, New York, 1969

—, *Unfinished Animal: The Aquarian Frontier and the Evolution of Consciousness*, Harper & Row, New York, 1975

Rothberg, D., and Kelly, S. (eds) *Ken Wilber in Dialogue*, Quest/Theosophical Publishing House, Wheaton, Illinois, 1998

Russell, P., *The Awakening Earth*, Ark/Routledge & Kegan Paul, London, 1982

Sabom, M., *Recollections of Death*, Corgi Books, London, 1982

Schucman, H., *A Course in Miracles*, 2nd edn, Foundation for Inner Peace, New York, 1976

Schutz, W., *Here Comes Everybody*, Harper & Row, New York, 1971

—, *Joy: Expanding Human Awareness*, Grove Press, New York, 1967

Segal, R. A., *The Gnostic Jung*, Routledge, London, and Princeton Univ. Press, New Jersey, 1992

—, *Joseph Campbell: an Introduction*, revised edn, Mentor Books, New York, 1990

Segaller, S., and Berger, M., *Jung and the Wisdom of the Dream*, Shambhala, Boston, and Weidenfeld & Nicolson, London, 1989

Selye, H., *The Stress of Life*, revised edn, McGraw-Hill, New York, 1976

—, 'Stress: The Basis of Illness', in E. M. Goldwag (ed.), *Inner Balance: The Power of Holistic Healing*, Prentice-Hall, Englewood Cliffs, New Jersey, 1979

—, *Stress Without Distress*, Dutton, New York, 1974

Shapiro, E., and D. (eds) *The Way Ahead: A Visionary Perspective for the New Millennium*, Rockport, Mass., and Element, Shaftesbury, Dorset, 1992

Sheldrake, R., 'Morphic Resonance', in S. Grof (ed.), *Ancient Wisdom and Modern Science*, State Univ.

of New York Press, Albany, 1984

—, *A New Science of Life*, Tarcher, Los Angeles, 1981

—, *The Presence of the Past*, Park Street Press, Rochester, Vermont, 1988

Shepard, M., *Fritz*, Dutton/Saturday Review Press, New York, 1975

Shroder, T., *Old Souls*, Simon & Schuster, New York, 1999

Simonton, C., and Matthews-Simonton, S., 'Belief Systems and Management of the Emotional Aspects of Malignancy', in S. Bliss (ed.), *The New Holistic Health Handbook*, Stephen Greene Press, Lexington, Mass., 1985

—, *Getting Well Again*, Tarcher, Los Angeles, 1978

—, and —, 'The Role of the Mind in Cancer Therapy', in R. J. Carlson (ed.), *The Frontiers of Science and Medicine*, Regnery, New York, 1975

Singer, J., *Seeing Through the Visible World: Jung, Gnosis and Chaos*, HarperCollins, San Francisco, 1990

Skinner, B. F., *About Behaviorism*, Knopf, New York, 1974

Smuts, J. C., *Holism and Evolution*, Macmillan, New York, 1926

Spangler, D., 'The New Age: The Movement Towards the Divine', in D. S. Ferguson, (ed.), *New Age Spirituality*, Westminster/John Knox Press, Louisville, Kentucky, 1993

Spence, L., *An Enyclopaedia of Occultism*, University Books, New York, 1960 (first published London, 1920)

Stace, W. T., *Mysticism and Philosophy*, Lippincott, Philadelphia, 1960; Macmillan, London, 1961

Starhawk, *The Fifth Sacred Thing*, Bantam, New York, 1993

—, 'The Goddess', in R. S. Gottlieb (ed.), *A New Creation: America's Contemporary Spiritual Voices*, Crossroad, New York, 1990

—, *The Spiral Dance*, Harper & Row, San Francisco, 1979

—, *The Twelve Sacred Swans: A Journey to the Realm of Magic, Healing and Action*, HarperSanFrancisco, San Francisco, 2002

—, *Webs of Power: Notes from the Global Uprising*, New Society Publishers, Victoria, Canada, 2002

Stevens, J., *Storming Heaven: LSD and the American Dream*, Atlantic Monthly Press, New York, 1987

Stevenson, I., *Twenty Cases Suggestive of Reincarnation*, American Society for Psychical Research, New York, 1966; 3rd edn Univ. of Virginia Press, Charlottesville, 1995

Stockton, E., *The Aboriginal Gift*, Millennium Books, Sydney, 1996

Storm, R., *In Search of Heaven on Earth*, Bloomsbury, London, 1991

Strelley, K., *The Ultimate Game: The Rise and Fall of Bhagwan Shree Rajneesh*, Harper & Row, San Francisco, 1987

Sulloway, F. J., *Freud: Biologist of the Mind*, Basic Books, New York, 1979

Sun Bear, 'Honoring Sacred Places' in F. Lehrman (ed.) *The Sacred Landscape*, Celestial Arts Publishing, Berkeley, California 1988

—, and Wabun, *The Medicine Wheel*, Prentice-Hall, Englewood Cliffs, New Jersey, 1980

Sutherland, C., *Transformed by the Light: Life After Near-Death Experiences*, Bantam Books, Sydney and New York, 1992

—, *Within the Light*, Bantam Books, New York and Sydney, 1993

Sutich, A. J., 'The Emergence of the Transpersonal Orientation: A Personal Account', *Journal of Transpersonal Psychology*, vol. 8, no. 1, 1976

—, 'The Founding of Humanistic and Transpersonal Psychology: A Personal Account', doctoral dissertation presented to the Humanistic Psychology Institute, San Francisco, April 1976

Swedenborg, E., *Apocalypse Explained*, Swedenborg Foundation, New York, 1996 (first published 1785–89)

—, *Arcana Coelestia, the Heavenly Arcana*, Swedenborg Foundation, New York, 1995 (first published 1749–56)

—, *Heaven and Hell*, Swedenborg Foundation, New York, 1976 (first published 1758)

—, *True Christian Religion*, Swedenborg Foundation, New York, 1997 (first published 1771)

Symonds, J., *In the Astral Light: The Life of Madame Blavatsky – Medium and Magician*, Panther, London, 1965

—, 'Madame Blavatsky', *Man, Myth and Magic*, vol. 10, BPC Publishing, London, 1970

Tacey, D., *Jung and the New Age*, Brunner-Routledge, East Sussex and Philadelphia, 2001

Tafel, R. L., *Documents Concerning the Life and Character of Emanuel Swedenborg* (three vols.), Swedenborg Society, London, 1890

Talbot, M., *The Holographic Universe*, HarperCollins, New York, 1991

Tarnas, R. T., *LSD, Psychoanalysis and Spiritual Rebirth*, unpublished MS, Esalen Institute, Big Sur, California, 1976

Tart, C. (ed.), *Altered States of Consciousness*, Wiley, New York, 1969

— (ed.), *Body Mind Spirit: Exploring the Parapsychology of Spirituality*, Hampton Roads, Charlottesville, Virginia, 1997

—, *Open Mind, Discriminating Mind*, Harper & Row, San Francisco, 1989

— (ed.), *Transpersonal Psychologies*, Harper & Row, New York, 1975

Thompson, G., *Mind Body Spirit Internet Guide*, Thorsons, London, 2001

Thompson, Hunter S., 'The "Hashbury" is the Capital of the Hippies', in *The Great Shark Hunt: Strange Tales from a Strange Time*, Summit Books, New York, 1979

Tillett, G., *The Elder Brother: A Biography of Charles Webster Leadbeater*, Routledge & Kegan Paul, Boston, Mass., and London, 1982

Travers, P., 'Gurdjieff', *Man, Myth and Magic*, vol. 42, BPC Publishing, London, 1970

Trenoweth, S., *The Future of God: Personal Adventures in Spirituality with Thirteen of Today's Eminent Thinkers*, Millennium, Sydney, 1995

Valarino, E. E., *On the Other Side of Life: Exploring the Phenomenon of the Near-Death Experience*, Plenum, New York, 1997

Valle, R. S., 'Relativistic Quantum Psychology', in R. S. Valle and R. von Eckartsberg (eds), *The Metaphors of Consciousness*, Plenum, New York, 1981

—, and von Eckartsberg, R. (eds), T*he Metaphors of Consciousness*, Plenum, New York, 1981

Van Dusen, W., *The Presence of Other Worlds*, Harper & Row, New York, 1974

—, *The Presence of Spirits in Madness*, Swedenborg Foundation, New York, 1983

Vaughan, F., 'The Transpersonal Perspective', in S. Grof (ed.), *Ancient Wisdom and Modern Science*, State Univ. of New York Press, Albany, 1984

Vernon, R., *Star in the East: Krishnamurti, the Invention of a Messiah*, St Martin's Press, New York, 2001

Virtue, D., *Angel Visions*, Hay House, Carlsbad, California, 2000

—, *Divine Guidance*, 2nd edn, Renaissance Books, Los Angeles, 1999

—, *Healing with the Angels*, Hay House, Carlsbad, California, 1999

Voigt, A., and Drury, N., *A Way Forward: Spiritual Guidance for our Troubled Times*, Red Wheel/Weiser, Boston, 2003

—, and —, *Wisdom from the Earth: The Living Legacy of the Aboriginal Dreamtime*, Shambhala, Boston, 1998

Walsch, N. D., *Communion with God*, Putnam, New York, 2000

—, *Conversations with God (Book One)*, Putnam, New York, 1996

Walsh, R. N., and Vaughan, F. (eds), *Beyond Ego*, Tarcher, Los Angeles, 1980

Washington, P., *Madame Blavatsky's Baboon*, Secker & Warburg, London, 1993; Schocken Books, New York, 1995

Watson, J. B., 'Psychology as the Behaviorist views it', *Psychological Review*, vol.20, New York, 1913

—, *The Ways of Behaviorism*, Harper & Bros, New York, 1928.

Watts, A., *The Joyous Cosmology*, Vintage Books, New York, 1962

—, *This is It and Other Essays on Zen and Spiritual Experience*, Pantheon, New York, 1960

Webb, J., *The Flight from Reason*, Macdonald, London, 1971

—, *Harmonious Circle: Exploration of the Lives of G. I. Gurdjieff, P. D. Ouspensky, and Others*, Thames & Hudson, London, and Putnam, New York, 1980

—, *The Occult Establishment*, Richard Drew Publishing, Glasgow, 1981; Open Court, La Salle, Illinois, 1976

Wechsler, R., 'A New Paradigm: Mind over Malady', *Discover* magazine, February 1987

White, J. (ed.), *The Highest State of Consciousness*, Anchor Books, New York, 1972

— (ed.), *What is Enlightenment?* Paragon House, New York, 1995

Whitmer, P. O., and Van Wyngarden, B., *Aquarius Revisited*, Macmillan, New York, 1987

Wilber, K., *The Atman Project*, Quest Books, Wheaton, Illinois, 1980

—, *A Brief History of Everything*, Shambhala, Boston, Mass., and Gill & Macmillan, Dublin, 1996

—, *Eye to Eye: The Quest for the New Paradigm*, Shambhala, Boston, Mass., 1988

— (ed.), *The Holographic Paradigm and Other Paradoxes*, Shambhala, Boston, Mass., 1985

—, *The Marriage of Sense and Soul: Integrating Science and Religion*, Random House, New York, 1998

—, *No Boundary*, Center Publications, Los Angeles, 1979

—, 'Psychologia Perennis: The Spectrum of Consciousness', in R. N. Walsh and F. Vaughan (eds) *Beyond Ego*, Tarcher, Los Angeles, 1980

—, *Sex, Ecology, Spirituality: The Spirit of Evolution*, Shambhala, Boston, Mass., 1995

—, *The Spectrum of Consciousness*, Quest Books, Wheaton, Illinois, 1977

—, *Up from Eden*, Doubleday Anchor, New York, 1981

Wilson, C. (ed.), *Men of Mystery*, W. H. Allen, London, 1977

Wolfe, T., *The Electric Kool-Aid Acid Test*, Farrar, Straus & Giroux, New York, 1968

Woods, R. (ed.), *Understanding Mysticism*, Image Books, New York, 1980

Zaleski, C., *Otherworld Journeys: Accounts of Near-Death Experience in Medieval and Modern Times*, Oxford Univ. Press, New York, 1987

Zaretsky, I. I., and Leone, M. P. (eds) *Religious Movements in Contemporary America*, Princeton Univ. Press, New Jersey, 1974

Zohar, D., *The Quantum Self*, Flamingo, London, 1991 (first published London and New York, 1990)

—, and Marshall, I., *SQ: Spiritual Intelligence*, Bloomsbury, London, 2000

Zukav, G., *The Dancing Wu Li Masters: An Overview of the New Physics*, Morrow, New York, 1979

List of Illustrations

Illustrations are listed by page number. Measurements are given in centimetres, followed by inches, height before width before depth, unless otherwise stated.

102a Ralph Metzner. Photo courtesy Ralph Metzner

102b Ram Dass. Photo © Lisa Law

103 Timothy Leary in the Brannan Street *Rolling Stone* Offices, San Francisco, 1969. Photo © Baron Wolman

106 The Apocalypse, 15th-century German illuminated manuscript. From *The Bomberg Apocalypse*. Bibliothèque Nationale, Paris

109 Dr Stanislav Grof. Photo courtesy *Nature and Health* magazine

111 Paintings depicting BPM I, BPM2, BPM3, BPM4. Courtesy Stanislav Grof

114 Acupuncture chart showing the series of points for controlling diseases on a standing figure. 18th century, Chinese

116 Acupuncture needles in a woman's ear and shoulder. Photo © Michael Donne/Science Photo Library

117 Yoga pose. Photo © Tony McConnell/Science Photo Library

118 Photograph of Canadian stress expert Dr Hans Selye, University of Montreal, 1962. Courtesy Hans Selye Foundation

119 Dr Lawrence Le Shan, 1997. Photo courtesy Dr Le Shan

120 Dr Carl Simonton, Zuma Beach, Malibu, 1999. Photo courtesy Simonton Center

121l Confocal image of normal brain tissue stained with antibodies to the receptor for orexin (stained green), a molecule associated with food intake and sleep. Photo © C. Guérin, C. Nolan, G. Davidson/Wellcome Photo Library

121r Dr Candace Pert. Photo courtesy Dr Candace Pert, Georgetown University Medical Center, Washington, D.C.

122 Dorothea Lange, billboard on US Highway 99 in California. Photo Dorthea Lange for the Farm Security Administration, March 1937, P & P Division, Library of Congress, Washington, D.C.

124 Shakti Gawain. Photo reprinted with permission from New World Library

125 Alexander Everett. Photo courtesy Alexander Everett

128 Deepak Chopra, Mardi Gras party at Manray Restaurant and Bar, New York, March 2003. Photo © Dan Herrick/Rex Features

129 Doreen Virtue. Photo courtesy Doreen Virtue

130 Massage at Esalen. Photo Daniel Bianchetta. Courtesy Esalen Institute, California

132a Edgar Cayce, founder of A.R.E. Photo courtesy The Association of Research and Enlightenment, www.edgarcayce.org

132b Egyptian priest from the *Book of the Dead of Ani*, (detail). British Museum, London

133 Neale Donald Walsch. Photo courtesy of

Conversations with God Foundation

135 The Maharishi Mahesh Yogi with the Beatles at his ashram, Rishikesh, India, 1968. Photo © Paul Saltzman (Contact Press Images) 2004

139 The chakras of the subtle body depicted as 7 lotuses, 17th-century painting, Nepal. Collection Stanislas Klossowski de Rola

140 Bhagwan Shree Rajneesh in Oregon. Photo Rajneesh Foundation International

141 J. Krishnamurti with C. W. Leadbeater and Nitya and Dick Clarke in Adyar, India, 1910. Courtesy the Krishnamurti Foundation of America

143 J. Krishnamurti in the Oak Grove, Ojai, 1949. Photo Johnson's Studio, Ojai. Courtesy The Krishnamurti Foundation of America

145 Mask. Eskimo, Alaska. Painted wood and feathers, 48 (18⅞) high. Private Collection

146 Joseph Campbell teaching at the Foreign Institute in Washington, D.C., 1957. Photo courtesy of Jean Erdman and the Joseph Campbell Foundation, www.jcf.org

147 Psychologist Dr Jean Houston. Photo courtesy www.jeanhouston.org

148 Jean Shinoda Bolen. Photo Lisa Levart. Courtesy Jean Shinoda Bolen

150 Starhawk, Holland, summer 2002. Photo © Bert Meijer

151 Goddess of Willendorf, *c*. 30,000–20,000 BCE. Red ochre on limestone, 11 (4⅜). Naturhistorisches Museum, Vienna

152 Ceramic from Colima, Mexico, 200 BCE –AD 100. Private Collection. Photo Peter T. Furst

153 José Benítez Sánchez, Huichol painting. University of Pennsylvania Museum, Philadelphia

154 Photo of Huichol shaman Ramón Medina Silva. Photo courtesy Peter T. Furst

157a Lynn Andrews, Hawaii December 2002. Photo courtesy Delia Frees

157b Sun Bear. Photo courtesy of Wind Daughter, The Bear Tribe. PO Box 16729, Mobile, AL 36616

158 Original school house on Vision Mountain. Photo courtesy of Wind Daughter, The Bear Tribe. PO Box 16729, Mobile, AL 36616

160 Brooke Medicine Eagle. Photo courtesy www.medicine-eagle.com

163 Shaman Priestess during a ritual dance. From F. Guirand, *Larousse Mythologie Generale*, 1935, Paris. Photo Kurt and Margot Lubinsky

164 Tellus Mater, the Earth Mother, surrounded by symbols of her fruitful abundance. Panel from the Altar of Augustan Peace, Rome, 13–9 BCE. Fototeca Unione, Rome

165 Wohow, Kiowa. The Taimay Power and the Sun Dance Lodge, 1876–77. Pencil and crayon, 22.2 x 28.6 (8¾ x 11¼). Missouri Historical Society, St Louis, Missouri

166 Clearing South East Asia tropical rainforest, Kalimantan. Photo © Wagne Lawler/Ecopix.net

168 Computer artwork of the atomic structure of a DNA double helix. Photo © Alfred Pasieka/Science Photo Library

169 *Diamond Mine* computer graphic image derived from the Mandelbrot set. Photo © Gregory Sams/Science Photo Library

170 Dr Rupert Sheldrake. Photo © Jill Purce

172 Fritjof Capra, 1977. Photo © Roger Ressmeyer

174 Professor David Bohm with Krishnamurti. Photo Mark Edwards. © Krishnamurti Foundation Trust Ltd

175 Danah Zohar. Photo courtesy Danah Zohar

176 Robert Venosa, *Mandala*, 1999. Oil on canvas, 64 x 64 (25 x 25). Courtesy the artist. www.venosa.com

185 Hieronymus Bosch, *The Ascent of the Blessed*, *c*. 1450–1516. Oil on panel. Palazzo Ducale, Venice

189 A. Andrew Gonzalez, *Unio Mystica*, 2002. Acrylic on clayboard panel, 61 x 45.7 (24 x 18). Courtesy the artist

195 Photo of Tlingit Indians at a potlatch, Sitka, Alaska, 9 December 1904. Courtesy Department of Library Services, American Museum of Natural History, New York (Neg. No. AMNH #328740)

196 Robert Monroe. Photo courtesy The Monroe Institute, Virginia

198 The Monroe Institute in Virginia. Photo courtesy The Monroe Institute, Virginia

199a Specially designed isolation booths for individuals to be monitored (CHEC Unit). Photo courtesy The Monroe Institute, Virginia

199b Monroe Institute researcher F. Holmes Atwater. Photo courtesy The Monroe Institute, Virginia

201 Pegasus rocket is launched from an Orbital Sciences Corporation jet, on the Celestis Earthview Founders Flight (Insert). Pegasus rocket as it heads into space (Main). Both photos courtesy www.Celestis.com

203 Subatomic particles. Photo © Mehau Kulyk/Science Photo Library

204 Shakyamuni Buddha, 11th–12th century, Tibet. Brass sculpture, height 40.6 (16). Zimmerman Family Collection

207 Fractal geometry, *Chaotic Attractors*. Photo © Mehau Kulyk/Science Photo Library

211 The Dalai Lama at a press conference, New York, 16 September 2003. Photo © Sipa Press/Rex Features

Every effort has been made to trace the copyright holders of the images contained in this book, and we apologise in advance for any unintentional omissions. We would be pleased to insert the appropriate acknowledgement in any subsequent edition of this publication.

Index